The Criterion for Distinguishing Legal Opinions from Judicial Rulings and the Administrative Acts of Judges and Rulers

World Thought in Translation

A joint project of Yale University Press and the MacMillan Center for International and Area Studies at Yale University, World Thought in Translation makes important works of classical and contemporary political, philosophical, legal, and social thought from outside the Western tradition available to English-speaking scholars, students, and general readers. The translations are annotated and accompanied by critical introductions that orient readers to the background in which these texts were written, their initial reception, and their enduring influence within and beyond their own cultures. World Thought in Translation contributes to the study of religious and secular intellectual traditions across cultures and civilizations.

The Criterion for Distinguishing Legal Opinions from Judicial Rulings and the Administrative Acts of Judges and Rulers

al-Iḥkām fī Tamyīz al-Fatāwā ʿan al-Aḥkām wa Taṣarrufāt al-Qāḍī wa'l-Imām

Shihāb al-Dīn Aḥmad ibn Idrīs al-Qarāfī al-Mālikī

Translated by Mohammad H. Fadel

Yale UNIVERSITY PRESS
New Haven and London

This publication was made possible in part by a grant from the Carnegie Corporation of New York. The statements made and views expressed are solely the responsibility of the author.

Published with assistance from the foundation established in memory of Philip Hamilton McMillan of the Class of 1894, Yale College.

Set in Adobe Caslon type by Newgen.
Printed in the United States of America.

Library of Congress Control Number: 2016961002
ISBN 978-0-300-19115-8 (hardcover : alk. paper)

A catalogue record for this book is available from the British Library.

This paper meets the requirements of ANSI/NISO Z39.48-1992 (Permanence of Paper).

10 9 8 7 6 5 4 3 2 1

For Reem and our beloved children,
Sarah, Laila, Fatima, and Ibrahim

Contents

Note on Transliteration and Usage

Throughout the text, I have employed a modified form of the *International Journal of Middle East Studies* transliteration system. I have, however, transliterated proper names throughout the translation. If an Arabic term, such as *mufti*, has entered the English language, I used the English spelling without transliteration. Dates are first provided by reference to the Islamic calendar, followed by the equivalent date according to the Common Era. Death dates are provided for individuals the first time they are mentioned in the text. I provide the original Arabic term in parentheses when translating a term of art.

Preface

As a graduate student at the University of Chicago, I became drawn to the study of Islamic law as a system of applied law, in response to the assumption of a prior generation of Islamic law scholars that Islamic law represented nothing more than a utopian ideal, not a practical system of regulating human society. Skeptical of this hypothesis, I decided to write my dissertation on Islamic law and legal process, focusing on post-twelfth-century Common Era jurists writing in Egypt, Syria, and North Africa and Andalusia (Muslim Spain). This seemed to be an ideal period to test the accuracy of the prevailing wisdom insofar as the jurists of this era were commonly believed to exemplify the derivative and utopian nature of later Muslim legal thought.

The decision to focus on Mālikī law was more serendipitous than a matter of considered deliberation, but having begun my study of substantive Islamic law in earnest using Mālikī texts, I took the path of least resistance and focused on Mālikī doctrines regulating legal process. My dissertation relied primarily on a fifteenth-century Mālikī treatise on adjudication, *Tabṣirat al-Ḥukkām*. That work in turn made repeated references to various works of Shihāb al-Dīn al-Qarāfī, including *al-Iḥkām fī Tamyīz al-Fatāwā ʿan al-Aḥkām*, the work translated here.

My serendipitous interest in Mālikism was the product largely of my experience studying Arabic at the American University in Cairo in 1988 as a student in the Center for Arabic Study Abroad Consortium. The director of the program that year was Sherman Jackson, who was still a graduate student at the University of Pennsylvania. My relationship with Professor Jackson began that summer in Cairo but grew over the subsequent years as I pursued the study of Islamic law in my graduate studies more systematically. In the course of those studies, Professor Jackson introduced me both to al-Qarāfī, who was the subject of his PhD dissertation, and to his teacher of Mālikī law in Cairo, Shaykh Hasan Salim Hasan Salih. Over the course of one summer and then one year in Cairo with the support of a Fulbright-Hayes dissertation-writing fellowship, I was able to complete the study of a basic Mālikī work of law, *al-Sharḥ al-Ṣaghīr*, with Shaykh Hasan. The work I did in Cairo studying Mālikī jurisprudence, along with Professor Jackson's groundbreaking work on al-Qarāfī, were crucial for my own dissertation on the study of the legal process in the Mālikī school and my subsequent research on Islamic law, including, but not limited to, this current translation and interpretation of al-Qarāfī's articulation of what it meant, from an institutional perspective, to have an Islamic polity. I am deeply grateful to Professor Jackson, both personally and professionally, for having encouraged me to study Mālikī law and for introducing me to Shaykh Hasan. It would have been extremely difficult (if not impossible) for an untrained graduate student to have navigated successfully the late medieval Islamic legal tradition that formed the subject matter of my dissertation, and ultimately led to this translation, without the initial assistance of a competent teacher.

My approach to the study of Islamic law, however, has also been deeply influenced by my formal legal education, which began shortly after I completed my dissertation in the fall of 1996, and my subsequent engagement with political liberalism, US constitutional law, and the relationship between religion and law in liberal states. Islamic law, from my perspective as a US-trained legal academic, is a site for exploring one approach to mediating and reconciling claims of the divine with those of humans, a task that is also fundamental to understanding the emergence of liberal political theory and constitutional regimes. Given my interests both in Islamic law and in political liberalism and liberal constitutionalism, when my friend and colleague Andrew March suggested I contribute a work on Islamic law to Yale's new translations series, World Thought in Translation, I could think of no better piece to translate than al-Qarāfī's *Iḥkām.* Although it is a work that reflects the centrality of divine law to the polity of his day, in it Qarāfī describes a complex legal system in which human law necessarily plays a crucial role, not only in the articulation of divine law through interpretation but also through human institutions that mediate between competing conceptions of divine law and the common good. In his own way, then, he is trying to solve some of the same problems that animated early Enlightenment political thought, albeit al-Qarāfī's approach is legalistic—and often, quite technically so. I offer this translation of his work, however, in the hope that it will render more accessible to a wider audience of readers a pre-Enlightenment Muslim thinker's approach to questions of divine and human sovereignty.

I would like to thank my friend Bilal Ibrahim, who, over a series of several days, sat with me as we undertook a line-by-line review of the Arabic text to insure the accuracy of my translation. I would also like to thank my two anonymous readers for the valuable comments they provided to my initial draft, as well as my University of Toronto colleague Alan Brudner for his graciousness in reading an earlier draft of the translation, and my old and dear friend Asifa Quraishi-Landes, of the University of Wisconsin Law School, for her detailed and thoughtful comments on this manuscript.

At Yale University Press, I would like to thank my editor, Jaya Aninda Chatterjee, as well as the series editors.

My wife and children have supported me throughout my academic career and the preparation of this book. I dedicate this work to them.

Translator's Introduction

One of the greatest difficulties facing both teachers and students of Islamic law is the paucity of translations of foundational Islamic legal texts. This is a result of a number of factors, not least of which is the relatively small number of scholars capable of producing high-quality English translations relative to the immense output of the Islamic legal tradition over the more than 1,200 years of Islamic law's literary history. Another important factor, however, has been a persistent bias among students of Islamic law, whether non-Muslims trained in Western universities or Muslims trained in the Islamic religious disciplines, to privilege earlier authors over later ones, on the theory that the earliest generations of Muslim jurists resolved all the fundamental questions of Islamic law. Twentieth-century scholars of Islamic law regularly expressed the assumption that no significant changes took place in Islamic law after the fifth Islamic century, or the eleventh/twelfth centuries of the Common Era, whether in regard to the theoretical principles of jurisprudence (*uṣūl al-fiqh*) or the substantive rules of law itself (*furūʿ al-fiqh*). In reaching this conclusion, they generally relied on the often-repeated but little understood proposition that "the gates of independent reasoning" had closed (*insidād bāb al-ijtihād*).

Scholars settled upon the fifth Islamic century, or the eleventh/twelfth centuries of the Common Era, as a decisive turning point for Islamic law insofar as the new regime of *taqlīd*, often disparagingly translated as "blind imitation," came to dominate the production and reproduction of Islamic law, replacing the previous legal norm of *ijtihād*, "independent reasoning," which, scholars believed, had given Islamic law a dynamic character for the first four hundred years of its existence. According to the orthodoxy of modern scholars, jurists operating under the regime of *taqlīd* could not, and did not, challenge the views of the early masters, but instead contented themselves with gathering the views of earlier generations of jurists, then systematizing them into abstract categories and, finally, producing elaborate commentaries on the views of the early masters, rarely going beyond them. Modern scholarship generally assumed that as a result of *taqlīd*, Islamic law lost the ability to adapt to changing social circumstances and, as a result, became increasingly irrelevant to social practice as jurists effectively withdrew from the social world into one of "ivory minarets" where they could safely study the ideals of their religious law without concerning themselves with the practical needs of Muslim societies. The law, having been perfectly elaborated (or very nearly so) by the earliest generations of jurists, simply needed custodians to guard it against corruption. It was the task of post-fifth-century jurists to guard the law against corruption, not to develop it in light of the ever-changing vicissitudes of social life.

In light of the prevailing historiography of Islamic law, it is no surprise that the earliest extant treatise of Islamic jurisprudence—Muḥammad b. Idrīs al-Shāfiʿī's *al-Risāla* (d. 204/820)—had been taken, until relatively recently, to have laid down the theoretical principles that forever guided the practical work of Muslim jurists thereafter. We now know better. The work of scholars over the past twenty-five years has demonstrated conclusively that Islamic law in the age of *taqlīd*, a period I will refer to as Islamic law's "postformative period," was at least as creative as that of the earliest periods of Islamic law, and that postformative jurists were far more than simply passive guardians of a perfect, albeit utopian, law who spent their lives debating and writing in a context of splendid isolation from the rough and tumble of social life.[1]

The conviction that the only works worthy of interest were written relatively early in Islamic legal history in turn influenced which works were selected for translation. As a result, for a long time, the only widely available translation of a work in Islamic theoretical jurisprudence was Majid Khadduri's translation of al-Shāfiʿī's *Risāla*.[2] More recently, thanks to the emergence of a new generation of scholars interested in the accomplishments of Muslim jurists in the postformative period, a wider variety of translations has begun to appear. A significant milestone in the translation of Islamic theoretical jurisprudence was the publication in 1992 of Bernard Weiss's commentary-cum-translation of *al-Iḥkām fī Uṣūl al-Aḥkām* by Sayf al-Dīn al-Āmidī (d. 630/1233),[3] a representative work of postformative Islamic theoretical jurisprudence that, in the centuries that followed al-Shāfiʿī, had taken a decidedly abstract and theological character, contrary to al-Shāfiʿī's express misgivings about speculative theology (*kalām*).

Shihāb al-Dīn al-Qarāfī and the Criterion for Distinguishing Legal Opinions from Judicial Rulings and the Administrative Acts of Judges and the Ruler

Al-Iḥkām fī Tamyīz al-Fatāwa ʿan al-Aḥkām wa Taṣarrufāt al-Qāḍī wa'l-Imām (The Criterion for Distinguishing Legal Opinions from Judicial Rulings and the Administrative Acts of Judges and the Ruler [hereafter, "the Criterion"])[4] by Shihāb al-Dīn Aḥmad b. Idrīs al-Qarāfī (b. 626/1228–d. 684/1285), translated here for the first time in English, is a work neither of theoretical jurisprudence nor of substantive law, but exists at the intersection of both. The Criterion aims to reconcile the idea of divinely revealed law with the fact that the practical norms of Islamic law can be applied only through the actions of particular human institutions. Al-Qarāfī, in this work, takes for granted the basic principles of theoretical jurisprudence (*uṣūl al-fiqh*) and the rightness of the already-existing rules of substantive law (*fiqh*) and attempts to explain how they operate in tandem within the political order of a normative Islamic state in which all public officials, acting under the authority of those rules and within their limitations, play distinctive roles in the elaboration, application, and enforcement of the rules. Al-Qarāfī's work therefore offers us a window into understanding how the author understood the state and society of his time as producing and reproducing a legal system that was, simultaneously, divinely revealed and humanly produced through the mediation of particular political institutions. The Criterion is a unique work in Islamic law insofar as it represents a systematic elaboration of the relationship between the theoretical principles and the practical rules of Islamic law, on the one hand, and a relationship to a particular normative conception of a state structure, on the other.

Before considering al-Qarāfī's theory of the relationship of Islamic law to the Islamic state, however, some historical background is warranted. Al-Qarāfī had been a relatively unknown figure in Western scholarship until Professor Sherman Jackson's work in the 1990s on al-Qarāfī rightly identified him as a major figure in postformative Islamic jurisprudence. This introduction builds on Jackson's analysis while offering a different interpretation of some of al-Qarāfī's positions.[5]

Al-Qarāfī lived in Cairo during the historically turbulent final years of the Ayyūbid state and the emerging new order of the Mamlūk state. During this period, which followed the final and complete collapse of the Fāṭimid caliphate in Egypt and the final destruction of the rump ʿAbbāsid caliphate in Iraq at the hands of the Mongols,[6] the distinctive institutions of the postcaliphal age were crystallizing throughout the Nile Valley and the Fertile Crescent.[7] Postcaliphal states during this period were ruled through an alliance of the military elite and urban notables, usually the merchants and religious scholars. In contrast to the ideals of the early ʿAbbāsid and Fāṭimid caliphates and those in the doctrinal works of the fifth century such as *al-Aḥkām al-Sulṭāniyyaa* (*The Ordinances of Government*), by the Shāfiʿī jurist Abū'l-Ḥasan ʿAlī b. Muḥammad al-Māwardī (d. 450/1058) and the Ḥanbalī jurist Abū Yaʿlā Muḥammad b. al-Ḥusayn al-Farrāʾ (d. 458/1066),[8] the caliphate had ceased to operate as a centralized state with provincial rulers tightly bound to the center. Instead, local dynasties emerged from the ranks of the leading members of the provincial military elite. These dynasties, of which the Ayyūbids were a leading example, tended to lack a strong central ruler, and, instead, the head of the dynasty at any given moment always faced the challenge of maintaining control of the state through a web of alliances with other leading members of the military elite, each of whom was in effective control of other regions and cities constituting the state's territory.

The postcaliphal order suffered from chronic instability throughout the Ayyūbid and Mamlūk periods as a result of continual competition among the military elite, whose temporary alliances would propel some to positions at the apex of the state while demoting others, oftentimes violently. The ʿAbbāsid caliph in Baghdad continued to be recognized as the nominal head of a unified Muslim community, at least until the Mongols, under Hulagu, sacked Baghdad in 1258 and put to death the then-reigning ʿAbbāsid caliph, al-Mustaʿṣim. Even before the sack of Baghdad, however, effective rule had devolved almost entirely into the hands of local dynasties, such as the Ayyūbids, with the caliph exercising effective control only over Baghdad and the Iraqi countryside. After the Mongol conquest of Baghdad and the execution of al-Mustaʿṣim, the Mamlūks established a "shadow" caliphate in Cairo and installed an ʿAbbāsid as nominal caliph who symbolically legitimated the Mamlūk political order.[9]

Beneath the veneer of instability at the top of postcaliphal states, however, civilian elites presided over what appears to have been a remarkably stable set of legal institutions that successfully discharged their functions despite the chronic instability found at the highest levels of the state. The most important of these legal institutions was the court, and its attendant officials, the judge (*al-qāḍī* or *al-ḥākim*), his assistants, and the witnesses. Alongside courts, the practice of giving legal opinions (*iftāʾ*) became formalized, and jurists responsible for giving legal opinions, *muftī*s, were able to claim substantial authority, even if they lacked coercive power. In addition to the judge and the mufti, numerous lesser officials existed, each of which played a role in ensuring the continued operation of the legal system. Lurking beneath the visible institutions of Islamic law during this period was the *madhhab*, traditionally rendered as "school of law," in the sense not of a physical structure, but rather as a doctrinal school of law, constituted by a common approach to the study of the law, and, even more important, a shared commitment to a particular set of authoritative legal texts and materials that constituted the foundational views of the school in question.

By the time of al-Qarāfī, four legal schools had come to be recognized as legitimate within Sunni Islam: the Ḥanafīs, the Mālikīs, the Shāfiʿīs, and the Ḥanbalīs. In the Ayyūbid-Mamlūk state, particularly in Egypt, the Shāfiʿīs were the most powerful school of law, at least in the early portion of al-Qarāfī's legal career, but the star of the Ḥanafīs was quickly rising. The early Mamlūk sultan al-Ẓāhir Baybars (r. 658/1260–676/1277) instituted a form of equality among the four different Sunni schools of law when he appointed four chief judges, one from each school, to hear disputes in the Mamlūk state.[10]

The *madhhab* was both a cause and an effect of the regime of *taqlīd*, for not only was it the effect of the labors of postformative jurists as they endeavored to systematize the teachings of earlier *mujtahid*s, or master jurists, but also it produced and reproduced the system of *taqlīd* by effectively regulating the ability of jurists to depart from established doctrines. The doctrines of the legal schools, then, in an important sense, provided a baseline set of norms that helped establish legitimate authority in the absence of stable centralized states. The stability in the quotidian institutions of the law served as an important counterbalance to the frequent changes that took place in the identity of the ruler and the governors of the state's cities and regions. No doubt the very instability of personal rule in this period made more urgent the articulation of a theory of institutional legitimacy, something the Criterion aims to accomplish.

The legal pluralism endemic in Sunni Islam of that period, however, also threatened to undermine the very stability that the law and its institutions purported to provide on a more secure basis than the oftentimes-short reigns of the various officials who filled executive offices, whether as head of state (*sulṭān*) or as lesser executive officials, such as provincial governors or rulers of towns (s. *amīr*/p. *umarāʾ* and s. *wālī*/p. *wulāt*). The adherents of the different doctrinal schools suffered from their own conflicts, stemming in part from principled disagreements on the content of the law, and in part from secular rivalries, such as competition for various public offices, whether that of a judge, professorship, head of a school, or other position in the bureaucracy. Managing legal pluralism was therefore both a political challenge for the Mamlūk state and a jurisprudential one. Al-Ẓāhir Baybars's decision to appoint a chief judge from each of the schools was the political response to this problem, and the Criterion was an important jurisprudential and constitutional response to the same problem.

In law al-Qarāfī was a Mālikī. Theologically, he was an Ashʿarī and showed particular interest in the work of the Transoxianan theologian and Shāfiʿī jurist Fakhr al-Dīn al-Rāzī (d. 606/1209).[11]

His Ashʿarism appears in some of the most significant arguments he makes in the Criterion. One of the most important influences on his legal thought was another leading Shāfiʿī, al-ʿIzz b. ʿAbd al-Salām (d. 660/1262), who was commonly known as *sulṭān al-ʿulamāʾ*, "the ruler of the scholars."

While al-Qarāfī's close relationship with some Shāfiʿīs led some historians to assume that he was a Shāfiʿī, al-Qarāfī's commitments to the Mālikī *madhhab* are indisputable. It appears, then, that his relationship to Shāfiʿī scholarship was largely a result of his interest in theoretical jurisprudence, comparative law, and theology, not a lack of commitment to Mālikī doctrine. Nevertheless, as his multivolume work on Islamic substantive law, *al-Dhakhīra*,[12] demonstrates, al-Qarāfī took a great interest in comparative jurisprudence, comparing and contrasting Mālikī views with those of the two other major legal schools in the Arab Middle East, the Shāfiʿīs and the Ḥanafīs. Indeed, in some cases, for example, in his discussion of the caliphate, he simply summarizes the views of the Shāfiʿī jurist al-Māwardī.[13]

According to Jackson, the primary motive that led al-Qarāfī to pen the Criterion was a crisis arising out of the mismanagement or misapprehension of the legal consequences of the legal pluralism that was endemic to the Arab Middle East in al-Qarāfī's day. The judicial power, as a formal matter of constitutional law, was vested in one person, *al-qāḍī* (alternatively, *al-ḥākim*), who received his appointment from the sitting ruler. As a practical matter, however, this judge (the "chief judge") exercised judicial power through the appointment of numerous lieutenant judges (s. *nāʾib*/p. *nuwwāb*) who heard cases on a daily basis as representatives of the judge. After a lieutenant judge issued his judgment, he would send his decision to the chief judge, who would then record the judgment (*tasjīl al-ḥukm*). Upon so doing, the lieutenant judge's decision would become final, and if the losing party did not voluntarily comply with the decision, the appropriate executive authority could enforce (*tanfīdh*) it coercively.

The Shāfiʿī chief judge of al-Qarāfī's day, known as Ibn Bint al-Aʿazz (d. 665/1267), consistently refused to register the judgments of lieutenant judges if their rulings contravened the Shāfiʿī view, even if the lieutenant judge's ruling conformed with that of the lieutenant judge's own legal school. Although Ibn Bint al-Aʿazz's name is never explicitly mentioned in the Criterion, Jackson argued that it was the threat to the integrity of legal pluralism that was the catalyst for the Criterion. In Jackson's view, then, al-Qarāfī's analysis of the relationship of Islamic law and the state was intended to serve two distinct but related goals. The first was to restrain the arbitrary power of the ruling military elite by explaining the proper role of executive authority in an Islamic constitutional system. The second goal was to protect the integrity of the *madhhab* by providing a systematic doctrinal refutation of Ibn Bint al-Aʿazz's stubborn refusal to uphold legal decisions contrary to that of the Shāfiʿī school, at least in circumstances when the ruling in question conformed with the established position of a recognized school of law.

Overview of al-Qarāfī's Argument

Jackson's analysis of al-Qarāfī, while certainly insightful, risks overemphasizing the immediate political circumstances surrounding the production of the Criterion, a reading that could reduce it to a polemical piece that would have become obsolete once the

Mamlūk sultan Baybars acted decisively to resolve the judicial crisis by appointing four chief judges, one from each Sunni doctrinal school. The fact that al-Qarāfī's arguments influenced subsequent generations of jurists, including jurists outside the Mālikī school, however, suggests that there is much more that motivated the work than a response to an overreaching and idiosyncratic Shāfiʿī chief judge. The reading I propose of the Criterion departs from Jackson's interpretation by offering an internal reading of its arguments that does not depend on facts external to the text itself to explain the author's purpose, but instead views the Criterion as a principled response to a series of jurisprudential problems internal to Islamic law that manifested with acute clarity at that particular moment in its history, problems that arose in the course of theorizing what it meant to apply a divine law through the human instrumentality of the state.

This approach to the Criterion appears to be consistent with the formal structure of al-Qarāfī's argument, which takes the form of an extended dialogue between al-Qarāfī and his scholarly peers as they debate and discuss a series of questions related to the formulation and application of Islamic law in the particular institutional context of the decentralized postcaliphal order. The dialogue proceeds across forty questions, the last consisting of a series of admonitions directed to his fellow scholars dealing with how they should interact with one another as well as with members of the public.

The dialogue begins with al-Qarāfī's interlocutor asking him to define the essence of a judicial ruling (*ḥukm*), one of whose attributes, the interlocutor observes, is that it is universally binding, which means that no one—all things being equal—is entitled to challenge its substantive content or reverse it. On the other hand, the ruling's domain was limited to its specific facts, and did not apply prospectively to future litigants, even if they found themselves in the same circumstances as that which produced the original ruling. Al-Qarāfī contrasts it with two other kinds of legal acts, that of giving a legal opinion (*fatwā*) and the administrative act or decree of a public official (*taṣarruf bi-l-imāma*). A legal opinion bound only those who accepted its truth, whereas an administrative act was universally binding, subject to the right of other public officials, provided they had proper jurisdiction, to revise the act or decree, or even repeal it in its entirety.

One of the most significant features of al-Qarāfī's analysis of the problems presented in the Criterion is that his arguments, instead of following the structure of either the theological proofs used in works of speculative theology or the jurisprudential proofs developed in accordance with the principles of theoretical jurisprudence, derive from the immanent practices and norms that had already become well-established features of substantive Islamic law in its postformative period. Accordingly, instead of attempting to explain why a judicial ruling is universally binding according to scriptural sources interpreted pursuant to the canons of theoretical jurisprudence, he relies on established legal precedents that demonstrate that Mālikī authorities, when faced with a case that had been subject to a prior judicial resolution, abandon their own view of the law in favor of the rule applied by the judge.[14] In contrast, if the case had not been subject to a prior judicial ruling, they remain firm in adhering to their own conception of the law (question no. 26).

Al-Qarāfī's attempt to define a judicial ruling—and explain the puzzle surrounding why it is universally binding and unassailable but limited to its particular facts—then leads to a series of other questions that cover a broad range of theological, jurisprudential, legal, and jurisdictional questions. Yet the moral power of a judge's ruling is clearly the central problem driving the work, with the other questions he answers in the Criterion functioning either to explain how it is possible for a judge's ruling to take on this moral function or to distinguish judicial rulings from other legally binding acts of public officials, which, despite their binding character, do not have this moral effect, even though there may be a superficial similarity between those acts and a judicial ruling.

The crucial feature of a judicial ruling according to al-Qarāfī's analysis, and the one that distinguishes it from a legal opinion, on the one hand, or an administrative act, on the other, is that it functions as an origination (*inshāʾ*) (question no. 1) of a particular rule that absolutely and irrevocably resolves the dispute between the two particular parties to that dispute. According to al-Qarāfī, because a judge's ruling is an origination of a particular rule rather than a declaration or communication (*ikhbār*) of a ruling, the judge's resolution of the case not only binds the litigants but also precludes other legal officials, specifically, muftis who hold views that differ from, or may even contradict, the judge's ruling, from challenging the legitimacy of the judicial outcome, even on a moral basis. This is so even though before the ruling, it would have been legitimate for muftis holding dissenting views to the one eventually adopted by the judge to issue legal opinions in accordance with their own views. This, as well as other epistemological features of a judicial ruling, distinguish it from a legal opinion—which communicates a universal rule (*ʿāmm*)[15] in a nonbinding fashion—and an administrative act or decree—which, although it consists of a binding command, is prospectively subject to revision or even repeal.

In taking this position, al-Qarāfī intervened in a long-standing controversy in Islamic theology and jurisprudence that questioned whether the outcome of a judicial proceeding had any effect on the moral obligations of the litigants.[16] One view was that it did not. Under this view God had established the rules of Islamic law, and accordingly, the judge's task was simply to apply the relevant rule to the case. Although the judge could apply a correct or an incorrect rule to the dispute, in all cases, his decision could not alter God's preordained determination of the case. On this theory, judicial rulings are binding not because they are constitutive in any meaningful sense of moral or ethical duties but only for the pragmatic reason that conflicts must be resolved.[17] The view al-Qarāfī endorsed was that in cases of genuine dispute as to the correct legal rule, the judge's decision constituted the rule governing the case. Accordingly, the judge's ruling created two moral obligations that did not exist prior to the decision: first, a moral duty on the part of the litigants to comply with the judge's ruling; and, second, a duty on third parties, including muftis who had held contrary views of the law prior to the judge's ruling, to uphold the judge's decision. These two duties arose simply by virtue of the judge's ruling, independent of his ability to coerce compliance with his decision.

Al-Qarāfī, in opting for this latter view, seems to have dissented from what had been the prevailing opinion within the Mālikī school, namely, that a judicial ruling did not change the moral status of the acts covered by the judgment. Why did al-Qarāfī believe it was crucial to establish that the judicial ruling is an origination rather than a declaration or a communication of the appropriate rule? A possible explanation might be that were a judicial ruling simply a declaration or a communication of previously existing rule, the judge would essentially be no different from a mufti, because, in each case, the case is being resolved by reference to the universal textual proofs (*al-adilla al-ʿāmma*) set forth in revelation.[18] If that is the case, there are no grounds for preferring the view of the judge to the view of the dissenting mufti, and while material interests of efficiency and convenience would counsel the necessity of enforcing the judge's decision, it would not provide a moral resolution of the conflict. By classifying the judicial ruling as an origination, al-Qarāfī solves this problem by holding that the judge's ruling constitutes a new, specific (*khāṣṣ*) proof of God's law that applies to that particular case (but only to that particular case). That everyone must defer to the proof provided by the judge's decision flows as the consequence of a universally accepted canon of construction from theoretical jurisprudence, namely, that specific textual proofs are given priority over universal textual proofs. Under al-Qarāfī's analysis, then, the dissenter is not allowed to challenge the moral propriety of the judge's decision because, in so doing, he would be relying on the universal textual proof provided by revelation that is not sufficiently strong to overcome the particular proof instantiated in the judge's decision (question nos. 16 and 17).

Al-Qarāfī's analysis raises a series of difficult questions, one of which is the implication that some rules of Islamic law come into existence after the death of the Prophet Muḥammad and through the mediation of (ordinary) human activity. The second question of the Criterion raises this very point, with the interlocutor asking al-Qarāfī, "How can it be said that God, sublime is He, gave anyone the power to create rules that bind God's servants? And does anyone other than God, sublime is He, originate rules?" To answer this question, al-Qarāfī does not turn to textual interpretation or theology but rather to well-established, immanent practices in substantive Islamic law, the devices of the vow (*al-nadhr*) and the conditional oath (*al-taʿlīq*).

In the case of the vow, an otherwise ethically commendable act becomes obligatory by virtue of the decision by an individual with requisite legal capacity to make a solemn vow obliging himself to perform that commended act. In the case of a conditional obligation, any person is authorized to make the occurrence or nonoccurrence of a thing, event, or condition an occasion to bind himself to perform or refrain from a particular act.[19] It follows, then, according to al-Qarāfī that "if it has been established that God, sublime is He, gave every person—even if he is uneducated and ignorant—the authority to originate rules for himself in the law without even a stipulation of necessity, it is, a fortiori, the case that He would give the authority to originate rulings to judges, given their knowledge and elevated status, in light of the necessity to restrain stubbornness, repel corruption, put out the fire of discord and resolve disputes." Theoretical jurisprudence also provides a proof in favor of his position, namely, the consensus that it is obligatory to follow the judge's decision, but this obligation "arose only after the judge's ruling, not prior to it, because the particular case, prior to the fact of the judicial ruling, was potentially governed by all valid legal opinions, each of which could have been subjected to all kinds of challenges and objections. We do not mean by 'origination' other than this feature of a judicial ruling, namely, its unassailability" (question no. 2).

Not all judicial rulings, however, are originations of a legal rule. Al-Qarāfī explains that in some cases, when a judge applies a universally acknowledged rule, his only role is that of a fact-finder who, if he is satisfied that the legally relevant facts (*asbāb*) have been proved (*thubūt*), simply enforces (*tanfīdh*) the applicable rule (question no. 30). In such a case, then, the judicial ruling, once the facts are proved, is not an origination but a mere application of the preexisting rule. Another example is when a judge applies a rule to resolve a case that, in fact, is not a legitimate rule of Islamic law. In such a case, the judge's ruling cannot constitute an origination of a specific proof of God's law because it does not rely on a valid rule of decision and is thus the equivalent of a legal error.

A judicial decision can constitute an origination of a rule only if two conditions are met: first, the legal dispute takes place in an area of law in which no common rule exists (*mukhtalaf fīhi*), and, second, the controversial opinion that forms the basis of the judicial ruling is itself based on a reasonable interpretation of revelation. Thus, he tells us not only that a judge's decision that is contrary to consensus "lacks any status" but also that "when a judge rules in accordance with a view that is poorly attested, his judicial ruling is given no consideration and must be repealed. Accordingly, when considering whether a particular judicial ruling is valid, one must consider whether the textual evidence for the judicial ruling is "reasonable" (question no. 1). Later, al-Qarāfī explains that there are four broad circumstances in which a judicial ruling in a controversial area of the law must be repealed: if it is contrary to consensus (*ijmāʿ*), universal legal principles (*al-qawāʿid al-ʿāmma*),[20] a univocal text of revelation (*naṣṣ*), or an a fortiori analogy (*al-awlā*).

For al-Qarāfī, then, the rules of Islamic law exist along four dimensions. First, there are universally acknowledged rules, such as the obligation of the debtor to pay his debt to his creditor, or that the thief's hand is subject to amputation. Second, there are controversial rules based on reasonable interpretations of revelation. Third, there are the universal rules that qualified jurists derive through the interpretation of revelatory indicants. These three classes of rules comprise what he calls those rules that are established simply by virtue of revelation (*mā taqarrara fī aṣl al-sharʿ*), and they constitute the body of legal doctrines that form the basis for legitimate legal opinions. Fourth, there are the particular rules "which He entrusted to individuals" to originate in accordance with specific procedural rules, such as vows, conditional obligations, and, according to al-Qarāfī, judicial rulings in controversial areas of law, provided the judge rules in accordance with a valid rule of law.

Rules that are established simply by virtue of revelation are discovered exclusively through the hermeneutical techniques and juridical principles set out in the principles of theoretical jurisprudence, and for this reason, one is justified in referring to them as prepolitical rules: neither their ontological existence nor our apprehension of them as morally obligated individuals (*mukallafūn*) is contingent on the existence of any particular political order. In the case of decisions that are originations of rules, however, the relevant decision maker must have been validly appointed to an office granting him the power to originate rulings in controversial areas of the law. Such rules are therefore explicitly dependent on the existence of a legitimate political order. Accordingly, one can appropriately contrast originations and, as shall be further explained, other rules of Islamic law produced via the mediation of political institutions, as political rules, from the prepolitical rules that are the product of learned interpretation of revelation and that constitute the specialized field of learning that constitutes substantive jurisprudence (*fiqh*).

I turn to the issue of appointment later. Here, I discuss in greater detail al-Qarāfī's requirement that a judge is limited to ruling in accordance with reasonable interpretations of revelation. In other words, only judicial rulings that are the product of reasonable interpretations of the law result in an origination of a particular rule that is, in fact, morally unassailable and universally binding.

As a negative matter, the relevant decision maker who purports to originate a judicial ruling must not apply a rule of law that violates consensus, a univocal text, an a fortiori analogy, or universal rules. This condition applies whether the decision maker is a master jurist or follows the doctrines of a master jurist, even though as a practical matter, of course, al-Qarāfī, as a postformative jurist, was writing in an era when judges largely, if not entirely, deferred to the views of one of the four Sunni schools of law. If a judge rules in such a fashion, his decision is automatically void, unless a valid countervailing consideration exists that justifies contravention of one of these four principles.

The clearest case of a countervailing consideration is a valid textual indicant that justifies the particular ruling, even if it contradicts universal legal principles. Al-Qarāfī provides several examples of extraordinary contracts that "contravene universal rules, texts and manifest analogy." Such contracts may nevertheless be upheld by courts in reliance on "particular textual indicants attesting to their validity," in light of the rule previously mentioned, namely, that the rules, texts, and manifest analogies that would invalidate those contracts are based on universal textual indicants, whereas particular textual indicants support the contracts at issue, so when there is a conflict between a universal indicant and a particular one, the particular is given greater interpretive weight. If, however, the countervailing consideration is weak, such as a poorly attested precedent from the Prophet or a companion, or absent entirely, such as the continued applicability of the presumption of the absence of obligation (*al-barāʾa al-aṣliyya*), then a judge's decision contradicting "universal rules, univocal texts and manifest analogy" must be overturned (question no. 29).

Al-Qarāfī does not limit valid countervailing considerations to particular textual indicants but also admits that circumstantial factors can function as a valid countervailing consideration. Al-Qarāfī gives two examples of rules that are valid despite the fact that they contradict universal legal principles based on circumstantial factors. The first is Mālik's opinion that the tax collector's estimate of a farmer's date crop is conclusive for purposes of assessing the farmer's tax liability, even if the harvested amount turns out to have been less than the tax collector's assessment. The second is the Mālikī rule that holds public artisans such as porters strictly liable for damage to the property of their customers, even though the usual rule is that if a person voluntarily gives his property to another, a bailment (*amāna*) is created, with the result that the bailee (*al-amīn*) is not liable for damage to the property in the absence of his negligence (question no. 33). Both of these rules contradict universal legal rules, but the particular circumstances of these two cases justify departure from the general principle in order to preserve the public good. Accordingly, nontextual indicants—at least for those doctrinal schools that accept them, like the Mālikī school followed by al-Qarāfī—such as "blocking the means" (*sadd al-dharīʿa*) and "unregulated benefits" (*maṣāliḥ mursala*) can also serve as valid countervailing considerations suitable to justify a departure from what is otherwise a univocal text, legal rule, or manifest analogy.

As a positive manner, if the judge practices *taqlīd* (which, as a practical matter, would be true for virtually all judges of al-Qarāfī's era in the Arab Middle East), his rulings that are in accordance with the judge's doctrinal school of law (*madhhab*) are almost always effective to originate a ruling that is unassailable and universally binding. In al-Qarāfī's analysis, reliance by a judge on the established rules of the doctrinal schools provides assurance that the interpretation of revelation is reasonable, and therefore that the judge's decision will be immune from repeal, except in the rare case when a school of law endorses a rule that contradicts universal legal rules, a univocal text, or manifest analogy and is not supported by a valid countervailing consideration.[21]

What does it mean for a judge to rule in accordance with the teachings of a doctrinal school of law? Al-Qarāfī is at pains to define what, precisely, is normative about the teachings of any doctrinal school. He begins by explaining that the normatively significant teachings of a doctrinal school are limited to pure doctrines of law that are themselves based on reasonable interpretations of revelation and are distinctive in one way or another to the school. Accordingly, rules of Islamic law that are held in common, such as the obligation to pray five times a day, to fast the month of Ramadan, or to pay debts, cannot be attributed to a doctrinal school and thus are not an object of *taqlīd*.

The pure rules of law consist of five parts: the substantive rule (*al-ḥukm*), or whether the action is obligatory, forbidden, permitted, commendable or disfavored; its legal cause (*al-sabab*), or the legal causes that produce the relevant legal effect; its conditions (*al-shurūṭ*), or the legal conditions that must be satisfied in order for the legal effect to come into existence; its impediments (*mawāniʿ*), or negative conditions whose presence precludes the legal effect of the rule from coming into existence; and, finally, the kinds of evidence (*al-ḥijāj*) that can be used to prove the existence of the previous three elements in a legal action (question no. 37).[22]

Factual assessments attributed by a doctrinal school to the master jurist or other authority whose views it follows, however, are not part of the normative teachings of a doctrinal school and therefore cannot be a legitimate object of *taqlīd.* To put this issue in terms familiar to an Anglo-American lawyer, *taqlīd* is limited to pure questions of law, whereas questions of fact and mixed questions of law and fact are not. The reason for the distinction is that a *muqallid* is permitted to defer only to the master jurist's legal conclusions as communicated in his legal opinions (s. *fatwā*/ p. *fatāwā*). Viewed from a positive perspective, the master jurist's expertise is limited to the derivation of substantive legal rules (*al-aḥkām*) from the relevant textual indicants provided by revelation (*al-adilla al-sharʿiyya*). For example, a *mujtahid*'s conclusion that territory incorporated into the Islamic state by force of arms (*ʿanwa*) is held in trust (*waqf*) for the benefit of the entire Muslim community—and thus is not eligible for private ownership—is a valid rule of law that may be applied by judges who follow the views of the master jurist who expressed the view; however, it would be impermissible for such a judge to adopt the master jurist's factual conclusion that a particular territory, such as Egypt, within the Islamic state was conquered by force of arms and was, therefore, legally held in trust.

Factual assessments cannot serve as valid objects of *taqlīd* because in such circumstances the master jurist is simply acting as a fact witness (*shāhid*), reporting knowledge that he obtained either firsthand or indirectly from another source. Such a report is distinct from a master jurist's report regarding the content of a rule of law (*fatwā*), insofar as the latter derives from his interpretation of the meanings of the relevant textual indicants provided by revelation. As a fact witness, the master jurist is no different from any other fact witness, and the admissibility of his testimony with respect to the occurrence or nonoccurrence of an element of a legal claim is subject to the same rules that apply to the admissibility of evidence generally. Because determination of the reliability of fact witnesses falls within the exclusive jurisdiction of the judge when he tries a claim brought by particular claimants, the master jurist's statements of fact are not a legitimate object of deference.

Al-Qarāfī's distinction between law and fact in turn partially underwrites another important dimension of his discussion of the relationship between adjudication and legal interpretation. A judicial ruling (*ḥukm*) is the union of both the legal rule originated by the judge and his factual findings regarding the existence (or nonexistence) of the relevant legal causes, conditions, and impediments. Because a legal judgment cannot come into existence until the judge makes these relevant factual findings, a judge's ruling is constituted differently from the legal opinion underlying his decision, which is derived exclusively from an act of textual interpretation without regard to the particular facts of any case. The fact that a judicial ruling unites the abstract with the particular further distinguishes a judge's decision from a mufti's legal opinion and buttresses his characterization of the judicial ruling as an origination of a particular rule.

His insistence that the judge's ruling is an origination, however, seems to be in tension, if not outright contradiction, with the theological view that the divine law is eternal, as is God. To defend against this objection, al-Qarāfī introduces an already well-established distinction in medieval Muslim thought that differentiated between mental speech (*kalām nafsānī*) and audible speech (*kalām lisānī*) (question no. 5). Muslim theologians first introduced this idea in connection with their disputes regarding the eternal nature of divine language as a solution to the paradox of the eternity of divine speech with its historical manifestation in particular human languages such as Arabic. For Ashʿarī theologians, only God's mental speech was eternal. In its eternity, it was pure simplicity, free of all contingent features such as sounds, parts of speech, and rules of grammar that characterize audible human speech. God's audible speech, the speech that is manifested in historical revelation, however, is created and takes on the contingent attributes of particular human languages such as Arabic. What this means as a practical matter is that revelation, viewed as an empirical phenomenon, is not God's eternal speech but only evidence of that eternal speech. Accordingly, the linguistic expression of divine revelation is not the substance of divine law but merely the evidence of the divine law that remains part of God's eternal, mental speech.[23]

Al-Qarāfī asserts that a judge, when he makes a legal judgment, originates a ruling that had not existed prior to the moment of his decision, but this is solely from the perspective of the judge, and not God; knowledge of the judge's ruling is eternal from the perspective of God, but it is an originated rule from the subjective perspective of the judge issuing it. Indeed, contrary to the case of God's knowledge of the ruling, which is eternal and everlasting, the judge's origination of the rule is a contingent and transient event, and it disappears in the instant he makes it. For that reason, al-Qarāfī assigns the origination to the judge's mental speech and describes the empirical manifestation of the ruling, whether by the judge's act of writing out his decision or by announcing it orally or having it suitably solemnized by appropriate witnesses, as a report (*ikhbār*) by the judge of the rule's origination in his mental speech. The origination may have taken place in the moment immediately prior to his communication of the ruling, or it may have taken place at a considerable time prior to its communication. What is crucial, however, is that the origination of the ruling takes place within the mental reasoning of the judge, his pure mental speech, and that is what gives the judge the subjective perception that he has introduced something new into the legal analysis that did not exist prior to his reasoning. The audible or written expression of the ruling, therefore, is nothing more than a manifestation of the conclusions previously reached by the judge's mental speech (question no. 8).

The judge's ruling constitutes a *particular* indicant of divine law that, according to al-Qarāfī, can validly stand in opposition to the evidence provided by the *universal* indicant relied upon by master jurists holding a contrary view of the case. Because principles of theoretical jurisprudence require giving effect to the particular in situations when the particular conflicts with the general, it then follows that all master jurists, and those jurists who follow their views, are obliged to accept the evidence of God's law as disclosed by the judge's ruling rather than insisting on the rule supported by the universal indicant that forms the basis of their legal opinion.

A judge's decision, then, is a more reliable source for knowing God's law in that particular case than the universal indicants found in revealed texts. It achieves its evidentiary strength, however, by its specificity, and accordingly, it cannot speak to other cases that have not yet been adjudicated. Accordingly, while a master jurist, or any of his followers, may not challenge the validity of a judge's decision—provided that it is based on a reasonable interpretation of revelation—on the basis of a contrary view of the law, they remain free to apply their own reasoning to cases that have yet to be adjudicated. Al-Qarāfī's theory that immunizes a judge's decision from repeal based on a different interpretation of the law at the same time affirms the continuing validity of the contrary rules followed by other doctrinal schools with respect to any other case that had yet to be conclusively and validly adjudicated by a judge. If the next case with facts similar to the first is heard by a judge with a view of the case contrary to the first judge, the contrary decision of the second judge too will enjoy the status of an unassailable and universally binding rule, but again, only with respect to that particular case.

The constitutional function of judges, however, is not limited to originating rules in areas of the law characterized by reasonable disagreement among the master jurists. Judges sometimes play crucial roles in areas of the law governed by uncontroversial rules if those rules are not self-executing. In such circumstances individuals are foreclosed from exercising these legal rights in the absence of a prior judicial ruling affirming that they may exercise such rights. Al-Qarāfī identifies three general contexts in which this is the case (question no. 32).

The first circumstance is a case where, although the legal rule may be clear, determination of the remedy, or its application in particular circumstances, requires factual investigation, circumspection, or both. An example of such a rule would be the right of a woman, in Mālikī doctrine, to obtain a divorce if her husband becomes bankrupt. Application of this rule requires a judge to ascertain that the husband has indeed become insolvent and that the wife possessed a valid claim for maintenance, it being the view of Mālik that a wife is estopped from claiming divorce on the grounds of bankruptcy if, at the time she married her husband, he was already insolvent.

While the right of a woman to obtain a judicial divorce in the event of her husband's insolvency is a controversial one, this principle applies equally to cases in which the substantive rule is a matter of consensus, but its application requires the exercise of empirical judgment. Accordingly, while jurists agree that it is appropriate to apply punishments to *taʿzīr* crimes (a class of crimes whose penalties have not been specified by revelation, in contrast to the *ḥudūd* crimes, the penalty for which revelation specified), only a judge is authorized to do so, even in cases where the conduct penalized is universally condemned, such as misappropriation of another person's property (*ghaṣb*), because judgment is required to determine the appropriate quantum of punishment.

The second circumstance is where enforcement of an otherwise uncontroversial rule by individual members of society would lead to disorder (*ḥaraj*) and perhaps even strife (*fitna*). The clearest examples of such rules are the scriptural penalties known as the *ḥudūd*. Although the law specifies these punishments with precision, along with the legal causes necessitating the punishments, if individuals were given unilateral authority to enforce such rules, chaos, bloodshed, and injustice would necessarily be the outcome. Accordingly, enforcement of these punishments is necessarily limited to public officials.

The third circumstance in which judicial intervention is required to authorize action is a case in which there are conflicting claims of rights between private persons and claims of God. Islamic law divides legal claims into two categories, one that belongs to private persons and a second that is said to belong to God.[24] For present purposes the chief difference is that the former may be waived by the human claimant, but the latter may not, because human beings lack the authority to compromise the demands God imposes on people as his servants. Claims of God are mandatory rules, whereas rights of private persons are permissive and amenable to compromise. Some cases may involve a conflict between a private claim and a mandatory rule of law. In these circumstances, a judicial decision is required to resolve the conflict. If the master of a slave, for example, were to effect a partial manumission of his slave, the slave would not be entitled to claim freedom without a judicial decision, because the case presents three conflicting claims. The first is the master's private claim to continued part ownership of the slave; the second is the slave's private claim to be free; and the third is God's claim for the liberation of the slave. Only a judicial ruling can resolve the competition between the private claims and the claims of God because it is only the judge, according to al-Qarāfī, who is authorized to represent God's claims.

Al-Qarāfī's theory of adjudication, then, provides four reasons judges are essential for the operation of Islamic law. The first is that the law itself is known only imperfectly, as evidenced by the presence of controversial rules. When there is a dispute in an unsettled area of the law, it is the role of the judge in these circumstances to originate a particular rule, in light of the universal indicants of the revealed law and the particular evidence of the litigants, which conclusively resolves their dispute, morally and politically.

The second reason judges are needed is related to what Anglo-American lawyers would call due process and fundamental fairness, and it is reflected in the juridical principle, shared by common law and Islamic law, that a person may not be the judge of his or her own case.[25] Thus, a woman whose husband becomes insolvent after her marriage may not declare herself divorced until a neutral judge ascertains the facts of her claim and gives the husband an opportunity to contest her claim. Here, the issue is simply that she cannot exercise her rights unilaterally because to do so would violate, or potentially violate, the rights of another party, namely, her husband. The judge in this instance functions as a neutral fact-finder who can ascertain the existence (or nonexistence) of the relevant legal facts.

The third reason judges are needed is to solve a collective action problem, or what is perceived to be a collective action problem, such as individual claims to public property, or the fear of conflict that could result from unilateral judgment, even in the application of uncontroversial rules of law.

The fourth reason is peculiar to Sunni Islam's hybrid structure of theocracy and secular (human) government. Because the judge is an authorized delegate of God, it is his responsibility to resolve conflicts between the private claims of human beings and the claims of God. Private individuals, such as a master who effects a partial manumission of his slave, can assert (or waive) only their own particular claims. When a dispute implicates a claim of God, the private rights of all are effectively suspended until such time as the case is brought before a judge who can conclusively resolve the conflicting claims, particularly God's claim in the dispute.

Al-Qarāfī's routine reference to the judge as God's delegate led Baber Johansen to suggest that for al-Qarāfī and the Mālikīs more generally, the judge, when ruling in controversial areas of the law, functions as a "legal prophet" who reveals God's law, as applied to that particular case, to humanity.[26] There is no doubt that al-Qarāfī locates the judge's authority to originate rulings in controversial areas of the law from the Prophet's authority to resolve disputes, provided that the judge exercises this power consistently with what God has revealed:

> He, therefore, when reporting his judicial ruling, is reporting to the people what he, himself, has decided, in reliance

> on the authority that God, Mighty and Elevated is He, has delegated to him via succession from the authority of God's Messenger, may God bless him and grant him peace, as set forth [85] in God's saying, sublime is He, "And make judgment among them based on what God has revealed." (Question no. 24)

Johansen's suggestion that the judge according to al-Qarāfī is the equivalent of a legal prophet must be qualified, however, by reference to al-Qarāfī's rejection of the notion that the judge is merely communicating or transmitting a rule from God, and his adamant insistence in attributing the rule to an act of the judge himself. Accordingly, al-Qarāfī explains:

> When he acts in a judicial capacity, he is similar to the judge's delegate (*nā'ib al-ḥākim*), adjudicating cases personally, originating obligations and releases in accordance with what the legal causes require in light of the factual evidence presented to him. He can exercise this authority because the judge who appointed him delegated that power to him. This is in contrast to the authority of a translator, who is obliged simply to explain the sense of the principal's words, but not to supplement them with anything from himself. *Just as the judge's delegate reports about himself that he originated an obligation, so too does the judge who is a master jurist in the revealed law: he reports that he originated an obligation in his capacity as God's delegate, Mighty and Elevated is He, on the earth and over His creatures, insofar as He has delegated to him the power to originate judicial rulings among His creation.* (Question no. 24, emphasis added)

Indeed, this notion of the judge exercising delegated power applied to the Prophet Muḥammad himself. Al-Qarāfī makes clear that even the Prophet Muḥammad, when he acted as a judge, exercised delegated power and was *not* transmitting to the litigants what would amount to divine speech:

> When he [i.e., the Prophet Muḥammad] acts as a judge, he follows God's command to him, Sublime is He, insofar as he originates rulings in accordance with the litigants' evidence (*al-ḥijāj*) and the legal causes (*al-asbāb*). *He is not, however, following God's command in the sense that he is transmitting that ruling from God, Sublime is He, because that which is delegated to him from God, Sublime is He, is not the same as that which is transmitted from God, Sublime is He.* (Question no. 25, emphasis added)

The judge's ruling has the moral effect of express revelation not because it is substantively revelation, but because the judge is exercising a power that has been properly delegated to him via a chain of authority that goes back to the Prophet Muḥammad himself in a manner that is substantively legitimate. The power to originate universally binding and unassailable rules is therefore contingent upon the party who purports to exercise that power possessing a legitimate delegation of authority *and* that party's exercise of that power in accordance with the substantive jurisprudential norms that guarantee that it amounts to a ruling that is in accordance with "what God has revealed."

Originating legal rules, however, is not simply the prerogative of any appropriately learned person with the requisite degree of moral integrity applying universal rules to the facts of particular cases. Only if the judicial power has been validly delegated to that person does he have this capacity. Accordingly, we need to understand how, in al-Qarāfī's view, a person becomes vested with such authority. His theory, it turns out, is derivative of his understanding of prophetic authority because, as he explains, public officials can possess only those powers that the Prophet Muḥammad himself had exercised during his lifetime.

Jackson has suggested that al-Qarāfī's theory of caliphal power set out in the Criterion was perhaps the first time that a Muslim jurist had attempted to reconcile the religious duty of Muslims to obey the Prophet Muḥammad while affirming only a qualified duty of obedience to the caliph as successor of the Prophet.[27] Al-Qarāfī developed his theory through a careful functional analysis of prophetic precedent, concluding that the Prophet's actions (p. *taṣarrufāt*/s. *taṣarruf*) always fell into one of four different categories, each of which had a different normative function for the formulation and application of Islamic law. These four functions were (1) his capacity as the apostle of God (*rasūl*), (2) his capacity as interpreter of revelation (*muftī*), (3) his capacity as judge (*qāḍī* or *ḥākim*), and (4) his capacity as head of state (*imām*).

Insofar as the Prophet was acting in the first capacity, he transmitted revelation to humanity pursuant to divine command:

> Messengership is God's command, sublime is He, to him, i.e., the Messenger of God, to communicate revelation to others. Accordingly, . . . when he acts as the messenger of God, . . . he is communicating and transmitting from God, Sublime is He. (Question no. 25)

When the Prophet acts in the capacity of God's apostle, he is simply an instrument for the communication (*muballigh*) of divine revelation. While revelation came to a conclusive end with the Prophet's death, the record of revelation, as manifested in the words of the Quran and the Prophet's Sunna,[28] continues to be transmitted until the end of time.

His conduct as a mufti, by contrast, consisted in his reporting to people "his understanding of the revealed indicants in respect of God's law" (question no. 25). Unlike his conduct as God's apostle, where the Prophet communicates precisely what God has revealed to him, when he acts as a legal interpreter, his conduct as a mufti is constituted through the Prophet's own subjectivity: he communicates to the people *his* understanding of the meaning of revelation. This in turn is precisely what muftis do after the Prophet's death: they communicate to the people their understanding of what revelation means. For this reason, al-Qarāfī compares the role of the mufti to that of the translator (*tarjumān*): his function is to transmit, faithfully, the meanings of one speaker—in this case, God—into the idiom of others who are incapable of understanding the first speaker's words for themselves. Because the Prophet's understanding of revelation is perfect, however, it constitutes authoritative communication of legal rules. Accordingly, his activity as a mufti is effectively assimilated into his function as messenger. This, however, is not the case for muftis who follow the Prophet: their interpretations of divine revelation are fallible and, accordingly, are binding only upon those who accept (*taṣdīq*) their interpretations as correct. The infallibility of the Prophet's interpretations of revelation, however, does not transform them from a human activity into one of mere transmission.

According to al-Qarāfī, when the Prophet acts in this capacity, and authorizes individuals to act in a certain way, he has effectively vested individuals with a legal right that endures until the end of time:

> As for his conduct . . . in giving legal opinions, messengership and communicating revelation from God, all of that is constitutive of revealed law which applies to human beings until the Day of Judgment. We are obliged to follow every rule that he has communicated to us from his Lord in accordance with the existence or non-existence of its legal causes, without regard to the ruling of a judge or the permission of the imam, because he, may God bless him and grant him peace, when acting in these three capacities, was communicating to us the connection between that rule and that legal cause. . . . In these cases he was not originating a judicial ruling from himself, nor was he acting in the capacity of an imam, i.e., making rules in accordance with his perception of the public good (*lā murattiban lahu bi-ra'yihi 'alā ḥasab mā iqtaḍathu al-maṣlaḥa*). . . . All of humanity is entitled to pursue these legal causes directly and individually and obtain the benefits of their legal effects without recourse to any judge to originate a rule, or to the current imam for permission to act on, and obtain the benefit of, these legal causes. (Question no. 25)

His conduct as a judge, by contrast, consisted of originating particular rules in reliance on the evidence that the parties to the dispute submitted to him *and* what God had revealed to him. His decision was not a transmission of divine revelation to the parties, but rather the product of his own judgment, a fact that al-Qarāfī asserts is confirmed by a statement attributed to the Prophet Muḥammad in which he warns prospective litigants that, because some are more eloquent in presenting their case than their adversaries, he may inadvertently rule against the party with the just claim:

> Judicial rulings, by contrast, are an origination and an imposition of an obligation that comes from him, may God bless him and grant him peace, in accordance with the conclusions he reaches regarding the existence or nonexistence of the relevant legal causes (*al-asbāb*) in light of the litigants' evidence (*ḥijāj*). For that reason he, may God bless him and grant him peace, said, "You bring to me your disputes, and it may very well be the case that one of you is a better advocate for his claim than his adversary. Accordingly, whoever wins his claim, but I award him something belonging to his brother, let him not take it, for I am giving him only a piece of Hell!" That indicates that judicial rulings are derivative of litigants' evidence and their ability to present it persuasively.[29] (Question no. 25)

While a legal opinion of the Prophet authorizes individuals to act in accordance with the rule communicated by the Prophet until the end of time, the fact that the Prophet awarded a right only in his capacity as a judge means that individuals are foreclosed from exercising such a right without first obtaining judicial ruling granting them that right:

> Whatever he . . . did in the capacity of a judge, like awarding ownership pursuant to a right of first-refusal; annulling marriages and contracts; [or,] divorcing women on account of

> the bankruptcy of their husbands . . . , it is not permissible for anyone to undertake any of these acts without first obtaining a judicial ruling from a sitting judge, in accordance with his practice . . . because he . . . did not permit these claims to be vindicated without a judicial ruling, so his community after him . . . is subject to the same principle. (Question no. 25)

Judges, therefore, have inherited from the Prophet the power to originate rules based on the litigants' evidence in accordance with the norms provided by revelation:

> He [i.e., the judge] is, therefore, when reporting his judicial ruling, reporting to the people what he himself has decided, in reliance on the authority that God . . . has delegated to him via succession from the authority of God's Messenger . . . as set forth [85] in God's saying, sublime is He, "And make judgment among them based on what God has revealed." (Question no. 24).

When the Prophet acted as head of state (*imām*), he exercised a function that was distinct from that of being a messenger, a mufti, or a judge, because the head of state exercises general police powers (*al-siyāsa al-ʿāmma*) whose function is "to direct the public and their affairs . . . [by] protecting them from harm, repressing the unjust, killing tyrannical oppressors, and securing God's servants throughout the state's domains (*al-bilād*), in addition to other matters of this nature" (question no. 25). Unlike apostleship or messengership, which entails communicating revelation; giving a legal opinion, which entails interpreting revelation; or giving a judicial ruling, which entails hearing litigants' evidence and determining whether they are sufficient to establish the applicable legal causes (*al-asbāb*) evidencing an entitlement, the head of state uses his own reasoning to lay down rules that achieve the public good (question no. 25). Accordingly, the reasoning involved in exercising the police power is different from that which is used in apostleship or messengership, acting as a mufti, or acting as a judge, insofar as exercise of the police power requires that the decision maker seeks the public good by considering the various empirical sources of evidence that disclose where the public good lies (question no. 4).

From the perspective of the legal system, actions undertaken by the Prophet in his capacity as head of state are known as administrative acts or decrees (*taṣarruf bi'l-imāma*), and are thus distinguished from his actions undertaken in the capacity of a mufti (*taṣarruf bi'l-fatwā*) and his actions undertaken in the capacity of a judge (*taṣarruf bi'l-ḥukm*). Actions that the Prophet took in the capacity of a head of state include, inter alia, actions such as "dividing spoils of war seized from the enemy on the battlefield; disbursing public funds in accordance with the public good; enforcing criminal penalties; organizing armies; fighting rebels; distributing public lands, whether agricultural or mines; and similar matters." Such actions therefore may not be undertaken by any particular individual unless the head of state first authorizes the action in question (question no. 25). Unlike a judicial ruling (*ḥukm*), which is unassailable and universally binding, however, a previous administrative act or decree (*taṣarruf bi-l-imāma*) may be modified, or even repealed in its entirety, by a decision of a subsequent officeholder. Unlike a legal opinion (*fatwā*), which binds only those who accept it as a truthful communication of divine law, a valid administrative act or decree is binding universally until such time as it is changed or repealed by a subsequent administrative act or decree.

The caliph or the imam, of course, inherits the Prophet's position as the head of state, which vests in him the authority to exercise the general police power in furtherance of the public good. According to al-Qarāfī, however, the caliph is also a mufti and a judge, which means that he is entitled to issue legal opinions as well as adjudicate cases. Far from expanding his power, however, recognizing him (and by necessary implication, lesser executive officials such as governors, rulers of cities, and so on) as having the powers of a judge and mufti in addition to that of the head of state paradoxically reduces his power in two respects. First, insofar as he is acting as a judge or as a mufti, his exercise of the judicial power or the power to give legal opinions, in each case, is subject to the same standards that applied to an ordinary judge or mufti. In other words, his legal opinions or his legal judgments, in order to be valid, would have to satisfy the same substantive standards of legitimacy that applied to all judges or muftis. Second, and much more controversially, Jackson argues that, according to al-Qarāfī's view, insofar as the caliph was simultaneously a mufti and a head of state, his actions ostensibly taken in his capacity as head of state could be recharacterized as a legal opinion, in which case individuals holding a contrary view would be free to ignore the caliph's commands.

Such a conclusion, were it correct, would have far-reaching implications for the ability of public officials to exercise the very power—the police power (*al-siyāsa al-ʿāmma*)—that had been entrusted to them, and indeed had justified the very existence of their offices as positions distinct from that of judges and muftis. Under this interpretation of al-Qarāfī, individuals could avoid a duty of compliance with an otherwise lawful act of the head of state (or those of another public official) by declaring the act in question to be a fatwa, which, by its terms, requires compliance only if a person accepts it as a true conception of revealed law.

Jackson relies on the following passage from al-Qarāfī's answer to the thirty-sixth question to support this conclusion:

> Among the acts of judges that are not judicial rulings are the legal opinions they give in connection with ritual and other matters, such as the illegality of marriage to certain women and the permissibility of marrying others, the ritual purity of certain bodies of water and the impurity of particular substances, and the obligation to wage war against non-Muslims, and other obligatory matters. None of these is a judicial ruling and accordingly anyone who does not accept that legal opinion is entitled to give a legal opinion in opposition to the legal opinion of a judge or the imam. [182] Likewise, if they command a good deed or prohibit an evil deed, and they themselves believe it to be good or evil, it is nevertheless permissible for someone who does not share that belief to refrain from doing as they command. (Question no. 36)

Commenting on this passage, Jackson writes that, because the Mālikīs and the Shāfiʿīs are of the view that "the overwhelming majority of the Prophet's actions were no more than fatwas . . . by analogy most of the statements of the caliph may likewise be treated as no more than fatwas."[30] Caliphal pronouncements on matters of ritual are obviously treated as legal opinions, and thus nonbinding, but Jackson also asserts that

> other matters, such as the obligation to wage jihad, are paralegal in that their resolution is solely a matter of discretion,

> not one of scripture identifying a causal relationship between a specific legal cause (*sabab*) and its corresponding legal ruling (*ḥukm*). According to al-Qarāfī's doctrine, caliphal pronouncements from either of these categories [i.e., ritual law and exercises of discretion disconnected from clear legal causes] constitute no more than fatwas.[31]

The difficulty with this reading of al-Qarāfī—aside from the fact that such a doctrine would not limit the caliph's power, but rather enfeeble it—is that it does not take into account the precise formulation of the thirty-sixth question. There, the questioner asked about which actions of judges and rulers are judicial rulings (*aḥkām*) and which are not, not which actions are fatwas and which are not. The fact that al-Qarāfī denies a particular action the status of a judicial ruling does not mean that it must be a fatwa; it could also be an administrative act. It is probably more reasonable to read these passages as simply denying that a ruler's decision to declare war constitutes an irrevocable and unassailable judicial ruling (*ḥukm*), without necessarily resolving whether such an action should be understood as a fatwa or as an administrative act. Al-Qarāfī's language would also make sense if we assumed that by denying that a declaration of war is a judicial ruling (*ḥukm*), he intended to classify such a decision as an administrative act, not a fatwa. Indeed, administrative acts are precisely paralegal in the sense described by Jackson; that is, they are based on the exercise of discretion rooted in an empirical assessment of welfare (*maṣlaḥa*). Clearly, they are not a claim arising out of scriptural interpretation, as would have to be the case were administrative acts to be viewed as fatwas, the defining feature of a fatwa being that it is an interpretation of scriptural indicants, not of the public good.

It would be odd indeed were a caliph or another executive official to declare war not on the basis of his asserted power as head of state but in his capacity as an interpreter of revelation! Indeed, al-Qarāfī makes clear in his analysis of the decision to go to war or to maintain peace with the enemy that the decision is based on an assessment of the community's well-being, not scriptural interpretation:

> The eighteenth kind [of act that is not a judicial ruling]: contracting a truce between Muslims and hostile non-Muslims. This is not a matter of legal controversy, but is permissible by consensus in accordance with its legal cause. Accordingly, the next head of state is free to determine whether the legal cause that justified contracting the truce remains in existence, in which case he affirms it, or not, in which case he cancels it. A truce is nothing more than an undertaking to cease hostility in circumstances of weakness. Accordingly, if it provides security, or canceling it results in attacks against the Muslims, it becomes unlawful to cancel it because it is contrary to the public good, not because it is a permanent peace treaty or categorical rejection of war. (Question no. 36)

Clearly, the decision to go to war or to maintain the peace cannot be understood to be a matter of scriptural interpretation. This decision is instead a matter of empirical judgment, something that places it squarely within the category of administrative acts that are binding because they are lawful commands of public officials, even if such acts are not unassailable and may be revised or repealed in their entirety by subsequent decision makers, or even the same decision maker.[32]

Moreover, Jackson's analysis does not appear to take into account al-Qarāfī's statement that, while affirming the right of dissenters to a caliphal fatwa to refuse to adhere to the caliph's view of the law, notes that a dissenter may nevertheless be under an obligation to adhere to the caliph's fatwa if "the imam calls him to denounce something, and opposition to him would amount to defiance, in which case obedience is obligatory for that reason, but not because it is a judicial ruling" (question no. 36). This suggests that even in cases of caliphal pronouncements that are unqualifiedly legal opinions and not administrative acts, dissenters may have an obligation to obey in order to further the public good.

Finally, al-Qarāfī's works in positive law seem to contradict the position that Jackson attributes to him in the Criterion. Al-Qarāfī, for example, states in his encyclopedic work in positive law, *al-Dhakhīra*, that jihad becomes obligatory upon the command of the caliph (*yataʿayyan bi-taʿyīn al-imām fa-man ʿayyanahu taʿayyana imtithalān li'l-ṭāʿa*),[33] a position that is well documented in other works of the Mālikī school, such as Ibn Shās's *ʿIqd al-Jawāhir al-Thamīna*.[34]

Outside of his reference to the possible duty to obey, for prudential reasons, a legal opinion with which one otherwise disagrees in certain exigent circumstances, al-Qarāfī's analysis generally leaves unanswered the relationship between administrative acts or decrees and the legal teachings of the various schools of law, and how conflicts between the two ought to be resolved. Suppose, for example, that the caliph prohibits reclamation of abandoned land (*iḥyāʾ al-mawāt*) without his prior permission. While such a command would be consistent with Ḥanafī teachings, the Shāfiʿī school holds that that no permission from the caliph is needed for a person to exercise his right to reclaim abandoned land (question no. 25). Al-Qarāfī, unfortunately, is silent as to whether a follower of the Shāfiʿī school in this circumstance is legally entitled to defy that command and act in reliance on the doctrine of his own legal school, or he is obligated to comply with the decision of the caliph or other relevant public official that is based in an exercise of the police power, even though he believes such a rule to be invalid.

For these reasons, Jackson's claim that al-Qarāfī's theory was intended, at least in part, to limit caliphal authority by authorizing jurists to recharacterize his actions as head of state as nonbinding fatwas is not convincing. Jackson's assertion that al-Qarāfī's theory also sought to prevent a politically powerful school of law from using its politically privileged position within the state to impose its own doctrines upon dissenters also seems overstated. Jackson argues that this is the effect of two doctrines that al-Qarāfī emphasized: the unassailability of a judicial ruling that applies a rule adopted by an established school of law, and the virtually absolute right of dissenters to follow the teachings of their own school in all cases that had not been resolved by a prior judicial ruling on the basis of a contrary rule.[35] Jackson's interpretation of these doctrines, however, does not take into account the fact that a hegemonic legal school could still impose its will by prevailing upon the rulers to appoint judges exclusively from its own ranks. Short of a claim that al-Qarāfī's theory imposed on the ruler an obligation to appoint judges from each of the different doctrinal schools, it is difficult to see how the unassailability of judicial rulings on its own represented a substantial obstacle in limiting the reach of rival legal schools that had achieved politically hegemonic status. Moreover, as the hypothetical involving a command prohibiting individuals from reclaiming fallow land demonstrates, there does not appear to be a sound basis in al-Qarāfī's writings to conclude that, in cases where a lawful governmental command contradicts a person's subjective interpretations of revealed law, al-Qarāfī proposes that there is a general right to ignore that command if it is not in conformity with a person's subjective apprehension of the law.

Jackson, however, is no doubt correct in emphasizing the importance of al-Qarāfī's functional understanding of the Prophet Muḥammad's mission and how that understanding in turn structured and limited the various powers of public officials in the Ayyūbid-Mamlūk polity of which al-Qarāfī was a part. Even if al-Qarāfī did not resolve systematically the relationship of the police power to the background principles of the jurists' substantive law, the very fact that the caliph's powers as judge and mufti were subjected to the same standards as other judges and muftis was itself a significant normative limitation on the powers of the caliph and represented an important achievement for Islamic constitutional law. Nevertheless, al-Qarāfī's achievements should be viewed not as superseding the doctrines of previous Muslim jurists such as al-Māwardī but rather as building on the doctrines set out in works such as *al-Aḥkām al-Sulṭāniyya* in order to define and delimit more precisely the legal powers of the various offices, something that al-Māwardī had failed to do in any meaningful fashion.[36]

Al-Qarāfī describes fifteen classes of public offices, beginning with that of the caliph himself, who enjoys, in theory at least, all the powers vested in the various lesser officers that al-Qarāfī describes, and concluding with paralegal officials, like official translators (*tarjumān*) and property appraisers (*muqawwim*), whose jurisdiction (*wilāya*) is limited to establishing relevant factual matters, such as preparing authoritative translations of either the judge's words or the litigants' words in cases where they do not speak the same language, or determining the value of property when it is in dispute.

On the basis of his description of the public offices of his day, we can identify three different kinds of political power. The first is the general police power, *al-siyāsa al-ʿāmma*, which is responsible for securing the public good, *al-maṣlaḥa al-ʿāmma*. The offices most closely connected with the police power are that of the caliph, the caliph's plenary minister, governors, ministers to governors (who may or may not enjoy plenary powers), and military commanders.

The second is the judicial power, *al-qaḍāʾ*. Ordinary judges exercise this power, which authorizes them to originate judicial rulings in controversial areas of the law and to enforce (*tanfīdh*) consensual rules, in each case, upon their proof in accordance with applicable evidentiary requirements (*ḥijāj*). Other offices, however, also enjoy these powers: most prominently, the five executive offices previously mentioned. Two other offices, however, also generally enjoy these two judicial powers: the jurisdiction over complaints (*al-maẓālim*) and lieutenant judges (*nuwwāb al-quḍāt*). The *maẓālim* judge differed from the ordinary judges insofar as this office granted its holder greater latitude in admitting circumstantial evidence and afforded him the authority to investigate claims proactively, whereas an ordinary judge was not given any investigatory role. Lieutenant judges differed from the appointing judge by the size of their dockets and the fact that they served at the pleasure of the appointing judge. The office of the market inspector (*wilāyat al-ḥisba*) also had the authority to originate judicial rulings in controversial areas of the law, but his jurisdiction was limited to disputes involving a public dimension, such as "the exterior windows of homes, stables for horses along public highways, and similar matters that are the subject of public regulation," but he notably lacked jurisdiction over contractual disputes, whether commercial or marital, whether governed by a controversial rule or a consensual one. Al-Qarāfī also mentioned specialized tribunals that were entrusted with exclusive jurisdiction over particular kinds of disputes, such as courts with jurisdiction over marriages or over the affairs of orphans. Here, the relevant decision makers enjoyed the two judicial powers of originating judicial rulings in controversial areas of the law and enforcing consensual rules upon their proof, but only on matters falling within their specialized jurisdiction. Arbitrators could also exercise the judicial power, but only after they had been duly appointed by the disputing parties, and only with respect to property claims, or claims that may be settled through a transfer of property. Arbitrators could not, therefore, originate or enforce rulings of criminal law or the law of personal status, such as marriage, divorce, freedom, or slavery. Tax collectors had judicial authority to originate judicial rulings in controversial areas of the law and enforce consensual rules, but only with respect to questions that fell within their taxing jurisdiction. Finally, although tax collectors who estimated the amount of crops that will be available at harvest time for purposes of assessing tax obligations do not enjoy even a limited judicial power, their estimates of farmers' crops were conclusive, and so their estimates were effectively originations of rulings for purposes of calculating the farmer's tax liability as of the date of the harvest.

The third power is that of enforcement, *tanfīdh.* It should be noted that al-Qarāfī uses this term in at least three senses. The first is when a judge (or someone exercising a judicial function) applies a consensual rule. Here, the relevant decision maker is simply finding the relevant facts (*al-asbāb*) and then automatically applying the rule that consensus identifies as applicable to the case once the relevant facts have been established. Because the rule is established by consensus, the judge does not play any role in formulating the law that applies to that case, and his role is therefore limited to fact-finding. This is in contrast to cases in which there is no consensus. There, to resolve the case, the judge must *originate* the applicable ruling even if there is no factual dispute to resolve.

Enforcement as fact-finding, however, differs from enforcement in its second sense, that of coercive enforcement of the laws, and is more properly viewed as part of the general police power.

As a general rule, judges lack coercive power to enforce their decisions. On this point, al-Qarāfī said:

> Judicial decisions are simply a matter of resolving litigants' disputes without regard to whether the judge possesses any share of the general police power (*al-siyāsa al-ʿāmma*). This is particularly clear in respect of a judge who lacks the power to enforce his decisions, as in the case of a weak judge ruling against a mighty king: he does no more than originate in his mind an obligation upon that mighty ruler, without the possibility of attempting to enforce it against him ever crossing his mind due to its impossibility for him. Accordingly, a judge, insofar as he is a judge, has no role other than to originate judicial rulings, while the power to enforce them is extrinsic to his role as judge. (Question no. 25).

Coercive enforcement of legal decisions, as part of the general police powers, is in the first instance the responsibility of the caliph, his ministers, and his governors—the first five classes of public officials that al-Qarāfī enumerated in his response to the thirty-third question. Judging, in the view of al-Qarāfī, therefore, is essentially a moral activity, and the empirical practicability of enforcement or nonenforcement of the ruling is irrelevant to the moral obligation of the parties to comply with the judgment. Indeed, al-Qarāfī clearly operates under the assumption that Muslims accept the moral conclusiveness of the judge's ruling, and therefore will generally comply with the judge's decision, even when it is contrary to their interests (question no. 32, [151]). As related to the judicial process, enforcement comes at the third and final stage of a lawsuit, the first being fact-finding and the second being the origination of the ruling (question no. 30, [138]).

The third and final sense in which al-Qarāfī uses enforcement is to describe the process by which a public official exercises the general police power in order to give effect to what the decision maker believes is the public interest. Thus, officeholders, when they are exercising the discretion delegated to them pursuant to the general police power, are said to be enforcing the public interest (*tanfīdh al-maṣāliḥ*) (question no. 33, fourteenth class of official).

Al-Qarāfī's tripartite classification of the kinds of legal activities found in the Islamic constitutional order—legal interpretation, adjudication, and police powers (which includes the power both to enforce valid law and to make rules in furtherance of the public good)—is functionally consistent with a notion of the separation of powers. Instead of designating particular offices as being defined exclusively by one of these three particular powers, however, al-Qarāfī distinguishes the exercise of these different powers by consideration of the different evidentiary premises that underlie the exercise of each. The lawmaking activities of muftis is a function of the interpretation of scriptural indicants; the judicial power is invoked when courtroom evidence, conjoined with a valid rule of law, forms the basis of decision; and the police power is invoked whenever empirical considerations of the public good form the basis of decision. In short, al-Qarāfī lays out a functional theory of the separation of powers that derives from an epistemological analysis of the different kinds of evidence each governmental function uses in its decision making.

One way to understand this epistemological approach to rule making is to compare it to a distinction familiar to Anglo-American lawyers: the difference between judicial fact-finding and legislative fact-finding. Courts, in resolving cases, are limited to such facts as can be established pursuant to the law of evidence, which places substantial limitations on the kinds of conclusions a court can reasonably reach and effectively limits courts' powers to making law interstitially. Legislative facts, in contrast, are not limited by rules of evidence, and accordingly, legislatures are permitted, indeed expected, to undertake expansive fact gathering as a background to any legislation they may adopt. Legislative fact-finding may involve inviting witnesses to appear before the legislature, but it does not require it. And while courts are precluded from considering hearsay and other kinds of indirect evidence, legislatures operate under no such limitation. Accordingly, courts produce rules under relatively strict epistemological limitations, whereas legislatures are given virtually unlimited discretion in determining the kinds of factors to use in promulgating legislation (provided that the factors used are not, for example, unconstitutional).

In al-Qarāfī's scheme, Islamic constitutional law provides three institutional means for rule making. The first is the judge, whose decisions are limited to the kinds of proof (s. *ḥujja*/p. *ḥijāj*) recognized as admissible under the Islamic law of evidence. Because this evidence is particular to the parties appearing before the judge, the judge's decision is, by necessity, particular. If the rule of law applicable to the dispute is uncontroversial, the judge acts merely to enforce the rule of law. But if there is uncertainty in the law, the judge acts as an interstitial lawmaker by originating a particular rule settling that case. The second is the master jurist, who establishes universal rules derived from his subjective interpretation of the revealed indicants (*al-adilla al-shar'iyya*). While these rules are universal law—unlike the law produced by judges, which is particular—they are nonbinding insofar as they are merely learned opinions (*fatwā*) that can be abandoned in favor of another learned opinion that one believes is more persuasive. From an epistemological point of view, the master jurist, in exercising his lawmaking powers, is not limited by the rules of evidence, but rather follows the methods set out in theoretical jurisprudence (*uṣūl al-fiqh*), which permit the master jurist to consider a broad range of indicants, revealed or otherwise (depending on the master jurist's method), which go well beyond those permitted to a judge. The universal character of the law produced by master jurists is thus reflected in the broader set of sources that are considered admissible in legal argumentation. Al-Qarāfī, for example, identifies approximately twenty kinds of arguments or sources that master jurists may use to produce universal rules, but he states that judges have available to them only about ten different modes of proof in litigation.[37] Finally, public officials exercising the police power (*al-siyāsa al-'āmma*) appear to be given the broadest interpretive range of all. Unlike either judges, who are limited by the rules of evidence, or master jurists, who are limited by the principles of theoretical jurisprudence, public officials can presumably consider any kind of evidence in their determination of what constitutes the public good.[38] Like master jurists, their epistemological freedom is largely a function of the fact that they make universal rules; however, unlike master jurists, whose rule making derives from interpretation of a fixed body of revealed indicants and aims to express an opinion about a fixed truth—God's law—the lawmaking of public officials pursuant to the police power is based solely on empirical, immanent considerations that are qualified by context in time and space. Accordingly, rules made pursuant to the police power, despite the fact that they are binding, are amenable to change in light of the fact that the evidentiary basis for those laws is constantly changing, unlike the case with the opinions of the master jurists, which may be opposed as erroneous or mistaken interpretations of revelation, but that in all cases claim to be *true* interpretations of an unchanging divine will.

Interestingly, al-Qarāfī justifies the greater discretion given to master jurists in the formulation of universal law relative to judges on the basis of the generality of the master jurists' task relative to the particularity involved in the latter's decisions. Because judging involves particulars, there is a heightened risk of bias and hidden conflicts of interest that require enhanced procedural safeguards, while the generality of the rule-making process followed by master jurists minimizes the risk of bias because the element of self-interest in universal lawmaking is de minimis (question no. 37 [206–7]). While he does not extend this argument to lawmaking pursuant to the police power, it seems that the same logic applies to explain why it is acceptable to permit wide latitude to decision makers when they exercise their public lawmaking powers: to the extent their powers are limited to making rules in respect of the public interest, there is little reason to suspect bad faith in how they will exercise that power.

Al-Qarāfī does not envisage the possibility that each of these epistemologically distinct powers could be vested exclusively in one particular office (or branch) of the state; instead, his constitutional theory contemplates the possibility that a single officeholder could legitimately exercise all of these powers simultaneously, provided, however, that in exercising these powers, the officeholder does so in accordance with the legal requirements that apply to the valid exercise of that power. A judge, for example, could simultaneously be a mufti and a judge insofar as he is capable of supplying the relevant legal norm that supplies the basis of decision.

But judges could also exercise police powers consistently with al-Qarāfī's framework: not only were some judges, as a historical matter, appointed to the position of market inspector simultaneous to their appointment as a judge, but also much of what judges did effectively amounted to exercise of the police power, such as specifying appropriate punishments for criminals under the doctrine of *taʿzīr*, pursuant to which the judge determined appropriate punishments, in light not of courtroom evidence but empirical considerations of the public good and the good of the individual defendant. Indeed, al-Qarāfī provides numerous examples of ordinary decisions of judges that are not judicial rulings at all but instead administrative acts dependent on empirical assessments, either of the public good or of the particular good of a litigant. Such actions are binding, but because they are administrative acts and not judicial rulings, they are prospectively subject to revision or repeal in light of changed circumstances (question no. 36), to say nothing of the fact that dissenters remain free to dispute their appropriateness.

Another contrast with a strict conception of separation of powers lies in al-Qarāfī's conception of the general legislative power:

in al-Qarāfī's description of the Islamic constitution, legislative power is shared between the legal schools and public officials who exercised the general police power. Legal schools promulgated generally applicable rules that were generally amenable to classification into the five elements identified by al-Qarāfī: the moral status of the act, viewed from the perspective of Islamic jurisprudence, which could be any one of the five categories recognized in Islamic jurisprudential theory; its legal causes; its legal conditions; its legal impediments; and the modes of proof admissible to establish the existence of the rules causes, conditions, and impediments. These rules were, for the most part, sufficient to provide individuals with a basis to act without the intervention of public authorities, but when a dispute erupted, judges, through their power to originate particular rules, were empowered to resolve conclusively particular disputes in controversial areas of the law. This power to originate particular rulings, however, was limited to the particular parties to the dispute but did not extend prospectively to other, similarly situated parties. Unlike a court of appeal in a common law system, then, a Muslim judge in al-Qarāfī's account did not make generally applicable law when he resolved a case in an unsettled area of the law; he could resolve only that particular dispute, and the background legal controversy persisted until a consensus among the legal class was reached. The power to make general laws that were derived from perceptions of the public good, however, was vested in the caliph and lesser executive officials, such as governors and rulers of cities. Unlike the schools of law, whose doctrines did not apply to anyone who rejected their authority, there was no such freedom to ignore the laws made by public officials, albeit there was a possibility that public officials could be persuaded to change their minds and revise their laws or repeal them in their entirety.

Epilogue

Al-Qarāfī's importance to the late medieval Mālikī tradition is evident from the ubiquitous citations to his views by subsequent generations of Mālikī jurists on a broad range of issues of substantive law within the Mālikī school. His influence, however, on how the Mālikīs understood the legal effects of a judicial ruling was decisive. Later Mālikīs came to agree that a valid judicial ruling not only resolved the dispute between the litigants for the purposes of the secular world but also removed any moral controversy that might have existed regarding the applicable legal rule prior to the judge's decision.[39]

Al-Qarāfī's influence, however, was not limited to his own legal school. His theories regarding the division of powers among judges, muftis, and rulers transcended the boundaries of the doctrinal schools, as evidenced by the extent to which even a Ḥanafī jurist writing on the judicial system of the late Mamlūk era quoted al-Qarāfī.[40] Shāfiʿī authors, however, seem to have been particularly open to the views of al-Qarāfī, and later Shāfiʿī authorities cited him with some frequency, at times expressly, but also without attribution.[41] Indeed, the Shāfiʿī theologian and jurist Tāj al-Dīn Ibn al-Subkī (d. 771/1369) even adopted wholesale al-Qarāfī's distinction between prophetic actions undertaken in the Prophet's capacity as a messenger, pursuant to which he communicates universal law to humanity, and as a secular lawgiver, pursuant to which he makes particular rules in accordance with the welfare of his community.[42] There is no better testament to the importance of a jurist in Islamic law than recognition by successive generations of jurists as an authority, an accomplishment that is magnified in the case of al-Qarāfī given the fact that his influence extended beyond the borders of his own school. The reach of his legal thought, particularly with respect to his understanding of the institutional framework governing the operation of Islamic law in Mamlūk society, justifies making the Criterion available to a wider audience. I hope that this translation will do precisely that.

The Criterion for Distinguishing Legal Opinions from Judicial Rulings and the Administrative Acts of Judges and Rulers

Introduction

[17] The servant in need of the grace of his Lord, Aḥmad b. Idrīs al-Mālikī, may God efface his sins, says: Praise is God's, the King, the Proprietor of all things, the One who has granted us the dominions of the earth as merely one of His several gifts; He is the Generous, the Benefactor, the One who disposes of all affairs, with either justice or generosity; He sent revelations and He introduced the means for obtaining His pleasing bounties, so that truth has become manifest, justice has become known and aggression has been removed. He magnifies the rewards of good deeds and effaces foul deeds; He is the King and the Judge, pouring forth generously gifts, and covering up our misdeeds; and He is the patron of forgiveness.

And the choicest blessings upon the best of His creation, a descendant of ʿAdnān—the wisest judge, the most upright ruler, and the greatest messenger—sent to both humanity and jinn.[1] May God bless him and grant him peace, and so too may God's blessings and peace encompass his family, his companions, his wives, and his helpers; blessings that deliver them to the gardens of the Abode of Security, and that earn us the greatest satisfaction from God, sublime is He [18].

To proceed: I have engaged, over the years, in various discussions with learned scholars about the difference between (1) a legal opinion (*fatwā*), which by its nature does not preclude a contrary, dissenting legal opinion; (2) a judicial ruling (*ḥukm*), which preempts dissenting views; and (3) administrative acts and decrees (*taṣarrufāt*) of the ruler (*al-imām*) and judges (*ḥukkām*). Scholars disagree, moreover, whether a declaration that the month of Ramadan has begun, if it is based on the testimony of only a single witness, binds those who accept no less than the testimony of two witnesses to establish the beginning of the month.[2] They also disagree whether a judicial sale of property belonging to an orphan implies a judicial ruling that the sale was valid, such that the sale is final and unassailable. And, when a judge rules that a prospective witness possesses integrity (*ʿadāla*),[3] may a subsequent judge reach a different conclusion, or is the first judge's determination a judicial ruling that may not be assailed? And there are many other cases that are similar to these.

I also asked what the essence of the judicial ruling referred to above was, and sought out a comprehensive definition for it. The only answer given, however, was that a judicial ruling is binding (*ilzām*), while a legal opinion is a communication (*ikhbār*) of a rule in a nonbinding manner. But, someone could object to this definition, and say, "If what is intended by 'binding' is the actual fact of compliance, the judge may be impotent to enforce the ruling by decree or imprisonment or otherwise, but his judgment is nevertheless a judicial ruling. The mere fact of compelling the losing party, however, is not a judicial ruling. But, if what is intended is that the judge communicates to the litigants, with regard to the rule of God that applies to their case, that it binds them, then a legal opinion is no different." [19]

But, in any case, a judicial ruling may decree the absence of an obligation such that no one is bound to do anything as a result of the decision, as is the case when the judge rules on the basis of an opinion (*qawl*) that denies the existence of an obligation, or when the specific case at hand is resolved by a finding that no one owns the property in dispute, and accordingly that there are no restrictions regarding its use. Defining a judicial ruling as something that imposes a binding obligation, therefore, is underinclusive.

I also asked whether a judge's judicial ruling is mental speech (*kalām nafsānī*) or audible speech (*kalām lisānī*),[4] and whether it is a communication of a preexisting rule or an origination (*inshā'*) of a rule that had not existed prior to the judicial ruling, but I could find no one who could answer these, and many similar questions, comprehensively.

Accordingly, I decided to compose this book, which provides a comprehensive treatment of these issues. I have composed the book in the form of a series of questions, in the manner that replicates the discussions that took place between my colleagues and myself. The answer immediately follows each question, pointing out the subtleties of these points and the issues that derive from them, as manifested in judicial decisions, legal opinions, and administrative acts of public officials.[5] I named this book the Criterion for Distinguishing Legal Opinions from Judicial Rulings and the Administrative Acts of Judges and Rulers, and it contains forty questions [20].

Question 1. "What is the essence of a judicial ruling that a judge issues, and that is unassailable?"

The Answer

"It is an origination of the freedom to act or the obligation to act with respect to legal questions governed by rules which are themselves subject to reasonable interpretation and disagreement, in respect of which disputes take place regarding the affairs of the profane world."

Our statement "origination of the freedom to act" takes into account one who might say, "A judicial ruling is the imposition of an obligation." A judge may be asked to rule regarding the status of land that lacks a living owner or living heir, in which case he rules that proprietorship of the land has come to an end and that it is now free for anyone to appropriate as private property. Another example is if the judge, being a follower of al-Shāfiʿī,[1] who believed that land remains free for appropriation as private property and is not held in trust, even if it had been conquered, and thus continues to be available for private ownership and use, rules that land seized from the enemy by conquest is free from any private or public claims of ownership [21]. This is in contrast to the opinion of Mālik and his followers,[2] who say that in this case the land is reserved for the benefit of the conquerors. The same analysis applies to the case of wild animals, bees, and wild birds—whenever possession takes place, private rights attach, but prior to capture, anyone may take them; so, too, when a judge rules that a possessor's rights have terminated, the judge originates a right for others to possess the land. Each of these cases entails a removal of obligation, even as it implies obliging the former owner to recognize the absence of his specific right in the property. But, this arises only by means of implication, and we are concerned in this context only with the primary entailment of the judicial ruling, not its secondary entailments. Similarly, we say that the primary entailment of the imperative mood in the Arabic language (*al-amr*) is the communication of an affirmative obligation, even though it also implies a prohibition of the contrary act, and that the primary entailment of a negative command (*al-nahy*) is prohibition, even though it implies that the contrary action is obligatory. But, when one speaks of the essential meanings of expressions, one must always refer to the primary meaning, not its secondary meanings that arise by implication.

Al-Kaʿbī[3] heedlessly ignored this principle, and as a result he said, "Permissible (*al-mubāḥ*)[4] acts are obligatory because their performance prevents the commission of forbidden acts, and shunning the forbidden is obligatory, so the permissible is obligatory" [22]. Accordingly, he reduced the ethical categories of the law to four and omitted the permissible on account of its secondary features, while abandoning its primary meaning.

The great majority of scholars, however, have affirmed the permissible as an ethical category based on what the essential, denotative meanings of expressions entail. Were it not for that, the recommended (*al-mandūb*) and the disfavored (*al-makrūh*) would also have become obligatory, because keeping busy performing them also prevents the commission of forbidden acts, as al-Kaʿbī asserted with regard to permissible actions. An obligatory action might become disfavored because its performance might prevent someone from performing a recommended act, and refraining from a recommended act is itself disfavored. An obligatory action might also become forbidden because its performance might prevent someone from performing a different obligatory act, and failure to perform an obligation is forbidden. In this way stupidity cascades, the foundations of the law are shaken, and it becomes impossible to establish the essential ethical judgment for any action. Indeed, not a single judgment could be made without affirming that its opposite might also be true, thereby invalidating the first judgment. This approach produces only deep confusion, and accordingly, one must investigate the essence of each concept on its own, and not take into account secondary implications or the contingent circumstances that might appear in conjunction with it.

Our statement "or the obligation to act" refers to when a judge rules against a party and obliges him to pay dower or maintenance to a wife or member of the family or to recognize another party's right of first refusal and similar matters.

Our statement "with respect to legal questions . . . reasonable interpretation": this qualification excludes a judicial ruling contrary to consensus, for it lacks any status [23].

Our statement "reasonable": this excludes legal controversy that is based on weak revelatory evidence. When a judge rules in accordance with a view that is poorly grounded in revelation, his judicial ruling is given no consideration and must be overturned. Accordingly, when considering whether a particular judicial ruling is valid, one must consider whether the revelatory evidence for the judicial ruling is reasonable.

Our statement "in respect of which disputes take place regarding the affairs of the profane world": this excludes questions of legal interpretation that arise in connection with ritual (*'ibādāt*) and similar matters. Such disputes are not on account of the profane world, but rather concern the affairs of the next life. Accordingly, it is no surprise that a judge's judicial ruling [24, 25, 26] cannot encompass them.

Question 2. "How can it be said that God, sublime is He, gave anyone the power to create rules that bind God's servants? And does anyone other than God, sublime is He, originate rules? Is there an equivalent to this in the revealed law of Islam (*al-sharīʿa*) or something else from it which may give some comfort or clarification on this issue?"

The Answer

This power is not a cause of astonishment or wonder, for God, sublime is He, has laid out the obligatory, recommended, forbidden, disfavored, and permitted acts through the words of His Prophet, may God bless him and grant him peace. God, glorified and sublime is He, revealed to him in His noble book, "Today I have completed for you your religion, and perfected for you My favor, and have accepted most favorably Islam as your religion."[1] Despite that, God also established as a fundamental feature of His law that an individual may create an obligation with respect to a matter that the revealed law had not previously made obligatory. Thus, any individual may transform any recommended act he wishes into one that is obligatory, even though the revealed law deemed the act in question to be merely recommended; God limited this authority to recommended acts and limited [27] the means to transform a recommended act into an obligatory act to one, the vow (*nadhr*).[2] The vow, then, is used to originate individual obligation with respect to an act which the revealed law renders merely recommended.

God, sublime is He, also established in His law that an individual may originate an obligation in another fashion. God, sublime is He, when He introduced the legal rules, He also introduced their legal causes (*al-asbāb*) and just as He divided the rules into two parts, those which were laid out in revelation itself, like the five obligatory prayers and similar matters, and those which He entrusted to individuals—and that is transforming a recommended act into an obligatory one via the vow, He also divided legal causes into two parts: those which are expressed in revelation itself, and those which He entrusted the origination of their status as legal causes to individuals. The authority to originate legal causes is general and is not limited to acts having a particular ethical qualification, recommended or otherwise. Instead, a person has authority to make any act—whether recommended, obligatory, forbidden, disfavored, or permissible, or even an act that is entirely free of any legal qualification—a ground for personal obligation, like the action of someone sleeping, or that of a distracted, mistaken, or insane person, or that of an animal, or even the motion of the winds and clouds and waters, as well as similar matters. God has no rules with respect to such actions, nor is there any communication from God entailing any kind of legal qualification with respect to such actions. Despite that, every individual, by means of one device, the conditional oath (*al-taʿlīq*), is entitled to make of any of these actions he wishes a legal cause for the divorce of his wife or the manumission of his slave, or for undertaking pilgrimage or any other act of devotion. Accordingly, revelation did not make entering a home, for example, a legal cause for the divorce of a wife or the manumission of a slave, but whosoever desires to do so, may make either one of them a legal cause effective to produce these legal effects [28].

The Lawgiver, in this context, has permitted anything and everything to be transformed into a legal cause, but He limited the manner by which this takes place, restricting it to the form of the conditional oath. In the previous case of the vow, by contrast, He limited both the subject and the means, limiting the subject to recommended acts and limiting the means to the vow. Thus, the vow, insofar as it can be used to originate individual obligations, is limited in both respects, while the conditional oath, insofar as it can be used to originate individual obligations, is limited in one respect and general in the other.

If it has been established that God, sublime is He, has given every person—even if he is uneducated and ignorant—the authority to originate rules for himself in the law without even satisfying a stipulation of necessity, it is, a fortiori, the case that He would give the authority to originate rulings to judges, given their knowledge and their elevated status, in light of the need to restrain stubbornness, repel corruption, put out the fire of discord, and resolve disputes. The vow and the conditional oath are therefore two examples from substantive law that should provide comfort to the skeptical, and indeed, the a fortiori proof, as has become clear, should also clarify this point.

As for a legal proof in favor of this view, it is the universal consensus (*ijmāʿ*)[3] of the master jurists[4] that the rule of God, sublime is He, regarding those questions that are resolved by interpretation is that rule which the judge applies in the specific case, as has already been mentioned, and it is an obligation for the entire community to adhere to that ruling. Consequently, it is forbidden for anyone to contradict it or overturn it. This feature of a judicial ruling arose only after the judge's ruling, not prior to it, because before this ruling the case was potentially governed by all valid legal opinions, each of which could have been subjected to valid challenges and objections. I do not mean by "origination" other than this feature of a judicial ruling, namely, its unassailability. The point has now become clear [29].

Question 3. "Can you provide an analogy from the universal rules of law (*al-qawāʿid*), in addition to what you have already mentioned, which could further clarify the previous point?"

The Answer

The relationship of the judge and the mufti in relation to God, sublime is He—and to God belongs the loftiest of similitudes[1]—is analogous to the relationship of the chief judge who appoints two persons, one of whom is his delegate with respect to judicial rulings, and the other is appointed to translate between the judge and litigants speaking a foreign tongue. The duty of the translator is to follow carefully the words and expressions used by the judge and to inform the foreigners of the sense of his words, without adding thereto or decreasing therefrom. That is the role of the mufti: if he is a master jurist who is an independent interpreter of the revealed law (*mujtahid*), his duty is to follow, assiduously, the indicants (*al-adilla*/s. *dalīl*) set out in revelation and, after having considered them all, to inform humanity of the meanings derived from them as they appear to him, without adding thereto or decreasing therefrom. If he is not a master jurist, but rather adheres to the views of a master jurist (*muqallid*), as is the case in our day, then he is a delegate of the master jurist. In this case he merely reports what the master jurist has taught to the person seeking the legal opinion. In this latter case, he is like the spokesperson for the master jurist whose teachings he follows, and the translator of his thoughts to the petitioner [30].

The judge's delegate, in contrast, originates judicial rulings with respect to particular disputes, sometimes by imposing obligations on litigants, and at other times by removing obligations from them, even though the appointing judge, who is the principal, has not personally confirmed his delegate's rulings; indeed, the principal has delegated that power to his delegate. Therefore, the delegate is dependent on the appointing judge from one perspective and independent of him from another perspective: he is dependent upon the appointing judge insofar as the appointing judge has delegated to him that authority to originate judicial rulings, and he has faithfully carried out the terms of that delegation; he is independent of the appointing judge insofar as he issues rulings imposing obligations on litigants and issues rulings removing obligations from them with respect to disputes for which the appointing judge had not issued a prior ruling—rather, the delegate is the first to judge with respect to that case.

This is analogous to the relationship of a judge to God, sublime is He: he is faithful to God's command, sublime is He, insofar as He has delegated to him that authority and he exercises it in accordance with its terms; and, he is an originator of judicial rulings because his ruling becomes mandatory and no one may challenge it, even though its mandatory quality had not been established in the law as it was revealed. Nor is its origination on account of the indicants which are used in the derivation of legal opinions, because it is obligatory to follow the preponderant inference that arises out of indicants found in revelation, but in the case of a lawsuit, a judge, as a matter of consensus, may rule on the basis of one of two views which are of equal strength, without giving preponderance to either one, or without even having knowledge of the revelatory indicants underlying both views. Instead, a judge rules in accordance with the factual evidence (p. *al-ḥijāj*/s. *ḥujja*) the parties submit to the court, whereas the mufti considers only the indicants found in revelation. Conversely, the mufti does not rely on the parties' factual evidence but considers only indicants found in revelation [31], which are the Book of God [i.e., the Quran], the Sunna,[2] and similar things, while the parties' factual evidence consists of eyewitness testimony, admissions, and similar things.

This, therefore, is the relationship of the judge and the mufti to God, sublime is He. But, a judge does not have the authority to originate arbitrary or capricious rulings; indeed, the opinion which he applies in his ruling must be the position of a master jurist that is itself well grounded in the revealed indicants, just as the appointing judge does not authorize his delegate to rule arbitrarily [32].

Question 4. "The difference between the mufti and the judge is now clear, but what is the difference between them and the administrative acts and decrees of the imam, the head of state (*al-imām al-aʿẓam*) of the Muslim community?"[1]

The Answer

The relationship of the imam to them is like the relationship of the whole to its parts, and that of a composite body to its constituent elements. The imam, as head of state, has the power to make judicial rulings and to give legal opinions in the manner set out previously. He may also, however, perform actions that are neither legal opinions nor judicial rulings, for example, by mustering armies, declaring war, taking possession of public property and spending it to further lawful aims, appointing governors, and executing wrongdoers. There are many things that are particular to him and in which neither the judge nor the mufti can share. Accordingly, every imam is a judge and a mufti, but neither of them can be described as the imam, the head of state of the Muslim community.

This is alluded to in the statement of the Prophet, may God bless him and grant him peace, "ʿAlī b. Abī Ṭālib[2] is the most judicious of you [33], but Muʿādh b. Jabal[3] is the most knowledgeable of you with respect to the lawful and the forbidden" [34, 35, 36]. He referred to the qualifications of Abū Bakr al-Ṣiddīq[4] for leadership of the community, may God be pleased with all of them, however, when he, may God bless him and grant him peace, said, "Tell Abū Bakr to lead the people in prayer."

The scholars said, "He, may God bless him and grant him peace, desired to receive a revelation from God that would declare Abū Bakr to be the imam after his death, but nothing was revealed to him; so, he, may God bless him and grant him peace, was inspired to allude to the community's well-being by appointing Abū Bakr to lead the communal prayer in his final illness, out of a firm desire to protect the well-being of the community through the subtle sign of Abū Bakr's appointment as prayer leader, while maintaining proper decorum with the Divinity by refusing to be explicit with respect to who should succeed him as imam. Thus, his nobility was perfected, and the well-being of his community was secured, may God bless him and grant him peace [37, 38].

The scholars said, "If Muʿādh was the most knowledgeable with respect to the lawful and the forbidden, he ought to have been the most judicious of the companions, may God be pleased with them, so what is the meaning of the Prophet's statement, may God bless him and grant him peace, that 'ʿAlī is the most judicious of you'?" They replied, may God be pleased with them, that "adjudicating disputes is a matter of understanding the various modes of evidence that litigants present in court. A person might be more knowledgeable regarding the lawful and the forbidden but not particularly skilled in understanding the tricks and deception that litigants use and therefore may not be able to reach the truth in the face of the different statements of the litigants." [39, 40, 41]

Judiciousness as a skill is something distinct from theoretical knowledge of the law, and it requires enormous perspicacity, intelligence, and intuition, as well as helpful experience and mighty assistance from God, sublime is He. All of this is needed *after* one obtains knowledge of legal opinions. It is the case, therefore, that a person may be a more competent judge even if he is less knowledgeable regarding legal opinions. Accordingly, there is no contradiction between his statement, may God bless him and grant him peace, that "ʿAlī is the most judicious of you" and his statement, may God bless him and grant him peace, that "the most knowledgeable of you with respect to the lawful and the forbidden is Muʿādh b. Jabal."

It has therefore become apparent that giving judicial rulings relies on litigants' evidence while legal opinions rely on revealed indicants, and that the administrative acts of the head of state—which are distinctive from and in addition to these two activities—rely on evidence pertaining to the community's common good, whether wholly or predominantly.[5] This activity, the determination of the common good, is something that depends neither on litigants' evidence nor on indicants found in revelation [42]. It has also become manifest that giving judicial rulings and providing legal opinions are inherent incidents to the office of the imam, and for that reason, the prerequisites for acting as imam, such as descent from Quraysh,[6] competence in managing public affairs and administration of the people's affairs, in addition to the other requirements that the scholars have set out in their discussions of this office, whether they are strictly conditions or are merely desirable, exceed those required of judges and muftis. And for this reason, the Prophet, may God bless him and grant him peace, said, "imams are from Quraysh," but he did not say, "Judges are from Quraysh." And this is only because of the generality of this office's power, and the complete effectiveness of its competence and independence, which are only a result of the greatness of its affair and its noble gravitas.

And this is the practice of the Lawgiver—whenever a matter is grave, numerous prerequisites are imposed. Take the example of marriage: because it is graver than sales, the Lawgiver imposed numerous prerequisites in regard to it which were not imposed in connection with the sales of goods, including requiring the attestation of the marriage by witnesses, the payment of dower, and other matters. The Lawgiver, by contrast, permitted the physical transfer of goods without attestation by witnesses or payment of any consideration; indeed, the Lawgiver even permitted gifts and charity and endowments and other kinds of actions involving private property, even though He prohibited all of this with respect to marriage because of what the latter entails in the preservation of humanity and the spread of progeny that proclaims God's oneness, sublime is He, worships Him, and submits to His majesty, in addition to what marriage entails in terms of companionship, love, tranquillity, and the good order of the profane world. God, sublime is He, alludes to these matters when He said: "Among His signs is that He created from among yourselves spouses [43] that you may take solace in them, and He made between you love and mercy."[7]

The Lawgiver also imposed restrictions on the sale of food that were not imposed on other commodities, including prohibiting the exchange of a large amount of food for a small amount of food, and the exchange of food in the spot market for food due in the future;[8] the Lawgiver also prohibited selling food before it was in the seller's possession. These restrictions were not imposed on the sale of other commodities because food is the means by which bodies are maintained and the means that assist human beings avoid sin and discharge their duties to God, sublime is He. The Lawgiver also imposed numerous restrictions on the exchange of gold and silver, including equivalence, simultaneity, and others, because they provide the measure of value for all property and establish values for compensation of destroyed and damaged goods and compensation for individuals when they suffer injuries.

Similarly, the Lawgiver imposed numerous conditions with respect to the office of the imam that are not required for other offices, because of its gravity. It must always be the case that if a station is lofty, reaching it must require satisfying demanding conditions and overcoming numerous obstacles along the way. Accordingly, it is much easier to become a local ruler than a minister, and a minister than the ruler of a region. Such is the custom of God, sublime is He, with respect to His creation and His law. Glory be to the Wise Organizer of the good order of the world, in all its details, large and small [44].

Question 5. "If the judge's ruling is an origination, is it mental speech or audible speech?"

The Answer

It is mental speech, and two considerations support that conclusion.

The first is that the law of God, sublime is He, with respect to a case, is nothing other than His speech which is subsistent in His essence, and the words (*alfāẓ*/s. *lafẓ*) of the Quran and the Sunna and other indicants are merely signs that point to the content of the rule, but they are not the rule itself. And a judicial ruling is also the law of God, except that He has delegated it to the judge. Accordingly, it is also mental speech insofar as it subsists in the mind of the judge, and it also subsists by God's essence, mighty and elevated is He. A judicial ruling should not be understood to be anything other than that which obtains in the mind of the judge; rather, the judicial ruling is precisely that which subsists in the judge's mind. Because He has obliged us to act in accordance with the judge's ruling, the rule of God, sublime is He, as originated by the judge, subsists in His essence just like the rest of God's rules, except that the ruling which subsists in the judge's mind is contingent, transitory in nature, and does not persist more than one moment of time, while the rule subsisting in God's essence, sublime is He, is necessarily extant from eternity, and in perpetuity, and is outside of time, like the rest of His rulings, sublime is He, as has been established in theoretical jurisprudence and theology [45].

The second argument which proves that the judge's ruling is mental speech is that when he rules, sometimes he communicates it audibly, saying, "Bear witness against me that I have ruled in this fashion," while at other times he may be asked about his ruling, in which case he moves his head or makes some other bodily motion from which it is understood that he has made a judicial ruling. At other times he writes it in the form of a letter to another judge or produces a document for the witnesses and says, "Bear witness against me in accordance with its contents," or the judge sends a written document to another region without either a verbal expression or bodily sign, and that document acts as evidence that he has issued a judicial ruling. These examples point to the fact that the essence of a judicial ruling is something other than his words, his writing, or his signs, and that something else is nothing other than his mental speech. These other, external things are simply evidence of his ruling, as is the case with all things that subsist in the mind, whether judgments, statements, or anything else. It has become clear, therefore, that the judge's ruling is mental speech, not audible speech [46].

Question 6. "If the judge's ruling is mental speech, is it a report concerning the content of God's rule, sublime is He, that is amenable to acceptance or rejection, or is it an origination of God's rule, that is amenable to neither?"

The Answer

The judge's ruling is not a report that is amenable to acceptance as true or rejection as false; rather, it is an origination which does not admit these possibilities. It is either the origination of an obligation or the origination of permission, and it is not said to whoever originates an obligation upon another or upon himself, or originates permission for another to perform an act: "You have spoken the truth," or "You have lied." The same holds for all commands, prohibitions, and optional performances;[1] interrogatories; optatives;[2] oaths; vocatives; and similar matters: none of these linguistic forms is amenable to acceptance or rejection because they all include the concept of a demand, either in the first instance, as in the case of commands and prohibitions, or in the second instance, as in the case of an optative.

The difference between an origination and a report is in three respects. The first is that a report may be accepted as true or rejected as false, whereas an origination is not subject to that, as previously mentioned. The second is that a report is derivative of the existence of its predicate with respect to time, whether in the past, present, or future [49]. The third is that a report does not bring about the existence of its meaning and does not entail its occurrence as an empirical matter, whereas an origination brings about the existence of the word's meaning and produces its legal effects, as occurs universally in all instances of originations, like divorce: because it is an origination, its legal consequence—the dissolution of the marriage tie and the rendering of the wife as forbidden to her husband—comes into existence immediately. The same is true for all the instances of originations: their effects come into existence as a consequence of their words and follow directly, something that is inconceivable with respect to a report [50].

Question 7. "What is the difference between an origination and a report?"

The Answer

The words pointing to the judge's ruling at times may be a report, such as when he says, "I have ruled in such and such a manner in such and such a case," because this expression is amenable to acceptance as true or rejection as false in accordance with what is known about the judge's particular circumstances and whether he possesses a good reputation for truthfulness. By "report" we mean nothing other than a statement which entails the possibility of acceptance as true or rejection false; at other times, it is a command, originating a demand, if he said, for example: "Bear witness against me that . . ." But, this is an origination seeking action from the witnesses to testify against him, and not an origination of God's rule, sublime is He; rather, it is a command to the witnesses, like other commands proceeding from him to them, as if he had said to the witnesses, "Take your seats to testify in such and such a place." Nothing in that is God's rule, sublime is He, which the judge originated; rather, this is a demand from him that is particular to him.

It is clear, therefore, that it is not the words of the judge, under either assumption, which originates the judicial ruling in that case at all, but rather it is a report that he has originated a judicial ruling, or it is a command that testimony be taken about it. As for the judicial ruling itself, it remains in his mind, subsisting in his essence as part of his mental speech, and something else points to it. Sure, it may be the case that the origination of the judicial ruling takes place simultaneously with the manifestation of that which evinces it. In this case the time of the ruling's origination is the same as the time that witnesses attest to it, but a lengthy interval of time, perhaps many years, may separate the two, if the judge, for example, rules on a case in his mind, but calls witnesses to attest to the judgment only after a lengthy time has passed [51].

Question 8. "Is the word that evinces a judicial ruling an origination or a report? And is there a difference between the word that evinces it and the words used by a witness? When the judge says, 'Bear witness against me that . . .' is that similar to the witness saying to the judge 'I testify before you that . . .'?"

The Answer

The judge's statement "I have ruled in this fashion," and "Bear witness against me that I have ruled in this fashion," is not an origination of the judicial ruling in that case, as has been previously explained. As for the witness's statement before the judge, "I testify before you that . . . ," and the judge rules that something took place in accordance with his statement, that is an origination of the testimony in front of the judge which does not admit either acceptance as true or rejection as false. Had it been a report, it would have not been permissible for a judicial ruling to result from the judge in that case, because it would be a promise from the witness that he will testify in the future before the judge regarding that case, and a promise to testify does not guarantee that the content of the testimony will be provided. Accordingly, it has become clear that the words used in the performance of testimony are an origination of the testimony, whereas the words of the judge, whether in respect of calling witnesses to attest to his judicial ruling or in respect of reporting his ruling, are in no case an origination of the judicial ruling. The difference between them is now clear [52].

Question 9. "Are statements like 'I sold' or 'I purchased' or 'You are divorced' the linguistic equivalent of a witness's statement 'I testify that such-and-such . . .' or are they rather the linguistic equivalent of the judge's statement 'Bear witness against me that . . .'?"

The Answer

A person's statement "I have sold that to you . . ." or "I have purchased that from you," or "You are divorced," or "You are free," and similar expressions, take the same analysis as the performance of testimony and are therefore originations. They are not like the judge's calling witnesses to attest to the fact of his judgment because these are expressions that bring into existence their legal meanings and are legal causes for their existence, like the performance of testimony, in contrast to the judge's calling witnesses to attest to the fact of his judgment; that is nothing other than a pure report or a demand that testimony be taken, as has been previously explained. Accordingly, the difference is clear [53].

Question 10. "If words are the origination, are all words capable of serving as an origination or not?"

The Answer

Some words are appropriate to produce an origination in one context but not appropriate in another context. This can be shown in the following fashion: the denotative linguistic form for the origination of testimony is the present indicative mood,[1] such that the witness says, "I testify." Were he to use the past tense, saying "I testified that . . . ," it would not be an origination, and the judge would not do anything as a result. As far as contracts are concerned, the appropriate form to be used, in contrast to testimony, is the past tense. The seller therefore says, "I sold you this good for one dirham." Had he said, "I will sell you this good for a dirham," it is merely a promise to sell, not a sale. Likewise, the purchaser says, "I bought," using the past tense, and were he to say, "I [will] purchase for such and such," using the present indicative mood, it would be merely a promise that he will purchase it.

As for the imperative mood, as in "Purchase it for such and such," it is not an origination. This concludes this discussion with respect to verbs.

As for active participles, the active participle has been used denotatively to originate divorce, manumission, and similar matters, for example, "You are divorced"[2] and "You are free." They are not, however, used to originate contracts, for example, "I am selling," or "I am purchasing," or "I am giving," and similar expressions. It is also not used [54] to originate testimony, for were a witness to say, "I am testifying that . . . ," it would not be an origination; this is as far as contracts and testimony are concerned. As for oaths, origination is valid here using the indicative mood, the future, and the active participle, for example, "I have sworn by God that I shall do such and such," and "I swear to God that I shall do such and such," and "I am imploring you by God that you must do such and such."

In short, only the past tense is used for originations in the case of contracts; only the present indicative mood is used in the case of testimony; and the oath uses the present indicative mood, the past tense, and other expressions as well, so it is the most general of cases with respect to the linguistic forms of origination [55].

Question 11. "If the judge's ruling is an origination of the divine rule, is it possible that any of the five ethical qualifications may be used in a judicial ruling inasmuch as God's laws encompass all five qualifications?" [47]

The Answer

It is inconceivable that the judge's ruling, although it is God's rule, sublime is He, could be based on any of the five ethical categories that constitute the law. Because the goal of judicial rulings is to bring an end to disputes between litigants, and to restore rights, a judge's ruling is limited to what brings about these ends. Accordingly, the ethical categories from which a judge's ruling derives is either obligation (like a judicial ruling declaring the ex-husband's obligation to provide maintenance for a divorced woman, for those who hold this view), prohibition (like a judicial ruling dissolving a marriage, which entails an invalidation of the prior invalid contract insofar as it gave rise to the erroneous belief that it was a valid marriage contract which rendered sexual relations permissible; it also entails a declaration that the woman has been restored to her original status as a prohibited sexual partner), or permissibility (like a judicial ruling declaring land to be free of ownership), freely available to all, as a consequence of the disappearance of living owners, as is the view of Mālik and others who share that view, or like wild animals taken in a hunt, bees and birds that have returned to the wild, and other examples, all of which may become the property of anyone who takes possession of them).

As for the categories of the recommended and disfavored, the judge can deploy them only in the context of a legal opinion, and not as the grounds for a judicial ruling. For example, if the judge is a Mālikī, and he orders the husband to give his divorced wife a parting gift, his statement is only a legal opinion and not a judicial ruling. The same analysis applies to similar cases where a judge orders a party to perform an action that is recommended but not obligatory. Accordingly, if the judge were to say, "It is better for you to do such and such" [56], or "It is worse for you to do such and such," that is nothing other than the judge giving a legal opinion, not a judicial ruling that concludes a legal dispute. The reason for this is that neither the recommended nor the disfavored—insofar as they are ethical categories—is capable of resolving a dispute. God accorded authority to judges to originate judicial rulings solely for the purpose of putting an end to disputes, and a dispute will never be concluded in the absence of a rule that obliges or permits, as has been previously explained, thus bringing an end to disputes in respect of spouses, maintenance, lands, and other matters, because the judicial ruling is a resolution of the dispute on the part of the judge. When a judge resolves a dispute with a judicial ruling, and rules in accordance with it, it is unassailable. The essence of the categories of recommended and disfavored, however, is an admixture of permission to act and permission to refrain from acting, a feature that renders the rules drawn from these two categories incapable of resolving disputes. One should not say, "Permission is also an admixture of permission to act and permission to refrain from acting, and this is its essence," for we say what we mean by permission is the categorical release that is concomitant to resolving the subject matter of the dispute by removing the previous owner's claim of ownership, so that its status as owned comes to an end, and there is no basis on which anyone else may be excluded from cultivating it; indeed, the previous owner and everyone else become equal with respect to the use of that place or those wild animals, and similar things [57].

Question 12. "If the word is an origination, must the word signifying the intended meaning occur simultaneously, as is the case with divorce, or is a delay in communication or calling witnesses to attest to it harmless with respect to the legal effect?"

The Answer

The judge's ruling need not be contemporaneous with the words that manifest the ruling; indeed, a delay between the ruling and calling witnesses to attest to it does no harm because the process of attestation is nothing other than a report of what has taken place in his mind, in contrast to the words of the divorcing husband or the manumitting slave owner. In these cases, the words must be simultaneous with the origination in the mind because the Lawgiver has made the conjunction of the two—I mean mental speech and audible speech—the legal cause of divorce in the well-attested opinion of Mālik. As for those who give no weight to mental speech in relation to audible speech in the case of divorce and manumission, audible speech suffices them without regard to the speaker's mental speech.

In accord with this latter doctrine, there is no need to consider the conjunction of mental speech with audible speech, given the sufficiency of the audible word in the view of those who hold that view. Conjunction takes place only between two things, but the audible word in the view of that person suffices, and it is a view contrary to the well-attested doctrine of Mālik. The opinion of another group of scholars is that an explicit formula of divorce is sufficient, and needs nothing else, meaning no particular mental state on the part of the speaker is required for the legal effect to arise.

Thus, the difference between the words of the judge after the judicial ruling and the words of divorce and other matters has become manifest: the words of the judge need not be contemporaneous with the judicial ruling in contrast to other things. Likewise, the correspondence of one judge to another, informing the latter of his judicial ruling, might take place immediately after his ruling, or it might take place sometime thereafter, because it is a communication, and communication and reporting can occur after the occurrence of the report's predicate [58].

Question 13. "Are the scholars in agreement with respect to the occurrence of origination, or is it a matter of controversy? If it is controversial, explain it, and what is the correct position?"

The Answer

The scholars have not agreed regarding the occurrence of originations in all cases, but they are in agreement with respect to oaths. Accordingly, when a speaker says, "I have sworn by God that I shall do such and such," it is a matter of consensus that it is not appropriate that one say to him either "You have spoken truthfully" or "You have lied." Evidence of a prior mental oath is not required to establish the truth of this expression; rather, he is originating the oath by his very statement: "I swore." There is no controversy about this; all scholars of the Arabic language, as well as others, have expressly agreed to that.

As for the linguistic forms used in contracts, the Shāfiʿīs and the Mālikīs have said that they are originations in the case of sales and other contracts. The Ḥanafīs, however, said they are reports, in accordance with their original denotative sense in the Arabic language [59]. They argue that the original usage of these forms is as reports, and that, when a speaker uses them, revelation necessarily assumes the existence of their meanings at a time prior to the unique speech act, in order to give credence to his statement.[1]

[60, 61] And, the Ḥanafīs argue that confirming the original usage is more appropriate than assuming a change in usage for two reasons. The first is that a change in meaning depends on overwhelming usage that results in an abrogation of the original denotative meaning (*al-waḍʿ al-awwal*) and the creation of a new denotative meaning, while assuming elision is appropriate when there is the slightest circumstantial evidence to support it. Assuming elision is more appropriate than that which depends on numerous premises and that which requires abrogation (*naskh*). The second is that the assumption that there is elision in the revealed law is something that is shared among the scholars; indeed, they agree that elision is ubiquitous in the revealed law, as I have shown in the book *al-Umniyya fī Idrāk al-Niyya.*[2] By contrast, change in the meaning of language is controversial. Reliance on an argument which has a shared basis is better than one that relies on controversial premises [62].

Question 14. "Does origination occur as a result of a word's original, denotative meaning in the Arabic language as posited by the Arabs, or is it a matter of linguistic convention?"

The Answer

The truth in this issue lies in the views of the Shāfiʿīs and Mālikīs, which means that the meaning of the phrase has changed from its original sense of a report to an origination, because customarily that is what immediately comes to mind when one hears these phrases. No one who hears the expression "I sold" or "I bought" understands anything other than the changed meaning, and that by use of this phrase, the speaker has originated a sale. When the meaning of a phrase which impresses itself immediately on the mind is contrary to that phrase's original denotative meaning, the correct position is that the word is taken to mean what first imposes itself on the mind, because that is the preponderant (*al-rājiḥ*) sense of the word. Adoption of the word's preponderant sense is obligatory, even if it is contrary to its original linguistic meaning. Consider the fact that nonliteral use of language (*al-majāz*) is contrary to the original usage, but when evidence makes it preponderant, it becomes obligatory to adopt it. So, too, particularization (*takhṣīṣ*), elision (*iḍmār*), and all matters that are contrary to the original linguistic usage: whenever the contrary usage becomes preponderant, it is obligatory, as a matter of consensus, to adopt it. Accordingly, it is obligatory for a reader to assume a change in the word's meaning because the changed meaning is, given linguistic custom, the word's preponderant sense [63].

Question 15. "Are mental speech and audible speech equivalent in this regard, or is this particular to audible speech?"

The Answer

The fact that a certain linguistic form is used for originations is sometimes a result of the original convention in the Arabic language, like the oath, and at other times it is the result of the customs of a subsequent generation of speakers, like the formulas for divorce and the like. For that reason, an express formula of divorce might be abandoned and become oblique (*kināya*), and an oblique formula of divorce might become widespread such that it becomes the substantial equivalent of an express formula with respect to its effectiveness in originating a divorce. For that reason, our view is that a speaker who says, "You are divorced," has no need to have a specific intention to originate a divorce, while one who says, "You are released," has not originated a divorce in the absence of a specific intent to originate a divorce: although the two expressions share the same triconsonantal root—*ṭāʾ*, *lām*, and *qāf*—and therefore share the same literal meaning, the speakers of the Arabic language have settled on the formula "You are divorced" for the origination of divorce and left "You are released" according to its original denotative meaning as a report. Accordingly, its use does not originate a divorce in the absence of specific intent to do so.[1]

As for the oath, the form used to originate an oath has remained unchanged from the pre-Islamic Days of Ignorance (*al-jāhiliyya*), through the founding of Islam to the present time. Accordingly, the linguistic convention of these two forms is different: one is denotative in the original positing of the language, and the other is customary.

As for the mental speech constituting an origination in the cases of the judge's ruling, and cases of divorce, manumission, and other matters that are originations, no linguistic convention applies, whether as part of a subsequent linguistic custom or the original positing of the language, for linguistic conventions are irrelevant to mental speech; linguistic forms apply only [64] to audible speech. Predicates, commands, and originations, as well as other linguistic forms, are found in mental speech simply as part of the essence of mental speech, not by linguistic convention. For this reason, all peoples, Arabs and non-Arabs, and indeed anyone who has mastered any of the different languages of mankind, understand equally the essence of predication, commands, optional commands, and all other grammatical parts of speech, and they do not diverge in this respect despite the divergence in their vocabularies and their stages of development. Accordingly, this proves that these grammatical features of language are essential and not conventional. Similarly, all species of belief (*iʿtiqādāt*), doubt (*shukūk*), and probability (*ẓanūn*), as well as all psychological states of persons, are found equally in all peoples, without any differences, something that can be true only on account of their having one essence, just as we say with respect to the particularities of various genera, such as blackness or whiteness, or tastes or scents, that these are not on account of extrinsic causes but rather can exist as they are only by virtue of their essences, even if none of them exists except through the power of God, sublime is He. For this reason, the scholars say that transformation of essences is impossible. Had these attributes been established solely by convention, their transformation would be conceivable, because whatever is fashioned by fiat is amenable to transformation and change from one state to another.

The questions, with the completion of these ten questions, have reached fifteen [65].[2]

Question 16. "What is the difference between the judge's ruling in a matter that is governed by consensus—since it is unassailable—and his ruling in a controversial area of the law, for that ruling, too, is unassailable? Consensus exists for both propositions. Is there one legal cause preventing a challenge of the judicial ruling in both cases, or are there several? If it is consensus, then the cause is one in both cases, but if there is another cause, what is it?"

The Answer

Consensus is an effective cause in both cases to render the judge's ruling unassailable, but the judicial verdict in controversial areas of the law enjoys an effective cause supporting its unassailability that is specific to it. The explanation for this is that God, sublime is He, when He gave judges the authority to originate judicial rulings in those questions of law that are derived from interpretations based on one of the views of the master jurists, He made it such that when they make a judicial ruling in accordance with one of those views, it becomes God's law, sublime is He, for that particular case.

Here is an example: Mālik said, "In my view revelation indicates that a man who says to a woman, 'If I marry you, you are thrice divorced,' and despite that marries her, she becomes thrice divorced immediately upon the marriage [66], and no subsequent marriage contract with her is valid until she marries another man, and is either divorced or widowed from him." Imagine that this man marries this woman, despite his statement, and lives with her in accordance with Shāfiʿī doctrine, which does not consider his statement of conditional divorce made prior to his marriage of that woman to be effective. He then divorces her once, which became a divorce of separation upon the conclusion of her waiting period. He then contracts a second marriage with her, and that contract is brought before a Shāfiʿī judge, who rules that this second marriage is valid. This judicial ruling, by necessary implication, entails a ruling that the man's conditional divorce was of no legal consequence,[1] and it becomes the equivalent of an express text (*naṣṣ*) from the Lawgiver that applies to this particular man who had made that conditional divorce, but to the exclusion of all other men who undertake the same conditional divorce, but in respect of whom no judicial ruling has attached declaring their conditional divorces to be valid and binding or invalid and of no legal consequence. This is because God, sublime is He, has confirmed the unassailability of a judicial ruling by means of consensus, and what God, sublime is He, has confirmed by consensus is known, by virtue of incontrovertible evidence, to be from the Lawgiver.

In this case, there is, without doubt, a conflict between the indicants that Mālik relied on to conclude that the subsequent marriages of those men who have conditionally divorced their wives prior to marrying them are invalid, and the indicant that obtains from this hypothetical judicial ruling. It is an obvious feature of the judicial ruling that it is more particular than the universal (*al-ʿāmm*) indicants upon which Mālik relies insofar as Mālik's indicants treat all cases of conditional divorce made prior to a subsequent marriage, while the indicant of the judicial ruling is limited to this specific case. But, whenever a particular (*khāṣṣ*) textual indicant conflicts with a universal indicant, the conflict is to be resolved by affording the particular priority over the universal. Were we to say, "This judge's ruling should be rejected," we would be violating that interpretive principle which mandates giving priority to specific indicants over universal ones, in addition to violating consensus. Were this to be the case, no weight at all would be given to the specific indicant which is in opposition to the universal one, and that is prohibited, in addition to the fact that consensus also prohibits ignoring the judicial ruling.[2]

It has thus become evident that there are two reasons that render judicial rulings made with respect to controversial areas of the law unassailable, while only one reason renders the judgment unassailable if it is governed by consensus [67]. Is it not strange how the unassailability of judicial rulings based on controversial rules is stronger than judicial rulings based on noncontroversial rules?

It has also become evident that the unassailability of a judge's ruling in controversial areas of the law is a result of a jurisprudential principle, namely, that a particular revealed indicant is given priority over a universal one. This is a good explanation of this issue, so pay heed [68].

Question 17. "When a judge gives a judicial ruling based on a controversial rule of evidence, like the testimony of a group of children, or one witness and the oath of the claimant, or based on customs whose legal relevance is controversial, like the habit of husbands with respect to the maintenance of their wives—'Is this a custom that places the burden of proof on the wife or not?'[1]—does the judicial ruling encompass the controversial rule of evidence or not? Does someone who rejects the rule of evidence have the right to reject a judicial ruling because of his belief in the invalidity of the rule of evidence used by the judge and say, 'This judicial ruling in my opinion lacks sufficient evidence, because the testimony of a group of children is tantamount to no testimony, and there is a consensus that a judicial ruling that lacks evidence must be rejected, so I reject that ruling,' or is that not permitted?"

The Answer

Rules based on controversial sources, whether textual or empirical, are of two types. The first is if the rule is poorly attested. A judge's ruling, if based on such a rule, must be rejected, because it is too weak to act as a valid countervailing consideration to universal legal rules. Such a ruling, then, would be contrary to universal legal rules, and whatever contradicts universal legal rules but is not supported by a valid countervailing consideration justifying its exceptional character must, as a matter of consensus, be rejected [69].

If the rule at issue, however, has a comparable basis in the revealed law to the contrary position, then in this case there are two controversies: the first with regard to the controversial rule of evidence used by the judge, and the second with regard to the substantive ruling that is a consequence of the evidence underlying the judicial ruling. In this case, if the judge gives the ruling in accordance with what the controversial rule of evidence entails, it becomes impossible to overturn the ruling because the evidentiary ruling merges with his substantive ruling on the case's merits. His judicial ruling based on one of the controversial substantive legal views, however, is not a judicial ruling with respect to which of the views regarding the rule of evidence is valid. Had it been so, further controversy regarding, for example, the permissibility of ruling on the basis of one witness and the oath of the claimant would be impossible on account of a judge having adopted it in his ruling. Nothing, however, can resolve the legal controversy regarding controversial rules of evidence other than a subsequent consensus which settles on one of the opinions. Accordingly, it has become manifest that a judicial ruling based on a controversial rule of evidence is not a ruling with respect to the controversial rule of evidence, but only a ruling in accordance with what it entails with respect to that particular case.

What clarifies this is that the judge did not intend to originate in his mind anything other than the consequence of the rule of evidence, not the rule of evidence itself. Indeed, a judicial resolution of the controversies regarding the rules of evidence is inconceivable, because resolution of such a dispute belongs to the affairs of the next life, not the affairs of this world.

Establishment of all the rules of the revealed law and theoretical jurisprudence all follow this rule: God, sublime is He, did not give anyone the authority to make a ruling based on one view of the law and thereby specify it as the one correct answer by means of a judicial ruling [70]. Instead, He gave judges the authority to give a legal opinion only with respect to the correctness of one of the views, but legal opinions do not preclude his opponent from giving a legal opinion in accordance with his dissenting view. This is in contrast to a judicial ruling, whose effect is to preclude his opponent from adhering to his own view of the law with respect to that case and compels him to accept the view adopted by the judge for his ruling.

As for the statement, "The judge has ruled without valid evidence," it is rejected. It is instead the case that controversial rules of evidence, if the rules are comparable to one other in strength, continue to be legally valid with respect to those who accept their validity, whether a judge or a mufti. Accordingly, the statement "He ruled without evidence" lacks meaning. That is the case only if he ruled on the basis of a rule that is poorly attested, as has been explained previously. If the controversial rule of evidence is comparable in strength to the contrary views, then no, it cannot be rejected [71].

Question 18. "Is it conceivable that a judge could make a judicial ruling that is based on a controversial rule of substantive law if the source for the decision is a matter of agreement, or is it inconceivable that he would rule in accordance with a controversial rule of substantive law except on account of contradictory and different sources for the rule, since by stipulation we are concerned with controversial rules? And how could it be that the substantive rule of law be controversial if its source is a matter of agreement? Indeed, if they agree on its source, they should agree on the substantive rule."

The Answer

Yes, it is conceivable that a judge can rule on the basis of a controversial rule of substantive law even though the basis for the rule is a matter of agreement. The opposite is also true: a judge can rule based on a noncontroversial rule of substantive law even though the basis for the rule is controversial, as a matter of both logical consistency and logical necessity.[1]

This is because if what is meant by "basis" is the factual evidence on which the judge relied in making his ruling, like witnesses, and similar things, and not the revealed indicants underlying legal opinions, like the Quran and the Sunna, it is conceivable that the evidentiary basis of the judicial ruling might be noncontroversial, whereas the substantive rule governing the substantive case is controversial, as is the case when two just witnesses testify before a judge that a man and woman suckled once from the same breast,[2] or that he had entered into a conditional divorce [72] with regard to the woman whom he subsequently married.[3] In these two cases, assume the judge rules to annul the first marriage and invalidate the second. The judicial ruling in both of these cases is controversial, even though their factual basis—and that is the testimony of two witnesses—is not.

The contrary can occur when the factual evidence is controversial but the substantive rule of law governing the case is not. For example, the right to retaliation or compensation for injuries is a matter of universal agreement, but most scholars deny that the evidence of one witness combined with the claimant's oath is sufficient to establish liability. This, however, is the well-established doctrine of Mālik, may God show mercy to him. Accordingly, both possibilities are conceivable if what is meant by "basis" is the factual evidence presented by the litigants.

If what is meant by "basis" is the revealed indicant which is the underlying basis of the master jurists' legal opinions, however, sometimes the substantive rule is controversial even though the basis in this second sense is a matter of universal agreement. Controversy may ensue in these circumstances, either because the opponent understands the indicant in a manner contrary to the way the other jurist understands it, or because he interprets it according to what it entails while the other believes it to have been abrogated, or because one of them believes it to be subject to a countervailing argument that the other does not accept as valid.

This is the case, for example, when the Ḥanafīs hold that the capital of a valid endowment (*waqf*) must not consist of movable property, in reliance on the statement of God [73], sublime is He, "God has not decreed either the *baḥīra* or the *sāʾiba*."[4] Abū Ḥanīfa reasoned that an endowment is a kind of *sāʾiba*. This controversy exists even though there is no dispute that the verses of the Noble Quran are a valid source of legal rules. This is also the case when Shāfiʿīs hold that a marriage continues to be valid, despite the occurrence of a conditional divorce prior to the time of the contract, in reliance on the Prophet's statement, may God bless him and grant him peace, "Divorce is the right of the one in possession of the woman."[5] And, they, the Shāfiʿīs, invalidate sales in reliance on the "option of the bargaining session,"[6] while Ḥanafīs and Mālikīs do not, despite their shared agreement regarding the validity of this report (*ḥadīth*),[7] and there are many similar cases.

It is also the case that sometimes the substantive rule might be a matter of agreement, but the basis for the rule is controversial, as occurs when there are two Prophetic reports applicable to the case, each one of which is valid according to the one upholding that rule of substantive law but invalid according to the other. In this case, they agree on the substantive rule of law in reliance on the two Prophetic reports but differ on which report forms the basis of the rule, each one relying on a different report.

It is therefore manifest that it does not follow that agreement with respect to the basis of either a substantive rule of law or a rule of evidence produces agreement with respect to the substantive judicial ruling or the general rule of law; nor is the converse true, that is, that disagreement with the basis of either a substantive rule of law or a rule of evidence produces disagreement with respect to the substantive judicial ruling or the general rule of law [74, 75].

Question 19. "The statement of the jurists 'When a judge rules in a controversial area of the law, his ruling is unassailable,' does that encompass the bases of the ruling that are the subject of legal interpretation and resolve whether they are or are not a valid indicant of God's law? And is it conceivable that a judicial ruling resolves these differences? And, is this principle unqualified, or are some controversial matters excepted from it? And if there are some exceptions, does that mean that some controversial bases of legal reasoning are also excluded from it?"

The Answer

The statement of the jurists cited in the question is not categorical but is qualified: in particular, the jurists have stated expressly that a judge's ruling cannot stand and must be rejected in four situations. These are if it is contrary to consensus, universal legal rules, a univocal text of revelation (*naṣṣ*), or an a fortiori analogy (*al-qiyās al-jalī*).[1] And some controversial issues of substantive law fall under these last three categories; otherwise, there would only be one category, that is, consensual rules. Accordingly, these last three cases, on the basis of their own rulings, are an exception to their unrestricted statement regarding the unassailability of judicial rulings in controversial areas of substantive law.

As for whether certain sources of law that are controversial are valid indicants of divine law or not, they are not intended to be included [76] within the general scope of their statement because what they intend are the rules of substantive law over which disputes occur among people for purposes of this world. Abstract disputes about what is, or is not, a proper indicant of the revealed law, as well as what is, or is not, admissible factual evidence in a trial, such as one witness and the oath of the claimant, and other matters, take place for the sake of the next life, not for a benefit that accrues to the disputants in this temporal life. Instead, these theoretical disputes are akin to disputes about rituals. And the goal of each of the disputants in these abstract controversies is knowledge of what has been established in the revealed law regarding the obligations of all persons until the Day of Judgment, not something that is particular to him. Accordingly, these matters cannot fall under the jurists' statement in any respect.

Finally, note that when the scholars say that a judge's ruling is rejected when it contradicts universal legal rules, univocal texts, or a fortiori analogies, that is true only when there is not a countervailing proof or consideration that otherwise justifies contradicting universal legal rules, the a fortiori analogy, or the specific univocal text. Otherwise, one might think that a judge who rules that a forward contract (*bayʿ al-salam*), a lease (*ijāra*), or an irrigation-cultivation partnership (*musāqāt*) is valid had ruled in a manner that contravenes universal legal rules, and thus his ruling should be rejected; however, because there is a preponderant countervailing consideration in each of these cases, it is no wonder that such rulings are not rejected.[2] It is important to know that judicial rulings are rejected only when they fall under one of the four categories mentioned, and there is no preponderant countervailing consideration, so know that [77].

Question 20. "Some jurists say that the reason judicial rulings based on controversial issues are unassailable is because were such judicial rulings to be rejected on the basis of a contrary legal opinion, disputes would not come to an end. Is that the reason for their unassailability, or is it because of something else?"

The Answer

The reason that precludes overturning one judicial ruling in favor of a contrary judicial ruling in contexts of legal controversy is not what you have attributed to this group of jurists. It is on account of a principle established in theoretical jurisprudence and the rules of the revealed law, which is that if there is a conflict between a particular text and a universal text, the particular text is given priority over the universal text. This has been previously explained in detail in the discussion of the difference between the judge's judicial ruling in an area of law governed by consensus and his judicial ruling in controversial areas of the law, even though consensus prohibits rejection of both. Derivation of rules from general principles of theoretical jurisprudence is always preferable to deriving them from particular substantive considerations. This is the practice of the greatest scholars, in contrast to weak-minded jurists whose expertise is limited to substantive law [78].

Question 21. "Is an actual controversy among the master jurists a condition for the unassailability of a judicial ruling, or is it sufficient that the case be one in which controversy could occur among the master jurists, even in the absence of actual controversy?"

The Answer

The occurrence of an actual legal controversy is not a requirement. If there is a gap in the law of the sort that would invite legal controversy, for example, and a judge rules in a fashion that is appropriate, his decision is unassailable, but if his ruling regarding a gap in the law is contrary to universal legal rules, then his ruling is rejected. There is no difference in the unassailability of a ruling in an area of the law with a gap and one in which legal controversy has already occurred [79].

Question 22. "Is it the case that a judge is permitted to rule only in accordance with that view of the law which he views to be preponderant, just as the master jurist is not permitted to give a legal opinion except in accordance with what he believes to be preponderant? Or may he rule in accordance with one of the views found in the law, even if it is not, in his opinion, the weightier view?"

The Answer

If the judge is a master jurist, then he is not permitted to rule or give legal opinions in accordance with anything other than what he believes to be preponderant. If, however, he is a follower of a master jurist, he may give legal opinions in accordance with the well-established doctrine of his school, and he may give judicial rulings in accordance with it, even if, in his opinion, it is not the weightier view, relying, in this case, on the reasoning of the master jurist whom he follows, just as he follows the views of the master jurist with respect to giving legal opinions.

As for simply following his caprice in giving judicial rulings or giving legal opinions, that is prohibited as a matter of consensus. It is true that the scholars have differed with respect to cases in which a master jurist finds that the revealed indicants are contradictory and equally strong, rendering him incapable of choosing which of the two is the weightier. In such cases some conclude that the contrary indicants cancel each other out, leading to no rule, while others say that he should simply choose one of the contrary indicants on the basis of his own preference [80] and give his opinion in accordance therewith.

In accordance with the view that he should choose one of the two and give his legal opinions in accordance with it, he may choose one of the two views and make a judicial ruling in accordance with it as well, even if, a fortiori, it is not preponderant in his view. This is so because a legal opinion is a universally applicable law that applies to all individuals until the Day of Judgment, whereas a judicial ruling applies only to particular cases. Accordingly, it is more appropriate that free choice in particular outcomes be adopted than in the case of universally applicable laws. This is what both substantive legal rules and general legal principles suggest. On the basis of this analysis, whether a judge issues judicial rulings in accordance with what he believes to be the weightier view or in accordance with the view of the master jurist whom he follows, he is not acting capriciously, and accordingly, both positions are valid. Indeed, the assumption is that, before giving his opinion or rendering his decision, he has expended all reasonable effort and has found that he is incapable of determining which view is weightier, and their equivalence has been ascertained. As for judging in accordance with what he believes is a weaker opinion, that contravenes consensus [81, 82].

Question 23. "When you say, 'The judge's ruling is an origination in the mind, and a vow, too, is an origination of a rule that had not existed in the texts of revelation,' do you mean that they are therefore equal in that both are originations and both are related to particular, not universal, law? Does that mean that there is a difference between them or that they are the same?"

The Answer

Although they are equal insofar as both are originations, they differ in respects. The first is that the fundamental pillar of the vow is the audible expression, for it is the legal cause that transforms a recommended act into one that is obligatory, whereas the legal cause of the judge's ruling is nothing other than courtroom evidence. Likewise, the judge's ruling does not require audible expression to come into existence [83], his subsequent statement about his ruling being only a report regarding how he ruled and a command for testimony to be taken in attestation of that judicial ruling. The second is that a vow is the origination of an obligation that binds the one who originates it, whereas the judicial ruling is an origination obliging or giving permission to another. The third is that a judge's ruling can consist of a removal of a legal obstacle, an invalidation of a right, or a declaration of permissibility, as is the case in a ruling invalidating ownership of lands after the disappearance of living proprietors. Thus, a judicial ruling does not necessarily result in an obligation. It may create an obligation sometimes, but other times it does not. Vows, however, always result in an obligation. The fourth is that the purpose of a judicial ruling might be prohibition, like the judge's nullification of a marriage, for its purpose is to prohibit the husband from engaging in intimate relations with the wife. The vow, however, never seeks prohibition, but instead seeks obligation. If one were to say, "If one were to take a vow to shun a particular act that is disfavored, he has effectively prohibited it for himself, in which case the object of the vow is prohibition," we would say to this that the intent is obligation, because cessation from disfavored conduct is recommended, so the vow transformed that recommended command into an obligation [84].

Question 24. "A master jurist, if he is a judge, gives legal opinions in accordance with his own views, and he gives judicial rulings in accordance with his own views. Accordingly, both reports are the result of his own interpretive efforts, so what is the difference between the two, particularly when there is an unprecedented case for which no prior legal opinion or judicial ruling has ever been given? In both cases, he reports the rule which binds the party with respect to that particular event. One cannot differentiate between the two by saying that the judicial ruling is binding but the legal opinion is not, because the conclusiveness of the judicial ruling depends on knowing it to be a judicial ruling and not a legal opinion."

The Answer

The difference is that, in connection with the legal opinion, he reports what he understands to be the preponderant meaning of what he believes to be the applicable indicant from revelation. Thus, he is in the position of a translator for God, sublime is He, in respect of the meanings that he discovers within revelation, like the judge's translator who reports to the people his understanding of the judge's words or writing. In the context of a judicial ruling, however, when acting as a judge, he is originating an obligation, or a release from an obligation, against the losing party, in accordance with what appears to him to be weightier on the basis of the applicable revealed indicant, and the occurrence of the legal cause in that particular case. He, therefore, when reporting his judicial ruling, is reporting to the people what he, himself, has decided, in reliance on the authority that God, mighty and elevated is He, has delegated to him via succession from the authority of God's Messenger, may God bless him and grant him peace, as set forth [85] in the saying of God, sublime is He, "And make judgment among them based on what God has revealed."[1] When he reports to the people a legal opinion, however, he is reporting to them what he understands to be God's law that he himself understood from God, mighty and elevated is He, as set out in the applicable indicants of the revealed law.

When he acts in a judicial capacity, he is similar to the judge's delegate (*nāʾib*), adjudicating cases personally, originating obligations and releases in accordance with what the legal causes require in light of the factual evidence presented to him. He can exercise this authority because the judge who appointed him gave him that power. This is in contrast to the authority of a translator, who is obliged simply to explain the sense of the principal's words, but not to originate anything from himself. Just as the judge's delegate reports about himself that he originated an obligation, so, too, does the judge who is a master jurist in the revealed law: he reports that he originated an obligation in his capacity as God's delegate, Mighty and Elevated is He, on the earth and over his creatures, insofar as He has delegated to him the power to originate judicial rulings among His creation. And, whatever he originates, it is as though it becomes a particular text revealed at that moment from the Lawgiver, mighty and elevated is He, with respect to that case. For that reason, it cannot be rejected, because a particular indicant is given priority over a universal indicant, as has been explained previously in detail. This, then, is the difference between a judge's ruling in accordance with his own views of the law and the legal opinion he gives in accordance with his own views of the law [86].

Question 25. "What is the difference between the conduct of the Messenger of God, may God bless him and grant him peace, when he gives a legal opinion and when he communicates (*al-tablīgh*) God's revelation to the people, and his conduct as a judge (*al-qaḍā'*) and head of state (*al-imāma*)? Do these differences leave varying effects on the revealed law and particular rulings, or are they one and the same in their effect? Is there a difference between messengership (*al-risāla*) and these three matters, that is, communicating revelation and giving legal opinions, adjudicating cases, and exercising public power, or are messengership and giving legal opinions one and the same thing? Whether or not you say that giving legal opinions and messengership are one and the same thing, is prophethood (*al-nubuwwa*) similar to messengership, or is there a difference between it and messengership in that respect? These are lofty concerns which are related to great and noble realities which must be clarified and explained with great care, for knowledge is ennobled by the nobility of its subject."

The Answer

When the Messenger of God, may God bless him and grant him peace, gives a legal opinion, he communicates from God, sublime is He, the content of his understanding of the revealed indicants in respect of God's law, blessed and sublime is He, just as we have said is the case about all muftis other than him, may God bless him and grant him peace. When he, may God bless him and grant him peace, conveys to the people what God has revealed to him, he exercises the very essence of messengership. Messengership is God's command, sublime is He, to him, that is, the Messenger of God, to communicate revelation to others. Accordingly, he, may God bless and grant him peace, when he acts as the messenger of God, conveys from the Truth[1] to humanity what he has received from God, mighty and elevated is He [87]. In that capacity, he is communicating and transmitting from God, sublime is He. The traditionists, those who narrate Prophetic reports, and those who memorize the Noble Quran in order to teach it to the people, have inherited this function from him, may God bless him and grant him peace, just as muftis inherited from him the task of giving legal opinions. Just as the difference between a mufti and a mere transmitter has become apparent to us, so, too, the difference between his, may God bless him and grant him peace, delivery of revelation from His Lord to the people, and his giving legal opinions regarding religion has also become apparent. The difference between the latter two functions and the former two is the very same difference, for giving legal opinions does not logically entail transmission, and transmission does not logically entail giving a legal opinion, insofar as the essence of transmission and giving legal opinions is concerned.

As for his conduct, may God bless him and grant him peace, in giving judicial rulings, it is distinct from both messengership and giving legal opinions. Giving legal opinions is only the interpretation of God's words, and messengership is simply the conveyance of God's words to the people. Judicial rulings, by contrast, are an origination and an imposition of an obligation that comes from him, may God bless him and grant him peace, in accordance with the conclusions he reaches regarding the existence or nonexistence of the relevant legal causes in light of the litigants' evidence. For that reason he, may God bless him and grant him peace, said, "You bring to me your disputes, and it may very well be the case that one of you is a better advocate for his claim than his adversary. Accordingly, whoever wins his claim, but I award him something belonging to his brother, let him not take it, for I am giving him only a piece of hell!"[2] That indicates that judicial rulings are derivative of litigants' evidence and their ability to present it persuasively [88].

So, when he, may God bless him and grant him peace, acts as a judge, he originates legal rulings, but when he gives legal opinions and acts as a messenger, he does no more than communicate the meaning of God's words [89], and convey the revelation he received from God to the people, respectively. When he acts as a judge, he follows the command of God, sublime is He, to him, insofar as he originates [90] rulings in accordance with the litigants' evidence and the legal causes. He is not, however, following God's command in the sense that he is transmitting that ruling from God, sublime is He, because that which is delegated to him from God, sublime is He, is not the same as that which is transmitted from God, sublime is He.

But there is also another way in which a judicial ruling differs from a legal opinion, and that is that a legal opinion is amenable to abrogation, whereas a judicial ruling is not. In contrast, a judicial ruling may be overturned if the invalidity of its legal effects becomes manifest while a legal opinion may not. The possibility of being overturned is a feature particular to judicial rulings, and abrogation is a feature particular to legal opinions.

This feature of legal opinions, that is, that they may be abrogated, applies to the Prophet's legal opinions in particular, may God bless him and grant him peace, and the legal opinions of his contemporaries, but only as long as he was alive with them. After his death, may God bless him and grant him peace, abrogation cannot be countenanced with respect to legal opinions because the revealed law became finally established with his death. This, in brief, is another notable difference between judicial rulings and legal opinions with regard to these two categories, even though it is not the case for each and every legal opinion, but whenever the difference between the two genera is established, the difference between their essences is known, and confusion ends [91].

As for messengership, insofar as it is only a message from God, it is not always amenable to abrogation, as is the case with revelation that merely conveys historical information. Such a report, however, may be subject to particularization, but not abrogation, in accordance with the valid view of the scholars. At other times a report is amenable to abrogation if it entails implicitly a rule of conduct. Accordingly, messengership is a broader category than giving legal opinions and is distinct from it. Therefore, the differences among messengership, giving legal opinions, and acting as a judge have become manifest.

As for prophethood, many people believe that it is an expression simply for revelation from God, sublime is He, to a prophet. But this is not the case because a person may receive revelation from God, sublime is He, without prophecy. Revelation came to Mary, the daughter of ʿImrān, may God be pleased with her, as related in the story of Jesus, upon whom be peace. The angel Jibrīl, upon whom be peace, said to her, "I am merely the messenger of your Lord, with news that He gives you a pure lad."[3] And the angel Jibrīl said in another context, "Indeed, God does give you glad tidings."[4] She was thus a recipient of revelation, even though Mary, may God be pleased with her, was not a prophet, according to the sound theological view.

One finds in the hadith collection of Muslim that "God, sublime is He, once sent an angel to a man who set out along a path to visit a friend of his in God,[5] sublime is He. The Angel came to the man along the roadside, and said to him [92], 'God, sublime is He, informs you that He loves you on account of your love for your brother in God, sublime is He'" (paraphrased).[6] Such a conversation, however, is not prophecy. Were God, sublime is He, to send an angel to one of us, informing him of the teachings of Mālik regarding a specific case of law, or of the location of lost livestock belonging to him, neither would constitute prophecy. Rather, prophecy—as the pious scholars have said—is that God, sublime is He, reveals to one of His creatures a *ruling* that was originated for him and that is particular to him, as was the case when God, sublime is He, revealed to His Prophet Muḥammad, may God bless him and grant him peace, "Recite in the name of your Lord who created; the one who created people from a clot."[7] This, that is, the command to recite, was an obligation particular to the Prophet Muḥammad at that moment.

The scholars said, "This is prophethood but not messengership. But when God, sublime is He, revealed to him, that is, Muḥammad, 'O enveloped one! Arise and give warning!'[8] [93] that revelation constituted messengership because it entails an obligation connected to someone other than the recipient of revelation."

For that reason the prophethood of Muḥammad preceded his messengership by a period of time. Accordingly, the scholars say, "Every messenger is a prophet, but not every prophet is a messenger," because every messenger has the particular obligation to communicate what has been revealed to him to others, but not all prophets have such an obligation. The difference between prophethood, messengership, legal opinions, and judicial rulings has thus become manifest.

As for his conduct, may God bless him and grant him peace, as imam, that is something that is in addition to prophethood, messengership, giving legal opinions, and acting as a judge, because the imam is the one to whom the universal police and administrative power (*al-siyāsa al-ʿāmma*) to direct the public and their affairs has been delegated. This authority entails responsibility for securing the people's well-being and protecting them from harm, repressing the unjust, killing tyrannical oppressors, and securing God's servants throughout the state's domains, in addition to other matters of this nature. And these matters do not fall under the categories of giving legal opinions, judicial decisions, messengership, or prophethood: giving legal opinions is solely a matter of reporting the content of God's law on the basis of the indicants found in revelation; and judicial decisions are simply a matter of resolving litigants' disputes without regard to whether the judge possesses any share of the universal police and administrative power. This is particularly clear in respect of a judge who lacks the power to enforce his decisions, as in the case of a weak judge ruling against a mighty king: he does no more than originate in his mind an obligation upon that mighty ruler, without the possibility of attempting to enforce it against him ever crossing his mind, because that would be impossible for him. Accordingly, a judge, insofar as he is a judge, has no role other than to originate judicial rulings, while the power [94] to enforce them is extrinsic to his role as judge. It is true that at times the power to enforce judicial rulings may be delegated to him, while at other times this authority may not be included in his jurisdiction, but it has become clear that having universal police and administrative power over all persons, which is the essence of being the imam, is different from giving judicial rulings insofar as it is a judicial ruling. As for the possibility of an imam who lacks universal police and administrative power, that is inconceivable unless "imam" is understood nonliterally, and here we are concerned only with primary meanings of terms. As for messengership, it is no more than communicating from God, Sublime is He, to others God's will, and this function does not require the delegation of general police and administrative power to him, that is, the messenger. How many a messenger of God, sublime is He, throughout history was sent with divine messages but was not tasked with anything other than communicating the message in order to establish God's proof before creation, without being commanded to consider the public good (*al-maṣlaḥa al-ʿāmma*).

Now that the difference between being an imam and messengership has become clear, a fortiori the difference between it and prophethood has become clear, for prophethood is particular to the one receiving revelation, without any consequences to others. The difference among all these categories has now become evident through their distinguishing features [95].

As for the consequences these differences have in the revealed law, they are various. Whatever he, may God bless him and grant him peace, did in the capacity of imam, like dividing spoils of war seized from the enemy on the battlefield; disbursing public funds in accordance with the public good; enforcing criminal penalties;

organizing armies; fighting rebels; distributing public lands, whether agricultural or mines; and similar matters, it is not permissible for any person to undertake any of these activities without the permission of the current imam, because he, may God bless him and grant him peace, undertook these activities exclusively in his capacity as imam, and these activities became licit only with the imam's permission. This, therefore, is established as part of the revealed law, in accordance with God's statement, sublime is He, "and follow him [i.e., Muḥammad], that you may be led aright."[9]

Whatever he, may God bless him and grant him peace, did in the capacity of a judge, like awarding ownership pursuant to a right of first refusal; annulling marriages and contracts; divorcing women on account of the bankruptcy of their husbands, a circumstance which renders discharge of the husband's maintenance obligation impossible; or adjudicating cases of husbands who swear oaths to refrain from sexual relations with their wives and the consequences of their renunciation of such oaths, it is not permissible for anyone to undertake any of these acts without first obtaining a judicial ruling from a sitting judge, in accordance with his practice, may God bless him and grant him peace, because he, upon whom be peace, did not permit these claims to be vindicated without a judicial ruling, so his community after him, may God bless him and grant him peace, is subject to the same principle [96].

As for his conduct, may God bless him and grant him peace, in giving legal opinions, messengership, and communicating revelation from God, all of that is constitutive of revealed law which applies to human beings until the Day of Judgment. We are obliged to follow every rule that he has communicated to us from his Lord in accordance with the existence or nonexistence of its legal causes, without regard to the ruling of a judge or the permission of the imam, because he, may God bless him and grant him peace, when acting in these three capacities, was communicating to us the connection between that rule and that legal cause, making clear the path between individuals and their Lord. In these cases he was not originating a judicial ruling from himself, nor was he acting in the capacity of an imam, that is, making rules in accordance with his perception of the public good. Rather, in these three cases, he merely reported from his Lord things like how to perform the daily prayers, pay the alms tax (*zakāt*) and perform different kinds of ritual, as well as the ways by which an individual may obtain private property, whether by contracts of sale, gifts, or other legal acts. All of humanity is entitled to pursue these legal causes directly and individually and obtain the benefits of their legal effects without recourse to any judge to originate a rule, or to the current imam for permission to act on, and obtain the benefit of, these legal causes.

Now that the different consequences that his conduct, may God bless him and grant him peace, as imam, judge, and mufti, had on the law has become manifest, you should know that his actions, may God bless him and grant him peace, fall into one of four categories. The first category is that in respect of which the scholars have agreed that it was an act in his capacity as imam, like granting land (*iqṭāʾ*), enforcing the mandatory rules of criminal law (*al-ḥudūd*), sending out armies, and similar matters. The second category is that in respect of which the scholars have agreed that it was an act in his capacity as a judge, like obliging the discharge of indebtedness, ordering sellers to deliver goods to their purchasers, ordering purchasers to pay the prices of the goods which they have bought, declaring marriages to be invalid, and similar matters [97]. The third category is that which the scholars have agreed that he was acting in his capacity as a mufti (such as communicating the obligation to pray and the establishment of public prayer, and the establishment of the pilgrimage rites, and similar matters). The fourth category is that in respect of which his action, may God bless him and grant him peace, partakes in features of all three of these categories, and accordingly, the scholars differed as to the proper classification of the act. There are several cases that illustrate this principle.

The first case is his statement, may God bless him and grant him peace, "Whoever reclaims wasteland becomes its owner."[10] [98] Abū Ḥanīfa said, "This was undertaken by him in his capacity as imam, may God bless him and grant him peace. Accordingly, no one is permitted to reclaim wasteland without the current imam's permission because it involves the creation of a right to private property. It thus resembles a grant of land from the public treasury to a private person, and such grants are conditional on the imam's permission. Accordingly, reclamation is subject to the same rule."

Al-Shāfiʿī and Mālik, however, said that in this case he, may God bless him and grant him peace, was acting in his capacity as a mufti, because most of his conduct entailed the communication of legal opinions from God. Accordingly, when there is doubt about the character of his action, it should be presumed to fall under this category, thereby giving effect to the most likely possibility, which is the circumstance particular to messengers of God, upon whom be peace. For this reason, reclamation of land does not require the imam's permission because it is a general legal rule granting permission to reclaim land, like the right to harvest wood and pasture from property held in common for private use, by virtue of the shared legal characteristic of acquiring private property by performance of the practical legal causes leading to the creation of the private property right.

As for Mālik's view that wasteland located close to settled land may not be reclaimed without the imam's permission, this is not because this rule derives from the Prophet's having made this rule in his capacity as imam, but rather it is the result of another legal rule, namely, that reclamation of land which borders settled land requires an impartial investigation to confirm the borders of the town's common land, just as impartial factual investigations are necessary to confirm the insolvency of a husband in a claim for the dissolution of a marriage.[11] Indeed, *anything* that requires procedures to confirm the existence of relevant legal facts requires the intervention of judges before such rights can be exercised [100].

The second case is his statement, may God bless him and grant him peace, to Hind bt. ʿUtba when she complained to him that Abū Sufyān,[12] her husband, was a miserly man who, despite his wealth, failed to provide her or her children with sufficient maintenance. He told her, may peace be upon him, "Take what reasonably suffices you and your children."[13] A group of scholars took the view that this was a legal opinion from the Prophet, may God bless him and grant him peace, because most of his actions were taken in that capacity, may God bless him and grant him peace. On this assumption, whoever happens to come across property belonging to another which is of the same, or even a different genus as the property that is the basis of his claim, may satisfy his claim from that property, provided that it is impossible for him to satisfy his claim from the obligor.

The well-established doctrine of Mālik, along with another group of scholars, is that one should not satisfy one's claim out of property that is similar to that which is owed to him if he happens upon it, even if it is impossible to satisfy one's claim from [101] the obligor, but they disagreed as to the rationale of the prohibition: is it because [102] in the story of Hind, he, may God bless him and grant him peace, had acted in the capacity of a judge, in which case it is not permissible for anyone to satisfy his claims against another without first obtaining a judicial ruling—these jurists taking this precedent as the basis for the permissibility of a judicial ruling against an absent defendant—while others viewed it as a precedent permitting a judge to decide a case based on his own knowledge of the facts, in view of the fact that she did not present any evidence for her claim, as al-Khaṭṭābī[14] and others have related? It was also said that this case involves nothing other than a legal opinion in view of the fact that Abū Sufyān was present in the same town, and it is inconceivable that a judicial ruling would be entered against a defendant when that defendant is present in the judge's town without the judge first giving the defendant notice of the claim. Accordingly, this statement was a legal opinion [103].

Finally, his statement, may God bless him and grant him peace, "Return trusts to those who entrusted you, and do not betray those who have betrayed you,"[15] conflicts with his statement in connection with the issue of Hind, and as a result, the two groups agreed as regarding the rule, that is, the prohibition against self-help, but they disagreed as to the rationale.[16] [104, 105]

The third case is his statement, may God bless him and grant him peace, "Whoever kills an enemy in battle is entitled to the slain warrior's possessions." [106] Mālik concluded that the Prophet, may God bless him and grant him peace, said this in his capacity as imam. Accordingly, it is not permissible for anyone to seize the belongings of a slain enemy without the specific permission of the imam prior to the battle, in accordance with the action of the Messenger of God, may God bless him and grant him peace. Al-Shāfiʿī, by contrast, concluded that this was a legal opinion, and he therefore concluded that the soldier who kills an enemy in battle is always entitled to take his possessions without need for prior permission from the current imam, because this is a ruling that simply results from the occurrence of its legal cause, as is the case with all other legal opinions. His conclusion was based on the previous principle, namely, that the Prophet's actions, may God bless him and grant him peace, were largely undertaken in his capacity as a transmitter of legal opinions, because his most basic function was that of messengership and the communication of God's will to humanity [107].

Mālik contradicted his usual principle in this case, making this case an example of an action undertaken in the capacity of imam, in contrast to the previous two cases, for several reasons. One of these is God's statement, sublime is He, "And know that whatever spoils you take, one-fifth belongs to God."[17] This verse entails that one-fifth of the possessions of slain enemies belong to God, mighty and elevated is He, with the remainder going to the victorious army. The verse of the Quran is mass-transmitted (*mutawātira*), while the Prophet's saying has been transmitted by only a few narrators (*āḥād*), and the mass-transmitted text must take priority over a report narrated by only a few sources.

The second is that permitting this behavior leads to the corruption of motives and might cause a person to fling himself against his enemy among the unbelievers in the hope of seizing his property, and if the nonbeliever kills him, while his intention in fighting is not pure, he might enter hellfire, destroying himself and his religion as a result. This is a great risk which justifies a refusal to give effect to this report, for reports can be set aside when they contradict universal rules, especially [108] when the report is not abandoned wholesale but is understood to apply to a particular circumstance, such as the decision of the acting imam, meaning, that if the imam permits it, it is valid.

The third is that construing this report as having been an act of the imam is the more reasonable inference, because one immediately understands by this statement of the Prophet, may God bless him and grant him peace, that he, may God bless him and grant him peace, said it only in that context which requires exhortation to combat, and for this reason, we say that whenever the imam believes that this rule is consistent with the common good, he allows it, but where it is not in the common good, he does not. By describing this as the action of the imam, we mean nothing other than this.

These are the reasons that led Mālik to contradict his normal method of treating the Messenger's actions, may God bless him and grant him peace, as legal opinions until the contrary is shown to be the case, because the greater part of his actions, may God bless him and grant him peace, were undertaken in that capacity. There are many similar cases to these, so one should be heedful of these issues; they will be found throughout the law, and one will discover that these principles provide great knowledge and an important basis for understanding the different views of the master jurists [109].

Cautionary note: no jurist should imagine that among the controversial legal issues is the dispute that occurred between ʿUmar b. al-Khaṭṭāb and Abū Bakr al-Ṣiddīq, may God be pleased with them, regarding the captives of Banū Ḥanīfa.[18] Al-Ṣiddīq, may God be pleased with him, permitted them to be taken as slaves, then, when ʿUmar b. al-Khaṭṭāb became caliph, he commanded that they be returned to their families. Had it been the case that al-Ṣiddīq, may God be pleased with him, had made a judicial ruling enslaving the Banū Ḥanīfa, they would have become property of the Muslim community, and it would not have been permissible for ʿUmar, may God be pleased with him, to cause a loss to them by manumitting them gratis. Indeed, Abū Bakr's action, may God be pleased with him, was nothing more than a legal opinion, and accordingly, it is no wonder that it was permissible for ʿUmar to contradict it, because it is a case governed by interpretation for which consensus had not arisen, and in respect of which no judge had ruled. So, know that many jurists find ʿUmar's decision to release these captives to the Banū Ḥanīfa problematic, on the view that Abū Bakr had enslaved them. Were it not for establishing these different principles, it would have been very difficult, in light of the apparent circumstances, to understand that decision, for what comes to the mind initially is that al-Ṣiddīq, may God be pleased with him, had given a judicial ruling [110].

Question 26. "When you say that a judicial ruling cannot be overturned, does that mean only that a subsequent judge cannot overturn it but that a mufti may continue to give legal opinions contrary to it, just as was the case prior to the judicial ruling, or does the judge's ruling preempt any legal opinion to the contrary such that the judicial ruling becomes the unanimous law of the case? If you say that the judicial ruling preempts contrary legal opinions, that seems to contradict what the author of the *Jawāhir*[1] says in the Chapter of Judgments regarding the repeal of judicial rulings, where he says:

> **'The fourth topic: a judicial ruling, although it must be given effect by other judges, does not displace [111] the rule that applies morally; rather, the latter remains binding in the same fashion as it did prior to the judicial ruling. This is because a judicial ruling does no more than manifest the applicable rule, and it is not an introduction of the rule. Accordingly, it is not permissible for a Mālikī to act upon a ruling from a Ḥanafī judge that awards him a right of first refusal based on the fact that he is the seller's neighbor (*shufʿat al-jār*), nor is it permissible for someone who knowingly proffers perjured testimony regarding his marriage to a woman—so the judge, in reliance on the reliability of the witnesses, rules that the woman is the man's wife and that intercourse with her is permissible—to have intercourse with her, or to persist in his marriage to her.'**

This is his text in the *Jawāhir*. With this language, how can one say that the judge's ruling preempts the contrary legal opinion when Ibn Shās says that 'the rule remains binding in the same fashion as it did prior to the judicial ruling' and that a Mālikī cannot act upon a Ḥanafī judge's judicial ruling awarding him a right of first refusal on the basis of the fact that he is the seller's neighbor? Had it been the case that a judicial ruling preempts contrary legal opinions, and the particular case instead becomes one governed by consensus insofar as the judge's ruling constitutes the law of the case, it would have been permissible for a Mālikī claimant to act upon the grant of the right of first refusal that Ḥanafīs award to neighbors. Accordingly, it is not possible to maintain the view that legal opinions change on account of judicial rulings that contravene them."

The Answer

It is true that a group of prominent Mālikī jurists have held the belief, as a consequence of the principle Ibn Shās mentioned, that a judge's ruling in controversial areas of the law does not change the content of the legal opinion that applies to the case. Accordingly, when a judge, for example, rules in a case, and reaches a conclusion of permissibility, a mufti who believes that the conduct at issue is forbidden should continue to opine in respect of that case in accordance with his view prior to the ruling. Therefore, the one who holds to this view says, for example, with respect to someone who believes that property held in common may not become the subject of an endowment, or that endowments are never legally valid [112], that he can continue, even after a judge has ruled that a particular endowment, consisting of commonly held property, or any other kind of endowment, is valid, binding, and has been duly executed, to give legal opinions permitting the sale of that property. This is so because he believes that the judicial ruling prohibits a subsequent judge from repealing the first judicial ruling, but it does not preclude giving legal opinions contrary to the judicial ruling or its secondary effects. So, too, he believes that if a man says to a woman, "If I marry you, you are divorced," and then he marries her, the fact that a judge then rules that the contract is valid, that the marriage continues in existence, and that the divorce is ineffective, a dissenter may continue to give legal opinions after that judicial ruling that she is forbidden to him in reliance on the legal opinion that considers the man's conditional divorce to be legally effective.

I believe that this position is contrary to consensus. I have not found the language quoted in *al-Jawāhir* in any other Mālikī authorities, even though I searched diligently and in great detail in the various legal treatises of our Mālikī colleagues. It appears that his expression, may God be pleased with him, suffers from some overbreadth, and that he intended only one of two questions discussed in the Mālikī school. The first is the case of a judicial ruling whose legal cause had not in fact occurred. In this case, the judicial ruling does not change the applicable legal opinion, like a judicial ruling of divorce in respect of one who did not in fact divorce his wife, either because the witnesses made an error or because they intentionally perjured themselves. Ibn Shās mentioned this case in *al-Jawāhir*, in this very context, as has already been mentioned. The same principle applies to a case of proportional retaliation (*qiṣāṣ*) or anything else, anywhere the legal cause is absent in fact. In such cases, the legal opinion that applied prior to the judicial ruling in our view continues to apply as it was prior to the judicial ruling, in contrast to the view of Abū Ḥanīfa.[2]

The second is a judicial ruling which contravenes universal legal rules, or specific texts [113]. Ibn Yūnus[3] said,

> ʿAbd al-Malik[4] said, "The meaning of Mālik's statement 'The judge's ruling cannot be overturned,' is limited to rulings that do not contravene the Sunna. If, however, it contradicts it, a subsequent judge should repeal it," like the case of a slave who agrees to work in exchange for a partial manumission, and the judge rules that this agreement is binding. A subsequent judge should repeal this judicial ruling, and whatever property the slave paid to his master should be returned to the slave, but the slave's partial manumission remains effective;[5] [114] or a right of first refusal in favor of the seller's neighbor in respect of real property, or after partition of real property; or giving judgment on the basis of a Christian's testimony; or granting inheritance to the paternal or maternal aunt or the clients of descendants; or anything that contravenes the practice of the people of Medina,[6] not having been held by anyone, save outliers among the scholars; or a judicial ruling that an absolute, triple divorce is only one divorce, and the man who effected it then remarries her, without her first having married another man and either been divorced or widowed from him, another judge may separate them.

These are approximately ten cases which Ibn Yūnus mentions where the legal opinion remains as it was and a subsequent judge should repeal any judicial ruling given in accordance with such rules. There remains the statement of Ibn Shās, the author of *al-Jawāhir*, "Although we say that another judge should not repeal a judicial ruling that enforces the neighbor's right of first refusal, a Mālikī is not entitled to exercise this right of first refusal, even if a judicial ruling awards him this right," even though Ibn Yūnus cited this case for precisely the proposition that a subsequent judge should repeal this judgment, so one can see an evident contradiction between the claims of the two authorities.

If the author of *al-Jawāhir* intended only these two questions, that is, where the judicial ruling is based on a clear factual or clear legal error, then the claim is valid, although his language, and his inclusion of the claim that another judge should not repeal the first judge's ruling undermines that conclusion, albeit the only examples he gives were that of the neighbor's right of preemption and a man whose wife is divorced from him as a consequence of perjured testimony. The fact that these were his only examples suggests that he intended only those two classes of cases, but at the same time, the fact that he also includes derivative claims, based on the principle that another judge should not repeal the first judge's ruling, contradicts this narrow interpretation of his language. This confusion is not found in other authorities, and in any case, numerous cases from the Mālikī school contradict his language.

The first of these is that of the alms-tax collector:[7] if he takes one sheep out of a flock of forty sheep which belong to forty proprietors[8] in deference to the view of the Shāfiʿī school, our Mālikī colleagues have said that the value of the sheep taken by the alms tax collector is to be borne pro rata [115] by all forty proprietors. They also said, however, that as a matter of their legal opinion, if the alms-tax collector takes the sheep without relying on any legal opinion, and he is not a judge, it is an act of injustice whose loss is not distributed among all forty of the proprietors, but instead the loss remains with the one from whom the sheep was wrongfully taken. Accordingly, their legal opinion changed out of regard to Shāfiʿī doctrine and the interposition of a judicial ruling, a fact which shows that a judge's ruling preempts contrary legal opinions with respect to that particular case, and renders that particular case as though it were a matter of consensus as a consequence of the judge's ruling resolving the controversy regarding the rule applicable to that case.

The second of these is in the *Mudawwana*, where there is a case of two men whose sheep graze together as one flock, one with 11 sheep and the other with 110. The author of the *Ṭirāz*[9] and others said in regard to this case, "The man with the 11 does not owe anything in terms of the alms tax unless the alms-tax collector takes it in reliance on the doctrine of a jurist whom [116] he follows in that question, in which case the two men share its loss pro rata."[10]

The third of these is in regard to the Friday congregational prayer, in respect of which Sanad said, "If the imam has appointed a delegate to lead the Friday congregational prayer, the prayer is not valid unless the delegate of the head of state acts as the prayer leader. This is because whether the Friday congregational prayer is a matter that requires the permission of the imam is a matter of legal controversy, so once a judge has ruled on the question in favor of that view, the Friday prayer can be valid only if the delegate of the imam leads the prayer."

All of these are examples of legal opinions changing as a consequence of a judicial ruling.

The fourth of these is the case of the seller and the purchaser swearing oaths affirming their contradictory claims regarding the terms of a contract: does this entail an immediate cancellation of the contract, on the theory that no proper contract had been formed, or does the contract remain in effect until a judge rules that it has been canceled? A derivative issue that arises out of this controversy is whether each of the parties [117] has the right to perform the contract in conformity with the other party's statement, until there is a conclusive judicial ruling resolving the controversy. In this latter instance, the legal opinion which permits one party to perform the contract in conformity with the other party's statement changed on account of a judicial ruling insofar as this option lapses upon a judicial ruling.[11]

The fifth of these is in the *Mudawwana*, regarding a man who manumits his slave while he is bankrupt, and at a later date, comes into wealth. In this case, the slave's value is to be appraised and the former bankrupt must pay that sum of money over to his creditors, unless there had already issued a judicial ruling freeing him from the obligation to pay the slave's value, in which case he is not bound to pay the slave's estimated value to his creditors. Accordingly, Mālik had first given a legal opinion requiring an appraisal and payment of that sum to the creditors; he then gave another legal opinion contrary to his first on account of a prior judicial ruling relieving the former master from this obligation. Thus, the judicial ruling changed Mālik's legal opinion.[12]

The sixth of these is in the *Mudawwana*, in the First Chapter of Manumission, regarding creditors of a bankrupt who manumitted his slaves but whose creditors repudiated his act of manumission; neither the creditors nor the master have the right to sell the manumitted slaves until the matter is brought before a judge. If, however, the master sells them, or the creditors sell them, and *then* the matter is brought before a judge after the master becomes solvent, the sale is rescinded and the manumission becomes effective on account of the subsequent occurrence of solvency. If the judge, however, had sold them, and *then* the owner who had manumitted them purchases them after becoming solvent, they are legally his slaves, despite his earlier manumission of those same slaves.[13] [118]

In this case the legal opinion changed as a result of the judge's sale of the slaves, something that necessitates an implied judicial ruling that they had remained enslaved and that the initial attempt at manumission failed. The legal opinion applicable to the creditors' sale of the slaves as well as that of the owner's sale of the slaves was that the sale automatically becomes rescinded upon the subsequent solvency of the bankrupt, whereupon the manumission becomes immediately effective. In the two cases, however, there is a sale, and in both cases, there is a claim of the creditors, and in both cases, there is the occurrence of solvency after bankruptcy, so there is no difference explaining the change in the legal opinion applicable to the case other than the intervening judicial ruling.[14]

In the seventh of these cases, Mālik said,

> If the quantity of dates on a tree are estimated and found to be sufficient to justify imposition of the alms tax, but when they are harvested they turn out to be less than the estimated amount, the difference between the estimated amount and the amount harvested is ignored, because the estimator (*al-khāriṣ*) has the status of a judge, and his estimate of the

quantity is final and conclusive; however, had the dates not been estimated, and it turns out that, at the time they are harvested, they are less than the minimum amount required to justify imposition of alms tax, then no alms tax is due.[15]

In both cases, the harvested quantity of dates is less than the legal minimum, but Mālik concluded that alms tax was due in the first case because the estimator's ruling entailed a judicial ruling that the quantity of the dates that would be harvested exceeded the legal minimum [119]. Mālik's legal opinion, therefore, changed on account of the intervening judicial ruling, despite the discovery of a factual error in the ruling. Because we are speaking more generally about the case of a judge whose ruling is not based on an obvious factual error, a fortiori such a judgment would produce a change in the applicable legal opinion.

The eighth of these is that which Ibn Yūnus reports on the authority of a group of our colleagues in the Chapter on the Reclamation of Uncultivated Land: "If two persons began to dig two wells such that each of them owns one of the wells, and after a dispute between them regarding the extent of land adjoining each well necessary to protect each well from the other, a judge rules that there is no harm arising from the location of the two wells, but later, harm is ascertained, the injured party will not be entitled to remove the harm, that is, the other well, for his right to claim that the other well is causing harm to his well lapsed on account of the judicial ruling."[16]

Their statement "his right has lapsed" is a legal opinion. Accordingly, the legal opinion changed on account of the judicial ruling. Had it not been for the judicial ruling, he would have been permitted to ward off the harm from himself, and we all would have given him such a legal opinion. Therefore, if the legal opinion changes, despite clear evidence that it was based on a mistake, a fortiori it changes when the judicial ruling is not obviously mistaken. This case, and the prior case of the estimated quantity of dates with respect to calculating alms tax, would not have been the subject of controversy among our colleagues were it not for the fact that the judicial rulings had been based on factual errors. Were there agreement, however, that no factual errors had been committed, there would have been unanimous agreement that the legal opinion should change [120]; the only controversy is whether such a ruling should be overturned because its factual basis is subsequently discovered to have been erroneous. It is clear, then, that there is no controversy that a judicial ruling whose factual basis is not obviously erroneous results in a change in the applicable legal opinion on account of the intervening judicial ruling.

Were one to say, "All that these cases show is that a subsequent judge should not repeal the prior judicial ruling, not that the legal opinion governing the case has changed?" we would say that "repeal of a judicial ruling is the responsibility of another judge, not that of the mufti. The mufti in these cases, according to everyone, is to report the content of God's ruling, sublime is He, that the petitioner can do this or that the petitioner cannot do that, or that he is obliged to pay alms tax or that he is not. Is this anything other than a pure legal opinion?" Indeed, there is no meaning to the concept of legal opinions other than saying, "This is lawful," or "This is forbidden," or "This is obligatory," or "This is not obligatory," or "This is permissible," or "This is not permissible," and similar statements. So, this is a change in the legal opinion without doubt, not mere restraint in repealing a judicial ruling.

The ninth of these is in the *Mudawwana*, "Neither an injured animal nor a male goat is satisfactory for the discharge of the alms-tax obligation; however, if the alms-tax collector believes that it is, then it is sufficient." [121] He gave the legal opinion that payment of an injured animal or a male goat is sufficient to discharge the obligation of the alms tax after the alms-tax collector takes the animal in question, and that if the alms-tax collector does not take the animal in question, that is, if the animal in question is paid voluntarily, then it does not discharge the obligation of the alms tax.[17] This is a change in the legal opinion on account of the judicial ruling, because the alms-tax collector, in Mālik's view, has the status of a judge.

The tenth of these is when Sanad said in the Chapter of Commingling, "If there are three associates, each of whom owns 40 sheep, and three sheep are taken from one of them, he can only recoup the value of two-thirds of a sheep from his partners because only one sheep is due on 120 sheep, of which he owes one-third and the other two, two-thirds. But, if the three sheep were taken in reliance on the view of those who give no effect to commingling, such as Abū Ḥanīfa, then he can recoup from each of his associates one sheep." So, the legal opinion has changed based on the judicial ruling. This is not an instance of refusing to repeal a judicial ruling, because repeal of a judicial ruling is something only a judge can do. As for a scholar saying, "You can recoup" or "You cannot recoup," that is nothing other than a legal opinion.[18]

There are very many similar cases to these in the Mālikī school, and I have sought to draw attention with this selection of cases only to make the desired point, namely, that this issue, as I believe, is a matter of consensus. In light of these examples, how is it possible for someone to persist in denying this point or to maintain the view that the legal opinion governing a case is unchanged by a judicial ruling? It has already been stated that God, sublime is He, has appointed judges as His delegates with authority to originate particular rulings in the context of disputes governed by a controversial rule.

Accordingly, when a judge rules [122], with the permission of God, sublime is He, and his ruling is validly attributable to God, sublime is He, that ruling of the judge is a specific textual indicant from God, sublime is He, arriving on the tongue of His delegate, who is His delegate on earth and the successor of His Prophet with respect to that particular case. It therefore becomes obligatory to exclude this case from the domain of the dissenter's legal opinion with respect to that particular dispute. The revealed indicant that the dissenter relies upon with respect to that case is universal, while this indicant from the judge is particular to some members of the genus which would otherwise be subsumed under the universal indicant relied upon by the dissenter. Accordingly, there is a conflict involving this member of this class between the particular indicant—the one provided by the judicial ruling—and the universal indicant which the dissenter believes applies to all members of the class. Priority, however, must be given to the particular indicant over the universal textual indicant, in accordance with what has been established in theoretical jurisprudence.

This principle is the secret which explains why another judge should not repeal prior judicial rulings, nor should a dissenter express opposition to the prior judicial ruling, not what some of the jurists believe, namely, that judicial rulings are unassailable only to put an end to conflict and dispute. A jurisprudential principle supports the argument that we made earlier, while what they believe lacks any jurisprudential principle to support it, and that which is supported by a jurisprudential principle is superior to that which relies only on prudential considerations. Even if we grant the validity of their argument, the two, the prudential argument and the jurisprudential principle, work together to strengthen the rule that judicial rulings are unassailable, whether by a subsequent judge or by a mufti holding a contrary view. Arguments may overlap, except that one ought not to ignore that explanation which the principles of jurisprudence support, unless there is a countervailing consideration outweighing it [123].

Question 27. "Is a judicial ruling indicated sometimes by way of an express statement of correspondence, at other times by indirect statements, and yet other at other times by implication, like other concepts, or is it indicated only by an express statement of correspondence? And, is it indicated sometimes by means of a statement while at other times by means of conduct, or is it indicated only by a particular statement, such as his statement, 'I have ruled that . . .' or 'Bear witness against me that I have ruled that. . .' And, if you allow for the possibility that the indicant of the ruling can be an action, would it be an action particular to judges or not?"

The Answer

The judicial ruling that the judge originates is indicated sometimes by an express statement of correspondence, such as his statement "I have ruled that this marriage is annulled." At other times, however, it may be indicated by an indirect statement, such as his statement "I have ruled that both of these marriages are annulled." The ruling with respect to the combination of these two marriages is indicated by an express statement of correspondence, whereas the ruling with respect to each of the two is indicated indirectly. Finally, it can be indicated implicitly through another statement, like his statement [124] "I have ruled that the sale of this slave whose previous owner had manumitted him while he was bankrupt is valid." It indicates by an express statement of correspondence the ruling regarding the validity of the sale, and by necessary implication the invalidity of the manumission, because it follows from the validity of the sale that the manumission was invalid, because it is impermissible to sell a free person. This is the explanation of the statements of judges.

As for a judge's conduct, it may sometimes indicate a judicial ruling by express correspondence. An example would be when a judge, without any accompanying verbal communication, sells a slave whom a bankrupt debtor had manumitted. The judge's willingness to sell him necessarily implies a judicial ruling that the manumission was invalid. Similarly, his willingness to marry off a woman who had been previously married prior to the contract which the judge effects on her behalf necessarily indicates a judicial ruling that her previous marriage had come to a conclusion, in contrast to the case where he marries off an orphan girl under his supervision, or sells goods belonging to her. Neither of these latter two actions indicate a judicial ruling in any way, not a prior ruling, or a future ruling, or a ruling simultaneous to his action. Accordingly, another judge may look into it, and if it fails to satisfy some requirements required by the other judge's legal doctrine, he may invalidate it.

As for a judge's conduct indirectly indicating a judicial ruling, this arises only in written documents. It is conduct, and when he writes a letter to another judge, "I have completed the manumission of these two slaves whose owner who had manumitted them in part," or "I have nullified these two marriages," the writing indicates the judicial ruling with respect to both cases by way of correspondence, but with respect to each one, it indicates the judicial ruling indirectly, because it is a part of what the writing [125] indicates. As for a judge's conduct which involves selling and similar matters, you will never find therein indirect indications of a judicial ruling. In such cases, the judicial ruling occurs only as a necessary consequence of his conduct, and the part of the consequence is not indicated indirectly. Indirect indications of a judicial ruling occur only when the part is indicated by correspondence, and selling does not indicate the occurrence of a judicial ruling by correspondence, but rather only by necessary implication. Writing, even if it is a type of conduct, is like an audible expression that indicates by correspondence, and for that reason, it is conceivable that indirect indication takes place with it. Take note of this, and distinguish between the two types of indications, and assume that writing indicates judicial rulings by linguistic convention in the same manner as audible expression, in contrast to sales and similar matters which indicate not by linguistic convention, but rather only by necessary legal implication.

It has now become manifest to you that a judicial ruling can be indicated by means of correspondence, indirectly, by necessary legal implication, by words, or by conduct, and that the act might be particular to judges, like selling a debtor's property, and it might not, like writing, because everyone is entitled to write about his circumstance and his actions. It has also become manifest to you that a judge's action may be completely free of any sign of a judicial ruling, and it might necessarily imply it. The preceding examples are sufficient to clarify these questions so pay heed [126].

Question 28. "Can a mufti repeal a judicial ruling or can only another judge repeal it? What about the jurists' statement 'The judge's ruling in matters of legal controversy is not denied or repealed'; does that apply particularly to judges, or does it apply to both judges and muftis?"

The Answer

Repeal of a judicial ruling can take place only from one who has the authority to make a decision in the matter that is subject to repeal, and the authority to originate a ruling in the controversial areas of the law is vested in judges. Accordingly, the repeal and the invalidation of judicial rulings are left to them as well. Because a mufti cannot originate a judicial ruling, he cannot repeal one, just like a trustee in charge of another's property has the authority to originate contracts involving his ward's property and so may rescind them. So, too, because the ward cannot originate contracts, he cannot rescind them. Likewise, for a woman: because she cannot originate her own marriage contract, she cannot terminate it. So, too, for a slave: because he may not marry without his master's consent, he may not terminate his marriage contract without his master's consent, unless the master has given him authority to marry, in which case he has the authority to divorce; because his master granted him authority to marry, he acquired the authority to originate marriage contracts and to terminate them by divorce [127].

This rule—that one lacking the power to make a contract lacks the power to terminate it—is one with many particular applications, and the Shāfiʿīs have used it against us Mālikīs regarding the case of the conditional divorce prior to marriage or ownership, when a man says, "If I marry you, you are divorced," or "If I purchase you, you are free." They said, "He did not own the rights of marriage, so he cannot possess the right to divorce," or "He did not have the power to originate a divorce, so he cannot enter into a conditional divorce." They make the same argument with respect to manumission, even though both the husband and the master of a slave each have the right to originate divorces and manumissions as a general rule by consensus when they have rights of marriage and ownership of the slave as a matter of fact.

A mufti, however, insofar as he is a mufti, lacks any of the powers necessary to originate a judicial ruling in the fashion that has been delegated to judges in any case, as has already been explained; accordingly, he lacks the power to repeal a judicial ruling in any case. This is no different from the fact that a woman has no right to marry herself in any case and so she lacks the power to divorce herself in any case. Accordingly, it has become manifest that everything a mufti does involves giving legal opinions, without repealing or judging in the fashion that has been delegated to judges, even though it is a kind of legal judgment insofar as it is based on a comprehensive interpretation of the textual indicants of revelation, like the judge's translator, as has previously been set out in explaining the difference between a judge and a mufti, and that the judge originates rulings while the mufti is effectively a translator of God's speech to humanity [128].

Question 29. "What is the cause for repealing judicial rulings in the four examples: contravention of consensus, universal legal rules, manifest analogy, and express text? What are some examples of these?"

The Answer

Consensus is a reason for overturning judicial rulings because consensus is infallible; it does not speak except the truth, and it does not judge except with truth. Something that contradicts it is, without doubt, false, and the revealed law does not uphold falsehood, so whatever contravenes consensus must be nullified. As for universal legal rules, manifest analogy, and express text, what is meant is that, even in the context of legal controversy, a judicial ruling that contradicts one of these principles must be overturned, but only if there is no valid countervailing consideration. If there is a countervailing consideration, then the judicial ruling, as a matter of consensus, is not overturned so long as the judicial ruling is in accordance with that countervailing consideration, such as a judicial ruling declaring the validity of a *commenda* (*qirāḍ*) contract, a partnership in an irrigated farm (*musāqāt*), forward contracts, contracts for the transfer of credit (*ḥawāla*) [129], and similar cases. These contracts contravene universal legal rules, express texts and manifest analogy, but particular indicants of revelation attesting to their validity are given priority over the contrary universal legal rules, express texts, and manifest analogies, because they are universal indicants in relation to those particular indicants, and in such a circumstance, the particular indicant is given precedence over the universal one.

Whenever there is not a valid countervailing consideration, whether it is completely absent, as when the interpretation was the product of fancy that lacks any basis in reality, or in reliance on the continued application of the presumption of the absence of obligation,[1] or similar considerations arising out of a failure to give due weight to the existence of those universal legal rules, express texts, and manifest analogies, or there is a countervailing consideration that is weak, like a report with a confused chain of transmitters, or similar considerations (for such things are not given any weight)—in either case, such a judicial ruling should be repealed because it contravenes the weightier countervailing consideration.

This is the reason for repealing judicial rulings that contravene one of these four considerations: the revealed law refuses to uphold such judicial rulings because of their weakness. And, just as such decisions are not accepted if they issue from a judge, so, too, it is not permissible to adhere to such views if a mufti expresses them, and it is sinful for anyone to act in accordance with them.

For this reason we say that it is not permissible to act on all judicial rulings, nor is it permissible to follow all the legal opinions of the master jurists. Indeed, every legal school includes views which, if examined carefully, would result in the conclusion that following such rulings is impermissible for the same reasons that judicial rulings which violate consensus, universal legal rules, manifest analogy, or express text must be overturned [130].

As for some examples, one is if the judge were to award the entirety of the decedent's estate to the decedent's brother and deprive the grandfather of any share. In this case, the Muslim community has two views: either the grandfather takes everything, or he shares it with the decedent's brother. No one has permitted exclusion of the grandfather from sharing in the estate. Were a judge to make such a ruling, on the view that the brother is a closer to the decedent than the grandfather, we would repeal that ruling, and if he were a mufti, we would not follow his opinion.

An example of something that contravenes universal legal rules is "Ibn Surayj's case," that is, when a judge rules to uphold a marriage to a woman to whom the husband had said, "If I divorce you [131], you are divorced before it thrice." He then divorces her three times or twice or once. The correct position is that he is bound to three divorces, so if she died or he died, and the judge awarded her the right to inherit from him or the right to inherit from her to him, we would repeal his ruling, because it contradicts general legal rules. One of the universal legal rules is the validity of the conjunction of a condition and its consequence, because its ruling appears only in it. A condition which cannot validly be conjoined with its consequence ought not to be recognized as a valid condition in the law. For that reason a judicial ruling in conformity with Ibn Surayj's case must be repealed.

An example that contravenes express text is a judge's ruling which awards a right of first refusal to the seller's neighbor, because a valid report limited that right to the seller's partner without granting a similar right to the seller's neighbor, and no valid countervailing consideration exists [132]. Accordingly, a ruling contrary to it must be repealed.

An example of a judicial ruling that contravenes manifest analogy is admission of the testimony of a Christian. Any judicial ruling based on his testimony must be repealed, because the testimony of an immoral witness is not accepted, and an unbeliever is worse than an immoral Muslim and, from the perspective of analogy, less entitled to occupy legal offices.[2] Accordingly, such a ruling would be repealed for that reason. You should include other examples in each case appropriate to it [133].

Question 30. "What is the difference between a judicial ruling, a judge's fact-finding, and the enforcement of a judicial ruling? Does a judge's fact-finding qualify as a judicial ruling or not? If we say that fact-finding is a judicial ruling, is it the judicial ruling itself, or something that necessitates it outwardly? And on either assumption, is the answer universally applicable to all instances of fact-finding or not?"

The Answer

As for a judicial ruling, its essential meaning has previously been defined as an origination of an obligation or a release in cases involving disputes related to matters of the profane world, and the relevance of these qualifications has also been previously explained. Fact-finding, however, involves the introduction of evidence in front of the judge confirming the empirical existence of the legal causes as a matter of probability in the mind of the judge. So, if the testimony of witnesses establishes that a master manumitted his slave in part, that a marriage took place without the permission of a guardian or was contracted with an invalid dower, that [134] a partner sold his share of partnership property to a nonpartner in a case involving a claim of the right of first refusal, or that she is a wife of the decedent so that she may inherit, and similar matters that relate to the establishment of legal causes, there is no doubt that proof may be made as to the existence of such matters, and whether or not doubt remains in the judge's mind about the existence of the relevant facts, he is still obliged to ask the other party whether he has impeaching evidence or contrary evidence. In these circumstances there are no grounds for anyone to dispute that such things do not qualify as a judicial ruling.

Once full proof of the occurrence of the legal cause has been produced, any suspicions regarding the evidence have been negated, and all legal conditions, along with any other relevant considerations, have been satisfied, there is no doubt that the judge is under an immediate obligation to rule because one of the litigants is acting unjustly, and the remediation of injustice is an obligation that must not be deferred. Because it is the judge's duty in this circumstance to make a judicial ruling, and by all appearances, he has done what is obligatory on him, the judicial ruling becomes a necessary consequence of his fact-finding. Accordingly, it is necessary to believe that establishment of the legally relevant facts is a judicial ruling, in reliance on the obvious circumstances. This is what is meant by the statement of Mālikī jurists that "the well-established position of the school is that a judge's fact-finding constitutes a judicial ruling." [136]

There is an isolated opinion among the Mālikīs, however, that the essential characteristic of fact-finding is different from the essential characteristic of judicial rulings, and because their essential characteristics differ, it is impossible to say that the occurrence of one necessitates the occurrence of the other, unless one can be logically certain of concomitance. But it is impossible to be certain of concomitance because it is possible that there remains some doubt in the mind of the judge that is unknown to us, and the absence of knowledge of something does not necessarily require the nonexistence of that thing. Accordingly, one must exercise caution until certainty is reached that it is a judicial ruling [137]. That a judge's findings of fact are not the same as a judicial ruling is clear with respect to disputes in which the judge is ruling by means of originating a rule in a controversial area of the law.

As for cases subject to a universally recognized rule of law, like the establishment of the obligation to pay the value of a destroyed object, the right to have an intentional murderer put to death in lawful retaliation, the establishment of the debtor's indebtedness, the contract of commenda, amputation of the hand as a punishment for theft, in none of these cases does the perfect establishment of the legal facts result in the need to originate a legal ruling; rather, the rules governing these cases are all established in the foundations of the revealed law as a matter of consensus. The role of the judge in these cases is limited to enforcement, and with the exception of enforcement, the judge and the mufti are equivalent. In this circumstance, there is absolutely no place for a judicial ruling the origination of which the Lawgiver has delegated to the judge. Indeed, these rules simply follow their legal causes, whether or not there is a judge. Yes, enforcement requires a judge, even though enforcement is not particular to him with respect to the enforcement of debts and similar matters. Accordingly, were it the case that the party who destroyed property paid its value, or the debtor the debt owed, or the seller delivered the sold good, there would be no need for someone to enforce the rule, whether a judge or otherwise [138].

The only reason a judge is required with respect to cases governed by a universally recognized rule is if these cases require deliberation, judgment, and investigation to ascertain the existence of the legal causes, like the nullification of marriages; or the circumstances are such that delegation of enforcement to the people generally would lead to strife and fighting, such as would be the case with respect to the mandatory criminal punishments and the discretionary ones, even though discretionary punishments are of the first category, meaning they need investigation and require judgment to determine the proportionate penalty relative to the crime, the criminal, and the victim. If the circumstances surrounding the application of a universally recognized rule lack these factors, there is no need for a judge to enforce the rule, and individuals may enforce it. It is never conceivable that origination of judicial rulings could take place in any of these cases.

As for the essential characteristic of enforcement, it differs from both the judge's finding of facts and his ruling, because it consists of ordering the seizure of the criminal and his imprisonment, or coercively taking property from the recalcitrant debtor and giving it to the entitled creditor, and matters similar to these. That is the essential characteristic of enforcement, and it comes in the third and final stage, with findings of fact coming in the first stage, and the judicial ruling between the two litigants coming in the second stage [139].

The difference between fact-finding, a judicial ruling, and enforcement has now become manifest. It has also been established conclusively that fact-finding is in no way the same as a judicial ruling; at times it may necessitate it, but at other times it might not. It might be the case that, once the legally relevant facts have been determined, its legal consequences are logically compelled while the outcome of other cases is not solely determined by the determination of the legally relevant facts, as was previously explained in connection with cases governed by universally recognized rules. It has also become manifest conclusively that the opinion which holds that fact-finding is a judicial ruling in all cases is an error. It has also become manifest that this view, that is, that fact-finding is a judicial ruling, must be particularized and that the scholars' statement to this effect must be interpreted so as to provide it a valid meaning, so take heed [140, 141].

Question 31. "Does the judge's tacit acquiescence with respect to a particular matter before him constitute a judicial ruling affirming that matter or not? Imagine a contract is brought before the judge and he ignores it, without any negative comment. Is that like the Lawgiver's tacit acquiescence when he sees someone do something and leaves him be (because the Lawgiver's acquiescence is an indication of the permissibility of that act), or is the judge's tacit acquiescence weaker in light of the fact that this takes place in a controversial area of the law, so he may choose to leave him be and not interfere with him insofar as that person is acting in a situation that this characterized by legal controversy, in contrast to the Messenger of God's acquiescence, may God bless him and grant him peace, because he, may God bless him and grant him peace, cannot maintain silence in the face of sinful conduct?"

The Answer

Acquiescence is prima facie evidence that the conduct in question is acceptable, but its persuasive power is weaker than either action or speech because it is merely a failure to express opposition combined with silence; however, in proper circumstances, it might even be consistent with condemnation. Consider the Messenger of

God, may God bless him and grant him peace: after he had communicated the prohibition of disbelief, and had communicated the command to faith, and those who believed accepted the call, and those who disbelieved rejected it, he did not, peace be upon him, continue to condemn the people of Mecca, or other nonbelievers at all times, nor did he send letters to the neighboring unbelieving kings every month, much less did he do so daily, after he sent to them his initial invitation to them to accept Islam [142]. The fact that he exercised restraint in condemning particular sins at particular moments of time, after he had already communicated their sinfulness, does not entail or imply that those sins had now become permissible. Accordingly, the intended meaning of acquiescence is ambiguous in a way that speech and conduct are not.

The acquiescence of a judge also suffers from that same weakness in respect of its meaning, as well as an additional weakness on account of other possibilities, for example, that the judge might refrain from ruling in connection with a case governed by a controversial rule because both legal opinions are equally permissible, and each is a way to God, sublime is He. In such a case it is not surprising that the judge could acquiesce to both rules without imposing either one. This is in contrast to the acquiescence of God's Messenger, may God bless him and grant him peace. His acquiescence with respect to a case can only signify the act's permissibility, unless it had been preceded by a prior condemnation sufficiently clear so as to guide people to God's rule, sublime is He, in respect of that case.

After it has been shown that the legal significance of a judge's acquiescence to an act is weaker than that of the Lawgiver's, one should know that, because acquiescence is an indicant of the law, albeit a weak one, our colleagues have differed in their views regarding how to understand the acquiescence of a judge in a particular case. Ibn Shās, the author of *al-Jawāhir*, says,

> If a woman makes a claim before the judge that she married herself to her husband without the permission of her guardian, and he acquiesces in it and gives effect to it, then later he is dismissed from his office [143], ʿAbd al-Malik b. al-Mājishūn said, "This is not a judicial ruling and another judge may invalidate it," while Ibn al-Qāsim[1] said, "No other judge may invalidate it, and his acquiescence to it is akin to his explicit ruling upholding it," and Ibn Muḥriz[2] preferred Ibn al-Qāsim's view.[3] [144]

This is in contrast to a case where the judge, after the case had been brought to him, says, "I do not recognize the validity of any marriage concluded without the permission of the guardian," but does not rule that any particular marriage is invalid. This is simply a legal opinion, and any other judge may make a judicial ruling in accordance with his legal views in connection with that case. The same is true if he were to say, "I do not rule on the basis of the testimony of one witness and the oath of the claimant." There is agreement that this is nothing more than a legal opinion.

Ibn Yūnus said:

> ʿAbd al-Malik said, "If it were to be said, 'The divorce that takes place after the husband gives his wife the option to terminate the marriage is a final divorce effecting separation, and the woman, if after being given the choice, elects to divorce herself, and then the first husband marries her again, without an intervening marriage to another man, and this

second marriage is then brought to a judge who believes this second marriage to be permissible, and so he acquiesces to it, a subsequent judge may invalidate the second marriage contract, and treat the initial divorce as a triple divorce.[4] And if he makes divorce or manumission conditional on marriage to the woman or acquisition of the slave, or he marries while in the ritual state required for pilgrimage, and a judge acquiesces in these acts, or he produces one witness to a murder before a judge who accepts the validity of group oaths to prove murder,[5] but the judge refrained from judging in accordance with that evidence, another judge may issue a ruling in all of these cases because what the first judge did does not constitute a judicial ruling.'"

It is as though Ibn Yūnus's quote of ʿAbd al-Malik is contrary to what the author of *al-Jawāhir* attributed to him.[6]

In brief, because a judge's acquiescence in the context of legal controversy encompasses two kinds of weakness, as has been previously explained, its legal significance has produced controversy among the scholars. Those who looked to its basic sense concluded that it appears to constitute a ruling in light of the judge's circumstances, but those who looked to its weakness, ignored it and did not believe that it constituted a judicial ruling, and they permitted others to repeal it [146].

Question 32. "What are the means by which one knows which legal acts are in need of a prior judicial ruling—meaning that an individual lacks the unilateral authority to determine the existence of the legal cause—and which legal acts are not in need of a judicial ruling, meaning that an individual has the unilateral authority to determine the existence of the legal cause and that is sufficient grounds for him to act?"

The Answer

There are three means by which legal rules that do not require a prior judicial ruling are distinguished from those that do.

The first of these means is when application of that rule requires deliberation, investigation, and exertion of effort from an insightful scholar, a fair arbitrator to confirm the existence of its legal cause and the extent of its legal consequence. Some examples follow.

The first example is divorce on account of the husband's bankruptcy. Application of this rule requires confirmation of the fact of bankruptcy, and whether she has a valid claim for maintenance against this husband such that bankruptcy can terminate [147] his marital rights—or was he someone whose apparent condition at the time she married him was consistent with permanent poverty? As Mālik said: "If she married a man who was an ascetic, she does not have the right to a judicial divorce on account of her husband's bankruptcy, because her marriage began in that condition."

The second example is application of the discretionary penalties of criminal law which require precision in determining the gravity of the crime and the relevant circumstances of the criminal and the victim, so that the punishment can be applied in accordance with these considerations without injustice.

The third example is judicial divorce in the case of a husband who has sworn an oath to abstain from sexual relations with his wife.[1] It requires exertion of effort and precision in determining the nature of that oath which was taken in respect of her: is it one that obliges him to take an action to resume marital relations or not; does his refusal to resume marital relations constitute harm to the wife or not; if the purpose of that oath was to injure her, should she be divorced from him against his will; or, did it have a beneficial, valid purpose, such that she should not be divorced from him against his will, as would be the case if he swore not to have intercourse with her out of fear that his nursing child might become ill should her milk be ruined were she to become pregnant as a result of intercourse, and similar considerations based on the husband's good-faith judgment [148]?

The fourth example is a man who swears an oath that he will administer a severe beating to his slave.[2] A judgment of mandatory manumission against the master's will in this instance is in need of a judicial ruling because it is not known whether the slave committed a crime that would justify the beating. Application of this rule also is in need of ascertaining whether the threatened beating, if carried out, would in fact rise to the level that the law considers abusive with respect to that particular slave's circumstances; whether the master, were he to carry out the terms of his oath, would be deemed to be sinful, it being the case that an oath to commit a sin is deemed to be immediately violated, thus resulting in the immediate manumission of the slave; or, would it be possible for the master to fulfill the oath without incurring sin, in which case involuntary manumission would not be required?[3]

The second of these means is when applying the rule to its facts is in need of a judicial ruling and the direct involvement of rulers because delegating the application of such rules to all people would result in civil strife, hatred, murder, fighting, and injuries to life and property. Some examples follow.

The first example is the mandatory penalties of criminal law. While they are determinate in themselves and thus are not in need of deliberation to determine their amounts, were all individuals entrusted with their enforcement, they would have rashly whipped fornicators and amputated those committing theft, and other crimes, and as a result fanaticism would become intense, fights would break out, and noble individuals would become enraged; civil strife would spread, and rancor would become severe. Revelation acted to prevent this risk by delegating these matters to public officials, and the people submitted to them, obeying willingly and unwillingly, and as a result, these great harms have been averted [149].

The second example is the division of battlefield spoils. Their proportions are known, as are the legal causes giving rise to entitlement, except that humans are by nature excessively covetous and competitive in their desire for precious things. Accordingly, every individual desires to have for himself precisely what every other individual desires, thus leading to the same harms mentioned previously in the first example. Accordingly, revelation prevented this by delegating the distribution of battlefield spoils to public officials. These matters, even though they are not amenable to resolution via a judicial ruling, are of a type that they require the intervention of public officials. I mentioned it for that reason in order to draw attention to why their involvement is needed and the appropriateness of this example to this discussion.

The third example is the collection of the poll tax from non-Muslims, and the land tax due in respect of conquered land and other lands, which revenues are the property of the Muslim community. Had the management of these public funds been left to the individual members of the community, disorder would obtain, and a baneful end would result.

The third of these means is when there is a substantial conflict between the claims of God and the claims of human beings. This conflict necessitates a judge, because the judge is God's deputy, sublime is He, on His earth, in succession of the Prophet Muḥammad, may God bless him and grant him peace. Accordingly, when he originates a judicial ruling [150] in the appropriate circumstance, his ruling becomes the law of the case, and submission to it is obligatory. Some examples follow.

The first example involves someone who manumits half of his slave. The remaining portion is not to be mandatorily manumitted in the absence of a judicial ruling because of the conflict among the claim of God, sublime is He, to manumission; the right of the owner in his property; and the right of the slave to work for himself. In addition, there is substantial dispute among the jurists whether the master can be compelled to complete the manumission.

The second example is mandatory manumission of a slave whom his master has mutilated. This involves a claim of God, sublime is He, to the slave's manumission; the claim of the master to his property; and the claim of the slave to his manumission, as was the case in the first example. If a judge rules, his decision becomes the law of the case, and whatever contradicts it becomes invalid, with peace returning to the people and rights being clarified.

The third example is the sale of a slave whom a bankrupt debtor has manumitted. This case requires a judge to intervene on account of the conflict among the claims of the creditors to the slave, insofar as he is property; the claim of God, sublime is He, to manumission; and the claim of the master to a right to be free of claims against him or to obtain an act of piety through manumission, to say nothing of the substantial dispute as to the proper rule which applies in this case. Indeed, al-Shāfiʿī's disagreement reached the point that he rejected the opposing view sternly, saying, "A debt is a generic obligation while manumission concerns a specific [151] slave, so there is no conflict." Accordingly, manumission does not become invalid in his view because the specific and tangible quality of the slave precludes his treatment as the equivalent of an intangible debt.[4]

But, if a judge upholds the validity of the sale, his ruling becomes the law of the case. Accordingly, title to the slave vests in the purchaser as a result of the ruling; the master who attempted to manumit the slave obtains the right to reacquire the slave if he repurchases him, and the purchase price is used to satisfy the bankrupt's creditors. With the judicial ruling, all parties to the dispute are satisfied with what issued from the judge, God's lieutenant, sublime is He, and the lieutenant of God's messenger.

These three circumstances are what necessitate the intervention of a judge or public officials. If none of these circumstances is present, the rule follows its legal cause, whether or not a judge rules in accordance with it. In accordance with this principle, legal rules fall into one of three categories: those which result from their legal causes by virtue of consensus and are not in need of a judicial ruling because none of the three reasons that gives rise to the need for a judicial ruling is implicated by application of the rule; those which are in need of a judicial ruling as a matter of consensus by virtue of the fact their application necessarily involves one of the three aforementioned circumstances that require a judicial ruling [152]; and those subject to disagreement, "Does it fall under the first category or the second?," by virtue of the fact that the case gives the impression that it might or might not include one of the three factors that give rise to the need for a judicial ruling. Accordingly, because of the uncertainty as to whether these factors are present in any particular case, there is uncertainty as to whether a judicial ruling is required in advance of applying that rule.

Specific examples of these three categories follow.

An example from the first category that does not need a prior judicial ruling are all ritual observances; all matters that are universally prohibited, such as drinking grape juice once it becomes intoxicating; matters that are controversially prohibited, such as the meat of carnivores; the rules regarding the purity of bodies of water for purposes of ritual washing; the obligation to repay debts and to restore deposits and misappropriated items to their true owners; and other such things.

An example of the second category is declaring a debtor to be insolvent after finding that his debts exceed the value of his property; judicial divorce of the wives of missing persons and others; and judicial dissolution of marriages on account of the husband's bankruptcy or abuse of or injury to the wife, and similar things.

There are several examples of the third category, that is, those cases for which there is disagreement with respect to whether a prior judicial ruling is required or not [153].

The first is taking possession of misappropriated property from the one who wrongfully took it if the true owner is missing; does this need a judicial ruling, or can an individual, on behalf of the true owner, take possession of it from the person who took it wrongfully? The scholars are divided on it.

The second is someone who manumits his share in a slave. Ibn Yūnus said, "Our colleagues agree that he immediately becomes manumitted after an expert appraiser determines his value without any need for a judicial ruling, because that is what is found in the Prophetic report." Others, however, have said that a judicial ruling is needed.

The third is manumission of a slave when he comes into the ownership of a master who is his relative, and the master is free and solvent. The well-established rule of the Mālikīs is that this does not require a judicial ruling, but it has been said that there must be a judicial ruling.

The fourth is manumission as a consequence of a master's abuse of his slave. Ibn Yūnus said, "Mālik said, 'Manumission in this case arises only after a judicial ruling,' while Ashhab[5] said, 'No judicial ruling is required; it follows immediately from its legal cause.'" [154]

The fifth is rescission of a contract of sale after both parties to the contract swear oaths.

The sixth is nullification of a marriage after both parties swear oaths (if someone accepts this view).

There should be added to this discussion as well the question of the Friday congregational prayer, even though the controversy does not involve its need for a judicial ruling, but rather whether the imam's permission is a prerequisite for its validity, but that is not a judicial ruling.[6]

The reason for the controversy with regard to each of these examples is the presence of conflicting factors, and the supposition that they are in need of a judicial ruling because of the presence of the legal causes giving rise to the need for a judicial ruling, and also the supposition that they are independent of and lacking the factors that give rise to the need for a judicial ruling [155]

This in summary provides a principle for when something needs a judge's ruling and when it does not—the existence of the legal cause being sufficient—and the different categories into which legal rules fall in respect of this principle. A summary of the reasons for this is provided comprehensively along with examples so that the jurist becomes capable of deriving from those examples the answers to other cases, having now become aware of the secret of this question [156].

Question 33. "What gives a person the capacity to originate rulings in controversial areas of the law, such that it is obligatory to enforce them and not permissible to repeal them? Is that something anyone can do or is this limited to those in respect of whom a particular cause attaches? And what is that cause? Is it one or of several types?"

The Answer

There is no disagreement among the scholars that not everyone enjoys that power and that it is limited to those in respect of whom a particular cause attaches, that cause being holding a particular office; not every office grants that power. There are many offices that do not include within it the power to originate judicial rulings; others include the power to originate all judicial rulings; and, finally, there are other offices that include the power to originate [157] some judicial rulings. Some offices expressly include the power to originate judicial rulings; some offices expressly exclude the power to originate judicial rulings; and the nature of some offices is such that they may or may not include this power.[1]

Public offices exist across a spectrum of powers with two extremes and a middle; the office of the caliph, which is the greater imamate, is the office with the greatest power; arbitration (*taḥkīm*), which comes into existence by an act of the two disputants, is the office with the least power; and between these two are many intermediate offices. I will mention fifteen of these offices in what follows (in descending order of power), giving examples and clarifying the laws that apply to them.

The first is the office of the imam, which explicitly confers upon the imam the power to originate rulings in all legal cases, whether monetary or criminal, and all other offices' authority are a part of its authority. Accordingly, its explicit terms include the judicial power as well as power to direct the community's general affairs.

The second is the plenary minister (*wazīr al-tafwīḍ*) of the imam. Ibn Bashīr,[2] one of our colleagues [158], said,

> "All matters may be delegated to the plenary minister, but the imam is distinguishable from him in three respects: the plenary minister lacks authority to appoint a successor to the incumbent imam, while the incumbent imam may choose whom he wishes as his successor, with the designated successor becoming the imam after the incumbent's death or removal, just as Abū Bakr al-Ṣiddīq, may God be pleased with him, did with his appointment of ʿUmar b. al-Khaṭṭāb, may God be pleased with him; the plenary minister may not resign from his office, while the imam may resign; and the plenary minister may not dismiss anyone whom the imam has appointed to a public office. This kind of minister is called a 'plenary minister.'"

Ministers themselves are of three classes, the most powerful being plenary ministers; executive ministers (*wazīr al-tanfīdh*), who have the power to carry out policy decisions, in the next rank; and advisory ministers (*wazīr al-istishāra*), who occupy the lowest rank. It is obvious that plenary ministers enjoy the authority to originate judicial rulings and other powers. This is by virtue of the office's explicit terms of appointment, insofar as the imam says, "I have appointed you as plenary minister," or "I have delegated to you plenary power of action," or similar language. If, however, the imam expressly states that his appointee is merely an executive minister, then when the imam issues a judicial ruling or exercises another public power, the executive minister must carry it out. Accordingly, such an officeholder lacks the power to originate judicial rulings, and the same is true of the advisory minister.

The third is the office of governorship over specific territories and regions, like the relationship of kings to the caliphs. The terms of this office expressly grant territorial governors judicial power, provided the officeholder has appropriate qualifications. It includes the judicial power as well as the power to exercise police powers, organize armies, distribute battlefield spoils, disburse money from the public treasury, and similar matters.

The fourth is the minister of a governor appointed over a specific territory. The scholars said, "He may not appoint a plenary minister except with permission of the imam, but he may appoint executive ministers. If, however, he has permission to appoint a plenary minister, judicial powers are included in the appointment, just like the minister of the imam, when he is a plenary minister." [160]

The fifth is appointment to the command of armies, administering the populace's affairs, and protecting its security, without the power to appoint judges or collect taxes. This office, in Mālik's doctrine, also includes the judicial power, for Mālik said in the *Mudawwana*: "The judicial rulings of the captains of the fleets are conclusive," which al-Qāḍī ʿIyāḍ[3] took to mean the public officers to whom the defense of coastal waters and of those who live on the coasts has been delegated [161]. There is no doubt that officers to whom the affairs of armies and other matters have been delegated are superior to them, so their judgments should be effective a fortiori, but the matter is a contentious one among the scholars [162].

The sixth is the judicial office. This office includes the power to originate judicial rulings but includes no other powers, in contrast to the preceding offices. It gives its officeholder the power to originate judicial rulings in controversial areas of the law, or those areas of the law that are amenable to legal controversy if the case is a novel one with no prior legal opinion or decision having been given in respect of it. It also gives its officeholder the power to enforce rules in areas of the law that are governed by consensus.

The seventh is the office of complaints (*maẓālim*). The first to introduce this office in Islam was ʿAbd al-Malik b. Marwān.[4] He dedicated one day each week to hear complaints from the populace [163], and he would refer the difficult cases to Idrīs al-Awadī.[5] This officeholder has the same powers as a judge, except that he is [164] freer than they are in admitting evidence, insofar as he may rely on circumstantial evidence to an extent not permitted for judges, as well as many other particular features that distinguish him from judges, as is set out in detail in the books of substantive law. This officeholder also has the power to originate judicial rulings in controversial areas of the law [165] and to enforce rules in areas of the law that are governed by consensus upon proof of their legal causes [166].

The eighth are the delegates of judges, whether over specific locales or without geographical restriction. These lieutenant judges are the equals of the appointing judges insofar as they have the power to originate judicial rulings in controversial areas of the law and to enforce rules of consensus when legal proof is provided that the legal causes have been satisfied. Their authority in this respect is the equivalent of the appointing judge, without any diminution [167] or increase, except that the difference lies in the size of the caseload—large or small—depending on the size of the region. The appointing judge also has the power to dismiss the lieutenant, but not vice versa. These differences, however, do not detract from the nature of the authority lieutenant judges possess.

The ninth is the market inspector (*al-ḥisba*). This office does not have the authority to originate rulings in all areas of the law. Instead, its officeholder is authorized to exercise judgment in connection with originating rulings with respect to the exterior windows of homes, stables for horses along public highways [168], and similar matters that are the subject of public regulation. He has no authority to originate rulings or enforce them with respect to either marital or commercial contracts. He has greater authority than the judge, however, insofar as he is authorized to investigate, *sua sponte*, violations of the law, even before a complaint is brought to his attention, while a judge rules only with respect to claims which a specific party brings to his attention; a judge, by contrast, does not seek out disputes that are not brought to his attention. He also has coercive power exceeding that of a judge because the market inspector should inspire awe, whereas the judge should inspire fairness. Accordingly, the market inspector's powers are broader than that of judges from one perspective, but narrower from another; the office enjoys some [169] judicial powers, not all, but it has coercive powers the judiciary lacks.

The tenth is particular offices that derive their authority from judges and other officeholders, like someone who is responsible only for authorizing and annulling marital contracts, or who supervises the exercise by orphans of their rights of first refusal, and thus has delegated to him the authority to repeal or ratify the exercise of such rights in accordance with what he believes is consistent with the law. This office is simply a branch of the judicial function, and its officeholder has the power to originate rulings in areas of the law not subject to consensus and the power to enforce those rules of law which are subject to consensus, but only with respect to cases falling under his jurisdiction. Nothing he decides that falls outside of that may be enforced.

The eleventh is offices that are derived from individual persons, and it is arbitration. Arbitration is lawful for monetary claims, but not criminal punishments, charges of adultery, and similar matters. Accordingly, it is also a form of judicial authority, so all the powers it has, judges have, but judges have greater power than arbitrators. Accordingly, he has the power to originate rulings in controversial areas of the law and to enforce laws that are subject to consensus, but only in claims involving property or that which is related to property. Ibn Yūnus said, "Saḥnūn[6] said, 'If he rules on a monetary claim, or a claim that is reducible to money, his decision is to be enforced [170], but if he rules on a matter of personal status, he has exceeded his jurisdiction and should be prohibited from doing so again.'"[7] [171]

The twelfth is tax collectors, those who collect the alms tax. They have the power to originate judicial rulings in controversial areas of the law and to enforce laws that are subject to consensus, but only with respect to properties that are subject to the alms tax. If their judgments fall outside of that, they are not enforced because of the absence of authority.

The thirteenth is the officer responsible to estimate the yields of date palms for purposes of assessing the alms tax.[8] This officeholder does not have the power to originate rulings in controversial areas of the law or to enforce laws that are subject to consensus. His authority is limited to estimating the amount of dates before their harvest, and what their amount will be once they are harvested and dried. Mālik treated his estimate of that quantity as conclusive and not subject to repeal, even if it is subsequently proven to have been erroneous. Analogy, however, would require that it be repealed once its error has been demonstrated, so long as it has not been enforced. I know of no dispute among the scholars that it is unlawful as a matter of consensus to enforce a judge's decision if it is known with certainty, prior to its enforcement, that it was an error.

Imposing the obligation to pay alms tax on an amount less than the minimum amount prescribed by law is itself contrary to consensus or contrary [172] to explicit text, if there is no consensus, and whenever it becomes clear that a ruling is contrary to consensus, consensus requires that it must be repealed. Mālik, however, was of the opinion that immunizing this official's decision from repeal is a matter of the public good, and benefits both the poor and the rich. As for the poor, preventing claims overturning the initial estimate ensures that the alms tax will be paid. As for the rich, this rule effectively gives them access to the remainder of their property and permits them to do with it what they wish. Were it not for the reliability and finality of these estimates, the law would have sequestered the owners' property, out of fear that they would consume its output, and then they would claim, "The crop was less than the estimated amount," and thus reduce or even eliminate entirely their alms-tax liability.[9]

General legal rules may be contravened for reasons such as this, just as Mālik imposed strict liability on the porter of food, even though contractors are generally treated as bailees of property given to them voluntarily by their owner.[10] He also imposed strict liability on craftsmen who work on materials given to them by their customers using their craft, like a tanner, and a weaver, and similar craftsmen. He did this, in each case, because the public good can be achieved only through that rule in light of the fact that people are tempted to pilfer food and to deny that they received property from a customer after it has been transformed as a result of craft.

The foregoing discussion clarifies the distinction between the powers of the officer who estimates the yield of date palms from the office of the expert appraiser: if the appraiser makes an error, whether by exaggerating the value of property or diminishing it, it is an obligation to use the correct valuation, in contrast to the officer who estimates the yield of date palms, because the question of the public interest underlying the finality of the decision of the officer who estimates the yield of date palms is absent with respect to an appraiser's determination of value and similar matters [173].

The fourteenth is offices that have absolutely no power to originate legal rulings, doing nothing other than securing public interests in accordance with their causes. Their power is similar to judges' power to enforce rulings but not to originate them, like the officer in charge of distributing battlefield spoils; delivery of the property claimed by victorious soldiers to them; distribution of expenses and grants from the public treasury to those individuals entitled to them; delivery of the alms tax to those classes of beneficiaries entitled to it; and similar matters, in which there is nothing other than enforcement and there is no occasion whatsoever to originate a judicial ruling.

The fifteenth is offices that neither have the power to originate a judicial ruling or to enforce a rule, such as the office of an appraiser, translator, scribe, physiognomist, the trustee of a slave girl when she is sold, the partitioner of property held in common, and similar officers. This class of officials also lacks the power to originate rulings or to enforce them, and whatever rulings they give are not enforced: because they have no authority to do these things, they are like private persons.

With this summary, the authority a person derives (and does not derive) from his office to make judicial rulings has become clear, and it has become clear that not all officers have this power to originate judicial rulings, but that there are many offices that authorize this power. In the case of some of these offices, the power to make judicial rulings is only a portion of their powers; in others, this power is only with respect to some particular matters; and with others, the office grants powers that in some respects exceed the judicial power but in other respects are less than it [174].

Question 34. "What is the meaning of the jurists' statement 'Every person is authorized to repeal his own judgment and is authorized to repeal the judgment of another if that other is not qualified to give judgment'? Is that limited to matters subject to consensus, or does it apply as well to controversial areas of the law, or does it apply to both categories, or is that statement not to be taken in its obvious sense?"

The Answer

It is conceivable that a person may repeal his own judgment in two circumstances. The first is that the case is not subject to a rule of consensus, and the second is that he is certain of his error. The correct rule, however, is that a subsequent exercise of legal judgment cannot repeal a prior exercise of legal judgment. In circumstances where a universally recognized rule applies, however, repeal of the ruling is not, in reality, connected to the judicial ruling, but rather is connected to the legal cause, meaning that what had been thought to be a legal cause was discovered not to have occurred in reality; that is, the judge committed a factual error. As for the legal status of that legal cause, it is impossible to transfer it from its condition, as when a judicial ruling is given against a defendant, finding him liable to retaliation in a context in which there is consensus among all that retaliation is legally required, but then it turns out that the defendant had not, in fact, killed anyone. In this case, the change [175] in the ruling touches nothing other than what was erroneously thought to be a legal cause, not that which results from it.[1]

The same principle applies when a successor judge reviews the legal rulings of his predecessor, when the preceding judge was either corrupt (*fāsiq*) or unqualified. It means nothing more than that, if the decision was in a controversial area of the law, the successor judge may change the judicial ruling itself, from binding to nonbinding, or from nullification to establishment, and similar things. He may also cancel what his predecessor believed was a legal cause, meaning that the second judge may refuse to recognize it as a legal cause in circumstances where its status as a legal cause is controversial.

As for a judicial ruling governed by a universally recognized rule, the only thing that should be investigated is its legal cause in order to determine whether its existence was appropriately proved or not. If the successor judge finds that its existence had been appropriately confirmed, he leaves the previous judgment as it is, and he has no means to change it. If, however, there are doubts with respect to the establishment of the legal cause, he may investigate it so that he may learn whether it had been established or not, in which case he either affirms the ruling or negates it [176].

Question 35. "The jurists' statement, 'If the witnesses retract their testimony, it does not lead to the repeal of the judicial ruling,' is problematic, because confirming a judicial ruling that lacks a factual foundation is contrary to consensus, and in this case the legal cause has not been established in light of the fact that the witnesses have retracted their testimony. Is this an exception from the general legal rule that whatever contravenes consensus must be repealed, or is there another way to understand this principle?"

The Answer

Whatever contravenes consensus must be repealed, but the reason for nonrepeal in this circumstance is the fact that the judicial ruling has been established in accordance with the statement of reliable witnesses and proof of the relevant legal cause. Moreover, the subsequent claim of the witnesses that they committed perjury is an admission on their part that they are immoral, but a judicial ruling cannot be overturned on the basis of the statement of an immoral witness. Accordingly, the judicial ruling must be preserved in accordance with its initial terms [177].

Question 36. "Some of the actions of judges have resulted in confusion in the minds of jurists regarding whether or not they are judicial rulings. Which judicial acts are not judicial rulings such that others are authorized to change or contradict them, if their opinion so requires? What is the criterion (other than calling it a judicial ruling) by which one may know that it is or is not a judicial ruling so that it may be subjected to review?"

The Answer

The actions of judges and public officials that are not judicial rulings are of many different kinds. I will mention, God willing, twenty kinds. These twenty cover most of their actions, so one may be safe from error with respect to them.

The first category is contracts, such as sales and purchases of property belonging to orphans, missing persons, or the insane; marriage contracts of orphans who have reached maturity or [178] women who lack capacity and have no male relative; lease contracts of property belonging to individuals lacking proprietary capacity; and similar matters. None of these acts is a judicial ruling, so others may review them. Thus, if they are discovered to have been concluded at below-market prices, or at less than the prevailing rental rate, or if a woman is married to a man not her social equal, these actions may be revised in accordance with applicable legal rules.

These acts, in connection with these things and usufructs, are not, in any sense, judicial rulings in themselves. Yet, they may constitute judicial rulings with respect to something else insofar as the validity of these acts depends on the invalidation of an act that preceded the present act of the judge, like his decision to contract a female's marriage after she had married another man (and that previous marriage was known to the judge) or the sale of a particular item to a person after it had already been purportedly sold to another person (and that previous sale was known to the judge), and similar matters. The establishment of these actions in respect of these contracts obviously entails a judgment invalidating those previous contracts.

The second kind: confirmation (*ithbāt*) of legal attributes such as the establishment of a witness's integrity or the impeachment of that witness before a judge; the eligibility of a person to serve as prayer leader or to be the caretaker of an infant, or to make a will, and similar matters [179]. All of these cases involve the affirmation of a legal attribute, and therefore there is no judicial ruling. Accordingly, other judges are not required to accept these decisions and may conclude that the witness whom the previous judge found to be upright is immoral if evidence to that effect is presented to him, or he may accept the testimony of that impeached witness if evidence of his integrity is presented to him, and the same applies to all these attributes, the affirmation of which or their negation are categorically not judicial rulings.

The third kind: establishment of the legal causes of monetary demands, such as establishment of the amount of the value of a destroyed good, or establishment of the amount owed by debtors, or establishment of the amount due for the maintenance of relatives or wives, or establishment of the fair rental equivalent with respect to usufructs of properties, and similar things. A judge's establishment of these legal causes is not a judicial ruling, and as a result, other judges are authorized to change the quantum of that rent or that maintenance payment as well as the other legal causes that give rise to monetary demands.

The fourth kind: confirmation of the litigants' evidence entailing the existence of the legal causes that give rise to entitlements, such as a judge's declaration that the party who was required to take the oath had indeed taken the oath, or establishment of which party produced which witnesses or confirmation of party admissions and similar matters [180]. These are the types of proof parties present to the judge in order to prove the existence of the legal causes that give rise to entitlement to their legal consequences, but it does not follow from the fact that a judge has affirmed them that they are judicial rulings. Indeed, others may look into it and affirm the decision or invalidate it. Indeed, if an irregularity is discovered, he should correct it, and that prior affirmation is no obstacle to the correction of an error in those proofs.

The fifth kind: confirmation of the legal causes, such as noon for the midday prayer, the sighting of the new moon marking the beginning of Ramadan, Shawwāl, and Dhū al-Ḥijja, which results in the obligation to fast, or to conclude one's fast or to perform the rites of the Pilgrimage, and similar matters, and all the times of prayers. All such confirmations are not judicial rulings; instead, they are like the affirmation of legal attributes. Accordingly, a Mālikī is not required to fast simply because a Shāfiʿī judge confirms the beginning of Ramadan on the basis of the testimony of a single witness, because it is not a judicial ruling but rather is only the confirmation of a legal cause. As for someone who does not deem that to be a legal cause, its legal consequences do not bind him [181, 182].

The sixth kind: among the acts of judges that are not judicial rulings are the legal opinions they give in connection with ritual and other matters, such as the illegality of marriage to certain women and the permissibility of marrying others, the ritual purity of certain bodies of water and the impurity of particular substances, and the obligation to wage war against non-Muslims, and other obligatory matters. None of these is a judicial ruling, and accordingly, anyone who does not accept that legal opinion is entitled to give a legal opinion in opposition to the legal opinion of a judge or the imam [182]. Likewise, if these officials command a good deed or prohibit an evil deed, and they themselves believe it to be good or evil, it is nevertheless permissible for someone who does not share that belief to refrain from doing as they command, unless the imam calls him to denounce something, and opposition to him would amount to defiance, in which case obedience is obligatory for that reason, but not because it is a judicial ruling. There is no obligation, however, to assist a judge in the performance of something that is contrary to our view, unless there are grounds to fear civil strife on a scale that revelation prohibits us from tolerating.

The seventh kind: the enforcement of judicial rulings issuing from judges regarding cases in which the judicial ruling came from someone other than the enforcing judge, by saying, "It has been established before me that it has been established before so-and-so, one of the judges, that such and such" has taken place.

This action of the enforcing official is in no way a judicial ruling. The same is true if he said, "It has been established before me that so-and-so ruled that such and such." This is not a judicial ruling on the part of the affirming official. Indeed, even if it were the case that he believed that judgment to be contrary to consensus, it would still be valid for him to say, "It has been established before me that it was established before so-and-so that such and such," because an invalid act or a sinful act might be established before the judge so that he may punish that judge or dismiss him for ruling contrary to consensus [184]. In brief, enforcement has nothing to do with a judicial ruling. Nor is there any help to be found in a judge's statement establishing that so-and-so ruled with respect to the validity of the previous judgment, so do not be deceived by judges' frequent resort to "established," for it is all the equivalent of one judicial ruling, and it is the first, unless the second judge says, "I have made a judicial ruling in accordance with what the first judge ruled."

The eighth kind: the actions of judges with respect to taking prophylactic measures and steps to protect the rights of entitlement holders, whether in respect of endowments, releases, requiring solvent guarantors, taking pledges for the benefit of creditors, determination of terms of imprisonment for prisoners, and the like. None of these actions, no matter how they occur, could be a binding judicial ruling, and another judge is authorized to change that and invalidate it through lawful means in conformity with what revelation deems to be consistent with the public good.

The ninth kind: the actions of judges with respect to different kinds of evidence, as when he says, "I will not admit your witnesses because you already swore an oath even though it had been within your power to produce your witnesses," or "I do not grant judgment on the basis of the testimony of a witness and the oath of the complainant," or "I do not offer the oath to the complainant if the respondent refuses to swear," or "I do not force the respondent to take an oath, because it is an oath whose only grounds is suspicion, and my doctrine rejects such oaths." [185] None of these decisions is a judicial ruling, and accordingly, other judges may do what the other refused to do.

The tenth kind: the actions of judges with respect to appointing lieutenant judges, scribes to record court proceedings, officials to partition estates, translators, expert appraisers, bailiffs overseeing judicial rulings in respect of orphans; appointing court officers and bailees to preserve the property of missing persons and the insane; appointing persons to invest the property of orphans, to lease their realty, to collect rents owing to them, to maintain their property, or otherwise preserve their well-being; and similar matters. None of these actions, in these contexts, is a judicial ruling, and other judges may repeal them and change them using lawful means, not for arbitrary reasons, personal interest, caprice, or frivolity.

The eleventh kind: the establishment of the legal causes that affect legal capacity to act with respect to property, like a judicial declaration of competency with respect to minor boys and girls, or removal of a declaration of incapacity from the bankrupt, slaves working for their freedom, and the spendthrift and the profligates,[1] or removing legal capacity, such as a declaration of the incompetency of youth who have not yet reached puberty, the insane, the bankrupt, the spendthrift, and similar individuals [186]. None of these is a judicial ruling that precludes reversal. Indeed, others can look into the legal grounds of these decisions, and whenever the opposite of what the first judge decided becomes obvious to him and certain, he can reverse the original ruling and decide contrary to it. Accordingly, he may release from interdiction a person who had been subject to an order of interdiction with respect to his monetary affairs, or he may subject a person to interdiction whom the first judge had released from interdiction, just as had been previously explained with respect to the integrity and lack thereof of witnesses, because this entails the affirmation of attributes, not the origination of legal rule.

The twelfth kind: actions of public officials with respect to spending public funds and determining the amounts of salaries; disbursements from state-owned real property or the state's share of movable property seized in war against a non-Muslim enemy; disbursements from the property of orphans which are under the control of judges for their needs; disbursements of salaries to judges, scholars, prayer leaders, persons who partition estates, and the heads of deserving households and the upright; and distribution of the rights to benefit from public property, whether agricultural villages or mines, to the soldiery or others. Another example is the immobilization of some public properties for the benefit of providing funds to certain lawful beneficiaries of the public treasury, despite the legal controversy this entails: is the relevant feature that it is spending of public money toward a lawful end, so that it is permissible, or is the relevant feature that this entails immobilization of the revenues deriving from a particular piece of public property for the benefit of a particular beneficiary who has no mandatory claim to that money, in which case it is illegal?[2] [187] None of these actions is a judicial ruling, and another judge may, using proper methods of legal judgment, reverse restrictions the first judge had imposed or place restrictions on what the first had left unrestricted, in accordance with what legal considerations require.

The thirteenth kind: declaring certain public lands to be reserved for common use (*al-aḥmiya*/s. *ḥimā*) so that livestock belonging to the state may graze there as well as other matters, such as what ʿUmar b. Al-Khaṭṭāb, may God be pleased with him, and other rulers after him did. Such decisions are not judicial rulings, and others who succeed the ruler may invalidate those decisions and regulate such lands in accordance with what the public interest requires.

The fourteenth kind: appointing commanding officers to various armies and units of the armies. The companions, may God be pleased with them, had determined to call back the army of Usāma b. Zayd,[3] but Abū Bakr al-Ṣiddīq, may God be pleased with him, ordered that it continue with its campaign, because the public good required that in his opinion, not because it would have been legally impossible to reverse the prior decision.

The fifteenth kind: designating which of the permissible punishments for highway robbery will apply to a specific highwayman is not a judicial ruling, and if it is brought before another judge [188] in his town who adheres to a school of law which holds that the law gives absolute freedom to the judge in choosing among the various punishments prescribed prior to the execution of the punishment, and the second believes that the public good requires a punishment other than the one designated by the first judge, the second judge has the authority to designate the punishment he believes is consistent with the demands of the public good because designation of a specific penalty is not a judicial ruling.

The sixteenth kind: designating the quantity of a discretionary punishment. If it is brought before another judge prior to its execution, and he has a contrary view, he may substitute his view for that of the first judge, because it is not a judicial ruling; rather, it is the exercise of judgment with respect to a particular legal cause, that is, a crime. Accordingly, if it appears to the second judge that the crime does not justify that punishment, he may rule in accordance with what he believes is correct. This is in contrast to specifying the fate of prisoners of war, whether to enslave them or something else, because it is a matter of disagreement among the scholars, with some saying prisoners of war must be executed, while our doctrine, the doctrine of al-Shāfiʿī, and the doctrine of Abū Ḥanīfa is that enslavement of prisoners of war is permissible, as is levying a tax on them and treating them as permanent residents of the Islamic state.[4] Therefore, if he chooses one of the two positions, it is a judicial ruling on his part in accordance with the view that he chose, and it is thus an origination of a rule in a controversial area of the law. The same holds true with respect to the five choices [189] the head of state is given with respect to prisoners of war: gratuitous release, release for a ransom, levy of tax and treatment of them as permanent residents, execution, or enslavement. Al-Shāfiʿī agrees with us regarding the five options, while Abū Ḥanīfa prohibited gratuitous release and release for a ransom. In short, the imam's choice of one of the five options with respect to the treatment of prisoners of war constitutes a judicial ruling with respect to the option chosen because it is the origination of a judicial ruling in a controversial area of the law.

As for the amount of a discretionary penalty, no difference of opinion exists in respect of it; instead, people have agreed that the nature of the penalty imposed in each case derives from the gravity or the triviality of the crime committed. The role of the imam or the judge in such cases is simply to answer that empirical question, and so no origination of a rule takes place by such identification or by enforcement of a consensual rule.

The same analysis applies when the imam elects to execute a highwayman who has committed murder; this is not an origination of a judicial ruling in a controversial area of the law because it is a matter of consensus, but it is rather the enforcement of a universally recognized rule. If he chooses, however, to execute a highwayman, not because he has committed murder, but rather because he is particularly dangerous because of his cunning and shrewdness, and his execution would further the public good, then he would be acting on the basis of a controversial rule of law [190]. Al-Shāfiʿī does not permit the execution of a highwayman who has not committed murder, nor does he permit amputation of a highwayman who has not amputated the limbs of his victims. Accordingly, this case is similar to that of prisoners of war: in this case one of the specific penalties available for the highwayman is being designated, either execution or amputation, and in accordance with this analysis, it is an origination of a ruling in a controversial area of the law which a subsequent judge may not repeal. So, too, designating land seized from the enemy by force of arms as available for sale or partition, or as being immobilized as public property belonging to the Muslim community, is an origination of a rule in a controversial area of the law.

The seventeenth kind: among these actions is the command to execute criminals and to confront the lawless. This is not the origination of a judicial ruling in a controversial area of the law. If it is not carried out, another judge or ruler, if the matter reaches him, is free to confirm its legal cause, unless the case involves a controversial rule of law, like the one who abandons prayer or the execution of heretics. In these cases, if he designates execution and rules accordingly, it is an origination of a rule in a controversial area of the law, and so a subsequent judge may not repeal it. This is in contrast to waging war against rebels in accordance with consensus, for that is a matter of agreement.

The eighteenth kind: contracting a truce between Muslims and non-Muslims. This is not a matter of legal controversy, but is permissible by consensus in accordance with its legal cause. Accordingly, the next head of state is free to determine whether the legal cause that justified contracting the truce remains in existence, in which case he affirms it [191], or not, in which case he cancels it. A truce is nothing more than an undertaking to cease hostility in circumstances of weakness. Accordingly, if it provides security, or canceling it results in attacks against the Muslims, it becomes unlawful to cancel it because it is contrary to the public good, not because it is a permanent peace treaty or categorical rejection of war.

The nineteenth kind: the contract of protection (*ʿaqd al-dhimma*) with nonbelievers; it may not be canceled, nor may it be changed, but not because it is a judicial ruling introduced by origination, like a judge's ruling that a controversial contract is valid, but rather because the revealed law recognized this contract as entailing a perpetual guarantee for the non-Muslim contracting party and his descendants until the Day of Judgment, unless the original agreement occurred in circumstances requiring its invalidation, like the contract of protection with a people whose religion may not be tolerated, such as heretics, apostates, and others [192]. When it is contracted with one who satisfies all its prerequisites, however, no one is allowed to change its terms, like a contract of sale and other contracts, whose legal effects are permanent. No one may invalidate it in the absence of a subsequent legal cause that entails its invalidation.

The twentieth kind: determination of the amount of tax due on agricultural land and customs duties imposed on foreign merchants. These matters are not judicial rulings but rather are based on considerations of present circumstances. If it subsequently appears to another decision maker that the circumstances are contrary to what the previous decision maker believed, he can adopt another policy. If it becomes clear that an agreement with a non-Muslim power is not beneficial to the Muslims, he can repudiate it, as is the case if a public official sells an orphan's property at a below-market price: it is to be repudiated.

Note: the judge's ruling in an area of the law determined by interpretation cannot be repealed and so, too, a ruling in a case governed by a rule of consensus cannot be repealed; a vow cannot be repealed, nor can conditional divorces, manumissions, and other conditional oaths; the contract of protection cannot be repealed, nor can other civil contracts. The legal causes precluding repeal of these cases, however, differ. With respect to a judicial ruling in a matter governed by legal interpretation, the legal cause is because of its status as a particular indicant [193]; accordingly, it must be given priority over universal indicants, as has been explained previously. With respect to a judicial ruling in a matter governed by consensus, the legal cause of its unassailability is the consensus that this particular legal cause necessitates this ruling, so it is impermissible to disconnect the judgment from the legal cause. With respect to a vow, the legal cause rendering it irrevocable is that a vow entails the origination of the obligation to perform what has been undertaken. With respect to the contract of protection, it is because it entails permanence as a matter of consensus, and so, too, civil contracts. Accordingly, the impossibility of repeal is common to both, but the causes differ [194].

Question 37. "What is the meaning of 'the doctrine (*madhhab*) of Mālik' and the 'doctrines' of the other master jurists that those who are not master jurists may legitimately follow? If one were to say that 'it consists of his statements that are true,' it becomes problematic in light of the master jurist's statement 'One is half of two,' as well as other mathematical and rational propositions. If one were to say, 'It consists of his opinions which are true with respect to religious matters, knowledge of which the Lawgiver commands,' it is false with respect to fundamental theology (*uṣūl al-dīn*) and theoretical jurisprudence, for these are matters, knowledge of which the Lawgiver has commanded, but that may not be attained through adherence to the opinion of another, whether Mālik or another master jurist.[1] And if one were to say, 'The doctrine of Mālik and of other master jurists which others may legitimately follow means the substantive rules of law,' it could be said in response, 'If one means all substantive rulings, that is false in light of those substantive rules that are known of necessity to be part of the religion, such as the five daily prayers; fasting in the month of Ramadan; the prohibition of lying, adultery and fornication, and theft; and other matters. It is not permissible to follow the opinion of another with respect to these matters because they constitute necessary religious knowledge, and everything that constitutes necessary religious knowledge is shared equally between specialists and nonspecialists, and some of these matters are part of the rules of substantive law.'

If you mean some but not all of the substantive rules, then what distinguishes those rules that others may follow based solely on the authority of the master jurist's opinion from those rules that may not? Even if this matter of substantive rules could be clarified [195], the attempt would still fail because the definition will not be comprehensive insofar as it does not include matters such as legal causes and their conditions, principles which are also derived from the authority of the master jurist; indeed, legal causes and their conditions are different from the legal rules, and for that reason, the scholars said that the legal rules are part of the discourse of obligation (*khiṭāb al-taklīf*), whereas the legal causes and their conditions are part of the discourse of convention (*khiṭāb al-waḍʿ*), so these are two different things. As a consequence of these questions, scarcely any of the feebleminded jurists, when he is asked about the scope of the doctrine of the master jurists whose authority he accepts, is able to give an answer in a precise fashion. These questions apply universally among all the legal schools where the opinions of the master jurists are followed."

The Answer

The elements of master jurists' doctrines that others may legitimately follow consist of five elements, no more. The first are the substantive rules of revelation derived through legal interpretation (*al-aḥkām al-sharʿiyya al-furūʿiyya al-ijtihādiyya*). The second are their legal causes (*asbābuhā*). The third are their conditions (*shurūṭ-uhā*). The fourth are their obstacles (*mawāniʿuhā*). The fifth are the evidentiary proofs (*al-ḥijāj*) that prove the existence or nonexistence of the legal causes, conditions, and obstacles.

Our statement "the legal rules" is meant to exclude essences [196], and our statement "revealed" is meant to exclude rational propositions, such as those of mathematics and geometry, and empirical propositions as well as other kinds of propositions. Our statement "substantive" is meant to exclude the dogmatic foundations of religion and theoretical jurisprudence because revelation has demanded of us that we attain knowledge of what is rationally necessary for God, sublime is He, what is rationally inconceivable for Him, and what is rationally conceivable. Revelation also demanded of us that we know theoretical jurisprudence in order to derive the substantive legal rules; these are part of the revealed law, but because they are foundational, adopting the conclusions of others with respect to them is not permissible.

Our statement "substantive" has excluded foundational rules, and these include both theological dogma and theoretical jurisprudence, even though revelation demands knowledge of both. Our statement "derived through legal interpretation" excludes those substantive rules which constitute knowledge of the necessary elements of religion. We intend by our statement "their legal causes" things like the sun crossing its zenith, indicating the obligation to pray the noontime prayer, sighting the new moon of Ramadan, which indicates that the month of obligatory fasting has begun, and that destruction of property is a cause of liability, and similar things which are a matter of agreement. Among the legal causes that are controversial is whether a single suckle prohibits marriage [197], as Mālik holds but not al-Shāfiʿī,[2] or whether bundling the sale of a commodity not subject to the rules of *ribā* with one that is,[3] such as the case of a bundled sale of dates and a silver coin, invalidates the contract, as is the view of Mālik and al-Shāfiʿī in contrast to Abū Ḥanīfa, or whether the addition of an impure substance to a liquid that is less than two *qulla*s[4] which does not result in any sensible change to the liquid causes it to become impure, as is the view of al-Shāfiʿī and Abū Ḥanīfa, in contrast to Mālik, who believes it does not, and similar cases. And "conditions" includes things like the passage of a year before the alms tax becomes obligatory and ritual purity prior to performance of ritual prayer. These are a matter of consensus, while others, like a guardian and witnesses in connection with the marriage contract, are a matter of controversy. And "obstacles" are like menstruation precluding performance of ritual prayer and fasting, and insanity and unconsciousness precluding legal obligation. These are matters of consensus, while others, like whether impurity on the body precludes ritual prayer, or whether indebtedness precludes the obligation to pay the alms tax, are controversial [198].

We mean by our statement "the evidentiary proofs that affirm the existence or nonexistence of the legal causes, conditions, and obstacles," what judges rely on as proof, such as eyewitness testimony, admissions, and similar matters, and it is also of two types. The first are those that are subject to consensus, like two witnesses with respect to monetary claims, four witnesses with respect to illicit sexual intercourse, and admissions in all cases when made by someone having legal competence in a proper fashion and which is not followed by a retraction. The second are those that are controversial, such as one witness supported by the oath of the claimant, the testimony of minors in murder and assault cases, admissions that are subsequently retracted, the testimony of two women with respect to matters to which women are exclusively privy, such as physical defects related to procreation, the birth of a baby, and similar matters, and affirming retaliation on the basis of group oaths, something al-Shāfiʿī rejects, and matters similar thereto. These modes of proof are used before judges to establish the existence of legal causes, such as murder, and conditions, such as social equality, and the absence of obstacles, such as the absence of a husband, and similar matters. Just as we follow the master jurists with respect to the legal rules [199], their causes, their conditions, and their obstacles, so, too, we follow them with respect to the proof required to prove those elements of a claim, as has been previously explained.

It is in respect of these five elements that non–master jurists defer to the views of the master jurists, nothing else, as can be discerned from an inductive analysis of their practice. Accordingly, whenever anyone is asked regarding which views of the master jurists he follows, let him mention these five elements in the manner described here, replying with this comprehensive principle. Any other answer, however, is defective, being either underinclusive or overinclusive.

Note: it is necessary to state that those rules which are a matter of consensus, and not unique to the doctrine of a particular master jurist, such as the permissibility of the commenda,[5] the obligation to pay the alms tax, and to fast Ramadan, and so on, constitute the universally recognized doctrines of the entire Muslim community. Accordingly, one should not say, "This is the doctrine of Mālik or al-Shāfiʿī," except insofar as it is something particular to him. That is the plain sense of the expression "the doctrine of Mālik." Is it not the case that were someone to say, "The obligation to pray five prayers a day is the doctrine of Mālik," it would sound strange and one would naturally reject it. Indeed, one necessarily grasps [200] the difference between that statement, and our statement, "The obligation to rub the limbs during ritual purification is the doctrine of Mālik," and "The obligation to pray the *witr*[6] prayer is the doctrine of Abū Ḥanīfa." The only thing that impresses itself on the mind with respect to these expressions is the particular expression without regard to what is held in common between early generations and later generations, and the ancients and the moderns. Likewise, no one would say, "This is the manner of the ascetics," except in regard to what is specific to them, not what they share with sinners and nonbelievers. It is not appropriate to attribute common ways of life to particular people except metaphorically; no literal attribution should take place except with respect to what is particular and distinctive.

So, too, legal doctrines are nothing other than authoritative conclusions of the legal reasoning of the master jurists; nothing should be attributed to a master jurist except that which is particular to him. Accordingly, it may be said, "The well-established legal doctrines are four," and the elaboration of the content of these four doctrines cannot take place except through articulation of what is particular to each one, not what they share. For this reason, a further restriction must be added to the previous discussion, so if someone were to ask, "What is the doctrine of Mālik?," one should say, "What is particular to him with respect to the substantive legal rules which are derived through Mālik's legal interpretation, and what is particular to him with respect to their legal causes, conditions, obstacles, and evidentiary proofs which affirm their existence or nonexistence." This is the appropriate understanding which is understood from ordinary linguistic usage, and the question is concerned only with that [201]. But, with this explanation, the question becomes even more mysterious, and the answer's distance from the question becomes even greater, but rare is the jurist with an answer.

Note: one should know that when non–master jurists follow individual master jurists with respect to legal causes, they should follow the master jurists only insofar as the master jurists have identified them as abstract legal causes, not with respect to the actual occurrence of those legal causes in the real world. There is a difference, therefore, in Mālik's statement "Homosexual sodomy necessitates the legal punishment of stoning" and his statement "So-and-so has committed homosexual sodomy." We follow him with respect to his first statement, but not the second. Indeed, the second statement is an instance of testimony, and if three others testified along with Mālik, the ruling would be established. In this respect he is the equivalent of other just witnesses, it making no difference that he—or any other scholar—is a master jurist in this context.

Likewise, we follow him in his view that a grave robber is subject to amputation, just like the ordinary thief, but we do not follow him when he says that "so-and-so is a grave robber." Likewise, we follow him in his view that an intention is a prerequisite to ritual purity, but we do not follow him when he says that "so-and-so had the proper intention." And we follow his view that [202] indebtedness precludes the obligation of the alms tax, but we do not follow him when he says that "so-and-so's debts exceed his assets"; rather, there must be an additional witness as proof in each of these cases. In all of these cases he is the equivalent of all other just witnesses,[7] and the fact that he is a master jurist is irrelevant to proving the occurrence of the legal cause at issue. Indeed, all that is required for this purpose is simply the integrity of the witnesses [203].

If someone were to say,

> We follow him [i.e., Mālik] when he narrates from Māʿiz[8] his confession of adultery, and that the Messenger of God, may God bless him and grant him peace, stoned him as a consequence. The same [204] holds for the woman from the tribe of Ghāmid who committed adultery.[9] We also follow him with respect to the one who stole the cloak of Ṣafwān and that the Messenger of God, may God bless him and grant him peace, amputated his hand as a punishment.[10] [205] All of these rules entail following Mālik with respect to the occurrence of the legal causes, and his narration of these events, by itself, is sufficient basis on which to formulate universal rules of law. The same is true if any other reliable scholar narrated them, and even if there were only one of them who narrated these precedents, we would still follow that reliable scholar and develop our general rules based on those precedents.[11] Accordingly, what you say, meaning, that following a master jurist does not entail following his views with respect to the occurrence of legal causes, is false. Indeed, most of the rules of Islamic law are built upon the occurrence of legal causes during the Prophet Muḥammad's lifetime, upon him be peace, whether unlawful divorces,[12] accusations of adultery, and other things, and everyone agrees that if a just scholar reports to us anything relating to such things, we must follow him with respect to it and derive from that report the appropriate rules. Master jurists do not have available to them a means to extract rulings from events and legal

> causes except if they follow what their narrators have reported about those precedents. Accordingly, it is clear that it is also an obligation to follow the master jurists with respect to their views regarding the occurrence of the legal causes, conditions, and obstacles, and not simply what constitutes the legal causes, conditions, and obstacles in the abstract,

then we would say that this is not of what we speak. Those examples are instances of historical reports (*min bāb al-riwāya*), and one narrator of a legal precedent is sufficient according the valid view of the scholars in that context, although some have required at least two independent narrators, and others have required four with respect to reports relating to precedents involving adultery. If we are satisfied with one narrator in the context of historical reports, it means that we [206] believe the narrator of the precedent with respect to the occurrence of that legal cause or that condition or that obstacle insofar as rules of general applicability, not limited to any particular person and applicable until the end of time, are to be derived from the occurrence of these normative precedents.

We do not believe him or give weight to his narration in applying the rule of that particular case which he narrated to other cases, so we do not stone anyone besides Māʿiz in reliance on his statement, nor do we amputate the hands of thieves until the Day of Judgment, on the basis of his statement about Ṣafwān's cloak. Accordingly, no particular judgments are ever established (except for that particular one which he narrated), except by means of legal proof and satisfaction of the minimum number of witnesses the law requires, which may include him but also may require others. It is important to understand this point, for many jurists trip and fall in this context.

This secret is what has caused many scholars of theoretical jurisprudence to say that multiple witnesses (or in lieu thereof other kinds of evidence) have been stipulated in cases of testimony (*al-shahāda*), whereas a single narrator is sufficient in narration (*al-riwāya*) because in particular cases the witnesses might be biased due to enmity against one of the parties. This bias might be hidden, and more generally, there may be many reasons to suspect the truth of testimony. The revealed law has accordingly stipulated a second witness to minimize the appearance of enmity and suspicion of bias. The possibility that a narrator would bear enmity [207] to the entirety of humanity for the rest of time, in contrast, is exceedingly implausible, and for that reason, the Lawgiver was satisfied with the narration of one upright narrator, because integrity justifies an inference of the narrator's truthfulness.

Accordingly, it has become clear that we follow the scholars only with regard to particular events when they narrate them inasmuch as they are of legal relevance beyond the particular case narrated. As for the particular cases themselves, we do not follow them in any way with respect to those cases; rather, it is the case that the narrator is simply one among many potential witnesses who is followed in one respect but not another, as has been already explained.

Now that it has been established that we do not follow the scholars with respect to the occurrence or nonoccurrence of legal causes in respect of their application to particular judgments involving those legal causes, you should know that there are many instances in the various doctrines of the master jurists where rules were established on the basis of non–master jurists erroneously following the conclusions of the master jurists with respect to the occurrence of legal causes in connection with the application of their particular rules to particular judgments. For instance, the Mālikīs reject the sale, lease, and exercise of rights of first refusal in connection with land conquered by force from the enemy, like Egypt, Mecca, Iraq, and similar lands. Mālik said, "Egypt was conquered by force," and as a consequence, the Mālikī jurists adopted the view that all sales, exercises of rights of first refusal and leases of land in Egypt are invalid, in reliance on his statement, "Egypt was conquered by force," and in reliance on his view that land conquered by force is not to be sold or leased, and neither claims of prior ownership, nor rights of first refusal are to be exercised in respect of it [208].

In this case, their deference to Mālik with regard to the status of sales, leases, and exercise of rights of first refusal occurring in conquered territory is a valid instance of deference to the master jurist's authority, because it is a case of deference to a master jurist with regard to a legal rule. And, their deference to him with respect to the general rule that conquered land is subject to those rules is also a valid instance of deference, because it is deference with respect to what makes something a legal cause, not whether the legal cause has in fact occurred. Their deference to him with respect to his view that Egypt, or Mecca, had been forcefully conquered, however, is not a valid instance of deference because it is deference in regard to the occurrence of a legal cause which does not result in the formulation of universal or particular rules [209, 210]. As for the fact that no universal rule applicable to all of humanity results from it, in contrast to the case involving the story of Māʿiz's adultery, the reason is because the formulation of the universal rules was only a result of the fact that they originated from one whose actions are a proof of the revealed law, and he is the Messenger of God, may God bless him and grant him peace.

Had it been the case that the actions of the one who stoned Māʿiz were not a proof, we would gain absolutely no benefit from its narration with respect to the formulation of universal rules.

The status of Egypt having been conquered by force, thereby invalidating the establishment of endowments, and invalidating sales of its land, does not derive from someone whose words or actions are proofs of the revealed law. Indeed, it was conquered during the era of the companions, may God be pleased with them, but it has not been established that they held that the sale of its land was forbidden. Had that fact been established, it would have been a legal proof. As for it not being constitutive of particular judgments, we have already explained that the transmission of the occurrence of legal causes does not produce the individual legal rulings that are particular to them, just as we do not stone Māʿiz on account of the report of one person, and similar cases [211].

The Mālikīs, however, uphold in their legal opinions and their judicial rulings the invalidation of contracts involving the land of Egypt and the invalidation of these rights, in reliance on Mālik's statement that it was conquered by force. Rather, it would have been better for them to be circumspect and refrain from such decisions, until either a sufficient number of witnesses, as established in their legal doctrine, came forward and testified to the fact that Egypt had been conquered by force of arms, or if it had been established that the rules applicable to forcible conquest had been authoritatively applied by a judge in these lands, or that the rules of forcible conquest had formed the basis of a legal opinion of someone whose action or statement is a legal proof, whether a prophet or a companion. Only then would the Mālikīs have been justified in giving such legal opinions and judicial rulings in particular cases.

Would that I knew the difference between Mālik's statement "Such and such a territory was conquered by force" and his statement "So-and-so was killed violently" or "unjustly" or "intentionally." Or "So-and-so's garment was unlawfully taken." Are these statements anything other than reports about the occurrence of a certain action modified by "violently" or "by force"? What will they do if Mālik says to them, "So-and-so was intentionally murdered." Shall they apply the law of retaliation to his killer solely on the basis of his statement, and apply all the rules related to that particular case and particular area of law, or will they refrain from applying those rules and treat it as testimony, and delay applying the substantive rules until another witness testifies or apply the group oath? What is the difference between that hypothetical case and whether a territory [212] was conquered by force of arms and his report about the occurrence of conquest in it?

Were they to say, "It is an instance of testimony," then one could reply to them that, "Mālik, may God be pleased with him, was not a witness to the conquest of Egypt, and testimony is not valid without direct knowledge." It is not plausible for them to say, "This is an example of testimony based on hearsay and widespread dissemination," because our Mālikī colleagues have enumerated all the cases which admit hearsay, and these are about twenty-seven cases in all, and they did not include this case as one of them. Where, in this case, is the authoritative citation from the school's legal texts that can be relied upon to show that Mālik testified on this matter in reliance on widespread hearsay?

Nor can they say that he obtained knowledge of this fact by virtue of widespread and concurrent reports that Egypt was conquered by force, and that when a witness has such knowledge, his testimony in accordance with that knowledge is admissible, whether or not he was an eyewitness to it, as the author of the *Muqaddimāt* has explained.[13] [213]

We would say to them that it is implausible that Mālik could have obtained such knowledge by means of widespread and concurrent transmissions, and indeed, the obvious facts of his personal circumstances contradict it. He, may God be pleased with him, was from Medina, not Egypt, and al-Layth b. Saʿd,[14] who was in Egypt, was of the view that Egypt had been incorporated into the Islamic state peaceably, not by the force of arms. Moreover, many scholars, historians, and transmitters of reports agreed with him in this respect to this. The people of a region are certainly better informed about the circumstances of their region than strangers are. Accordingly, had there been widespread and concurrent transmission that Egypt had been conquered by force of arms, Egyptians would be more likely to have such knowledge than Mālik [214]. Moreover, because they are adamant in reporting a view contrary to his, that fact alone indicates that transmission of these events did not reach the level of a mass-transmitted report with respect to Mālik, but rather reached him only through the solitary report of someone whom he deemed trustworthy. Accordingly, he reported only what he believed, not what he knew regarding the status of Egypt.

Let us grant for the sake of argument that Mālik had knowledge that Egypt had been conquered by force of arms, but in that case one could say in response, "Al-Layth and those who agree with him, a fortiori, also had knowledge, so the testimony of Mālik and those who agree with him contradicts the testimony of al-Layth and al-Shāfiʿī and those who agree with them." In this case, there is a contradiction among the witnesses, and were one of the jurists to be so impudent as to claim that Mālik and those who agree with him are more reliable, it could be said to him, "Is this a case in which a judge may make a ruling based on which of the contradictory witnesses is more reliable?" for the Mālikī rule is that judgment based on the more reliable of the two sets of contradictory witnesses is permissible only in claims involving money, and this is a question and legal cause which has nothing to do with money but rather the legal status of Egypt [215].

Were they to say that he transmitted the testimony of someone else, one could say to them that a condition for the transmission of another's testimony is that the eyewitness permits the derivative witness to bear it on his behalf, but is there any evidence in the possession of Mālikī judges that the original eyewitness, whose testimony Mālik is transmitting, gave permission to Mālik, may God have mercy upon him, to transmit from him? In any case it is not permissible for a judge to rule on the basis of the testimony of a derivative witness until the conditions for bearing that testimony have been proved, as well as all the circumstances in connection with that event.

This principle applies to all legal cases before judges; all legally relevant facts must be proved before the judge, in accordance with the appropriate legal means used to prove those facts. Some legally relevant facts require eyewitness testimony; some are satisfied with the report of a derivative witness. These are all complex matters, so give it careful attention and know that this is not particular to our doctrines; indeed, the Shāfiʿīs have a similar issue with respect to the land of Iraq and others, so they are subject to the same criticism that applies to our position [216].

So if you pay careful attention to these discussions, you will realize with certainty that non–master jurists should not defer to everything that has been transmitted from the master jurists. Rather, deference is permitted only with respect to those five things that were summarized previously, and what goes beyond that is not entitled to deference. Deference may take place with respect to matters of transmission, if it is transmitted from someone whose conduct or statements constitute legal proofs; it might also take place in the case of testimony with respect to the occurrence of legal causes, conditions, and obstacles. Some matters, however, are not proper subjects of deference, narration, or testimony, and that is what they mention in the sciences of theoretical jurisprudence and theology and other sciences with respect to empirical, rational, and other truths, and these different divisions have all been briefly explained in the best fashion in what has preceded [217].

Question 38. "What does it mean when we say in our legal opinions 'wiping the entirety of the head is obligatory when performing ablutions,' 'singing is forbidden,' 'the meat of predatory birds is permissible to eat,' and other controversial legal opinions like these? Does that mean that wiping the entirety of the head is obligatory for everyone, or only Mālikīs? If one says, 'Only Mālikīs,' is it not the case that the revealed indicant which establishes that rule signifies that this is a universal obligation applicable to all? If so, how can it be limited? And if one says, 'It applies to all,' does that mean that Shāfiʿīs are in a constant state of disobedience because they are insistent in not complying with this obligation, and insistence on abandoning an obligatory act is licentiousness and rebellion? Does it follow that al-Shāfiʿī is a licentious sinner in the view of Mālik and the Mālikīs and that Mālik and his party are sinners in the view of al-Shāfiʿī because they refrain from reciting 'in the name of God, the Beneficent, the Merciful' as part of the ritual prayer, and similar matters? The same problem arises in connection with all the legal doctrines of the master jurists, and as a consequence, none of them can escape the charge that it is sinning against God by abandoning something that its opponent deems to be obligatory. That conclusion seems very implausible [217], but so does the notion that revealed indicants that are otherwise universal by their terms can be read as having been particularized, for that is the essence of arbitrariness. Both of these are shameful paths from which there appears to

be no exit, so how can we overcome them? And, what do jurists rely on when they give a legal opinion that something is obligatory? Do they intend by that universality or particularity, or does any of this cross their mind at all, and they are completely heedless of these weighty matters?"

The Answer

A question that prompts a legal opinion appears in one of four contexts. Sometimes, there may be a question whether wiping the entirety of the head is a generic obligation for all persons subject to the revealed law, without regard to the doctrine of any particular master jurist. Sometimes the question is limited to the obligation of the person who follows the doctrine of the master jurist whose view is that it is obligatory. Sometimes the question is limited to the obligation of the person who follows the view of the master jurist who dissents from the view that it is obligatory. Finally, the question may be limited to the obligation of a master jurist who has yet to consider the problem [219].

The first is if the question is about the obligation in itself. In this case we universalize the legal opinion, because the applicable indicant signifies in itself that it is universally applicable to all persons until the Day of Judgment, in all places and all times, so long as there is no justifiable basis to follow a contrary view of a dissenter who relied on a revealed indicant that contradicts this textual one: if there is, however, then the dissenter's evidence repels the effect of our textual indicant from that dissenter, because that contrary textual indicant is weightier in the dissenter's opinion, and God, sublime and glorified is He, has obliged everyone to act on the basis of what each believes to be probable.

The second is if the question is concerned about the obligation of a person who defers to the views of a master jurist who says it is obligatory. In this case we tell the questioner that it is obligatory. There is nothing surprising in this because the master jurist to whom the questioner defers believes it to be obligatory on account of an indicant that is preponderant in his view. And, the questioner has undertaken to defer to the doctrine of this master jurist. Accordingly, he is bound by what he has undertaken for himself. For this reason, if the master jurist himself whose legal interpretation led him to the conclusion that this is obligatory asked us this question, we would tell him that God's law, sublime is He, for him, and for those who follow his teachings, is that it is obligatory. This is on account of his belief regarding what is likely to be true, and because his probable beliefs are the grounds of his obligations and the obligations of all those who defer to his view. Accordingly, whoever defers to him derives his obligations from those of the master jurist in these matters.

The third is if the question about wiping the head, for example, is asked by a person who follows the teachings of al-Shāfiʿī, who denies that it is obligatory: we tell him that it is not obligatory, because there is a consensus within the community of Islam that the rule of God with respect to a master jurist, and with respect to those who follow him, is whatever rule he reasonably believes to be the rule of God, when that rule's legal cause takes place [220].

Our statement "when its legal cause takes place" excludes a master jurist who has reached a probable judgment with respect to the rules of the alms tax but he has no property, and so is under no obligation to pay the alms tax, or with respect to the rules of marriage, but he has no dependents to marry off, or with respect to the rules of adjudication, but he does not occupy a judicial office. Because consensus exists on that point, were we to give him a legal opinion contrary to the views of the master jurist whom he follows, we would be violating consensus. Accordingly, this is a rule governed by consensus, and no one is permitted to contradict it.

The equivalent to this question is the case of ten people, each using independent judgment to determine the direction of the Kaʿba for ritual prayers. Each one, however, reaches a conclusion different from the one reached by the nine others. Moreover, each of these ten has followers, none of whom is capable of determining the prayer direction for himself, and so each group follows one of the ten. Indeed, each of the ten who is knowledgeable in determining the direction of prayer, whose probable judgments disagreed with respect to the proper direction for prayer, and each of whom chose a direction other than the one chosen by the others, if he asked the nine others who disagreed with him, "Is it forbidden for me to pray to the direction which I believe the Kaʿba probably lies, or not?" they would tell him, "It is obligatory for you and for those who follow you, to pray to the direction which you believe the Kaʿba probably lies, and it is not forbidden to you, but it is forbidden for us [221] to pray to that direction, and so, too, those who follow us, because we believe that the Kaʿba does not lie in that direction." Accordingly, there would be a consensus among those ten that God's rule with respect to each of them is to pray to the direction to which their individual judgment led them.

The same principle applies to legal judgments generally. Marriage to a woman without the permission of a guardian, or eating the meat of predators, for example, may be prohibited to some but permissible to others, just as God has made eating the meat of carrion permissible to those under duress but prohibited to those who eat it voluntarily. The differences in the mental states of the master jurists are therefore like the different circumstances of those under duress and those exercising voluntary choice in respect of compulsion and choice. On account of the differences in the two conditions in the two contexts, God, sublime is He, has established two contradictory rules. This is plain truth without any ambiguity.

Accordingly, when we are asked about the Shāfiʿīs and whether they must wipe the entirety of the head as part of ritual ablutions, we say no, and we give Ḥanafīs a legal opinion that wiping one-quarter of the head is obligatory for them, and we give legal opinions based on our doctrine that are contrary to our doctrine to every group whose master dissents from our doctrine in accordance with what the dissenting master jurist believes and which is contrary to our views, because the validity of the views of dissenters, for those who accept them as authoritative, is a matter over which there is a consensus.[1] [222]

There are four situations, however, which are excluded from this principle, and these are the circumstances in which a judge's ruling must be overturned: if the judicial ruling is contrary to consensus, universal legal rules, express texts, or manifest analogy in circumstances where, with respect to the last three criterion, there is no valid countervailing consideration. Accordingly, if we have a probable belief that the master jurist who has dissented from our position has adopted a view that falls into one of the four categories described earlier with respect to that case, then in that circumstance we will give a legal opinion to his followers in accordance with only our view, not their master's view (that falls into one of these four circumstances), because his dissent is not counted as a valid legal opinion. It cannot be deemed to be a universal law for those subject to the law's moral obligations, because that which we would not uphold had a judge ruled in reliance on it—despite the fact that a judicial ruling would normally render it unassailable—we should not, a fortiori, uphold in the absence of a judicial ruling adopting it. For the same reason, those who have permitted persons to pick and choose among the various substantive doctrines of the master jurists excluded these four cases, and said, "It is permissible to follow one doctrine among the four and also to pick and choose among them on condition that by so doing, one does not violate consensus, universal legal rules, manifest analogy, or express texts, to the extent that there is no valid countervailing consideration." [223]

The fourth is if the question about the obligation to wipe the head is asked about a person who is a master jurist who has the capacity to engage in independent interpretation of the law, like al-Shāfiʿī and those like him. We would not give him a legal opinion at all, whether of obligation or nonobligation. We would instead tell him:

> The rule of God, sublime is He, with respect to you is that you exert your utmost ability and interpret the revealed indicants of the law, its sources and circumstances, and whatever probable conclusion you reach, that is God's rule with respect to you and those who follow your teachings, so long as you do not contradict one of the four matters that necessitate the repeal of a judicial ruling when a judge violates them. If your judgment contradicts one of these four matters, but you did not realize this, you continue to be obligated to follow your probable opinion, even if it is contrary to consensus itself.

Al-Ghazālī stated [224] in the Chapter on Legal Interpretation in *al-Mustaṣfā*, "There is a consensus that if a master jurist unknowingly violates consensus, he is obligated to continue to act in accordance with his opinion, even though it contradicts consensus, until he discovers that he has violated consensus."[2] [225]

We would also say to him, "If you discover that you have contradicted one of these four matters, you are obliged to revise your opinion," but we would still refrain from giving him a substantive opinion, whether of obligation or nonobligation. We would give the same answer to his followers, meaning that if they are unaware that the master jurist whom they follow has contradicted one of these four matters, then God's law with respect to them is that they continue to follow the opinion of their master jurist; however, if they discover that he has contradicted one of these four matters, it becomes prohibited for them to adhere to his views. Instead, they are free to follow any of the other views of the master jurists.

In such a circumstance it becomes obligatory to act in accordance with the combined teachings of two master jurists, or to adopt the teachings of the second master jurist in their entirety, provided that it is one of the valid doctrinal schools of law. A person who is not a master jurist cannot do without adopting a valid opinion with respect to wiping the head because he needs it for his daily prayers, and the hypothetical involves the assumption that he cannot find a valid answer within the teachings of the master jurist he follows. In such a case, he must choose between two options: either to continue to follow the teachings of his master jurist, with the exclusion of this one case, but adopt the teachings of another master jurist with respect to this one case, or to abandon the teachings of the first master jurist whom he followed and adopt the teachings of another master jurist in their entirety.

All those who claim that it is prohibited [226] to adopt views from different master jurists should pay attention to this example and admit an exception to his rule prohibiting adoption of particular views from different master jurists. Sometimes, there is a necessity or pressing need to do so that cannot be avoided.

This is an example of how muftis should give legal opinions with respect to all possible teachings: sometimes the opinion is general, sometimes it is particular, and sometimes it is contrary to the position that the mufti himself believes to be true. Whoever is ignorant of this and gives legal opinions is ignorant of something profoundly important for the office of the mufti. Sometimes, ignorance of these points may lead him, imperceptibly, to contradict consensus in the opinions he gives when subtle matters such as these, which can scarcely be found in the books of scholars, are presented to him. How many a matter cannot be found expressly in books and is incapable of transmission but is found only implicitly in various general legal rules, and is grasped by only a handful of jurists, not most of them [227]!

A difficult issue of unusual depth: the followers of the Shāfiʿī school reported that al-Shāfiʿī, may God be pleased with him, was asked this question, but I could not find his answer to it reported by any of his followers. The question is that the followers of the various master jurists are permitted to follow one another in prayer, even if each one of them believes that his fellow, who holds a different view of the rules of prayer, has done something which, if he were to have done it, would have rendered his prayer invalid, for example, he wipes only part of his head as part of his ritual ablution prior to prayer, omits stating "in the name of God, the Merciful, the Compassionate," prior to his recitation of the opening chapter of the Quran in his prayers, or does not rub his limbs while doing ritual ablution prior to prayer, and so on.[3] Similarly, it is permissible for a master jurist to pray behind other master jurists, despite these differences regarding the requirements of prayer. It is also related that consensus upholds the permissibility of that position, and that consensus preceded the disagreement that subsequently occurred with respect to it.

In contrast, there is a consensus to the contrary with respect to master jurists regarding the purity of containers, the direction of prayer, the ritual purity of clothing which has become commingled with impure substances, and questions similar to that, in circumstances when the conclusion of one master jurist with respect to these matters conflicts with the conclusion of another. In these cases, it is not permissible for one master jurist to follow the other, or to follow him in prayer because he believes his prayer to be invalid on account of their disagreement on one of these questions [228].

What is the difference between these two areas of the law? No answer attributed to al-Shāfiʿī, may God be pleased with him, has been reported. One of the later followers of the Shāfiʿī school answered this question by arguing that, with respect to the first category, had the ruling been one of prohibition, that would have reduced attendance of congregational prayers, given the breadth and quantity of disputes in regard to these detailed matters, in contrast to the second category, in which controversy is much more rare. Accordingly, the rule prohibiting following another master jurist when controversy takes place with regard to that latter set of questions would not result in this evil. But, this is a weak answer, for were it the case that the benefit to be gained from permitting one master jurist to follow another is not invalidated on account of their differences in legal judgment, then the same reasoning should apply in both cases, and if not, then permission to follow should be prohibited in both categories of cases, because the difference that is asserted, and the discussion in support of it, lack any objective evidence to support it.

The correct answer is that proper juristic analysis is based on the principle that God, sublime is He, has decreed that, in respect of the issue of wiping the head, and other similar questions, that the applicable rule is the one which the master jurist's reasoning reaches, and He made this a universally applicable principle of law that is valid in itself, just as He permitted a person facing the prospect of starvation to eat carrion but prohibited it to one who would eat it willingly. Consensus in this case recognizes that there are two different rules for the two different groups, those acting under necessity and those acting out of free choice. God, sublime is He, also decreed that, with respect to the two conflicting opinions [229] of the master jurists, that they are like the two circumstances of necessity and choice in the case of a legally competent person who eats carrion.

As for the case of the two master jurists who differ with respect to the direction of prayer and similar issues, they are both in agreement that there is a particular rule that is applicable to their case, and it is the actual direction of the prayer and the actual purity of the garment. They also both agree that abandoning the rule, if it becomes clear, would constitute an error. Accordingly, each of them believes that his fellow is acting in a manner contrary to consensus, although he cannot be certain. But, in cases where one has a probable belief that a position is contrary to consensus, it is forbidden to follow that view. It is for that reason that individually transmitted reports which are contrary to consensus, universal legal rules, or express text are given no effect, even though the belief that the report is invalid is only a probable inference. This is a principle that is itself the subject of consensus.

In the case of wiping the head and similar questions, one of the master jurists believes that his colleague contradicted a relevant piece of evidence which he believes, but is not certain, is dispositive. His conclusion is countered by another opinion beside it with respect to whether the evidence, whether textual or analogical, is in fact dispositive. As for the consensus which we believe was violated in the matter of the direction of prayer and similar questions, there is absolutely no countervailing consideration beside it, and so it is impossible to defer to one who is contradicting consensus in our view, whereas in the first category, there is a symmetry of opinions, and so it is possible [230] that each opinion could be conclusive with respect to the master jurist who holds it.[4] For that reason his view can be recognized as an established universal rule that applies to that master jurist and those who follow him until the Day of Judgment, regardless of the position we take on whether every opinion of master jurists is correct.[5]

A similar case would exist where two followers of Shāfiʿī who hold the view that the droppings of riding animals, such as camels or horses, are impure, and are trying to determine whether a particular garment has become impure as a result of contact with impure droppings. If they disagree as to whether the garment is pure or impure, it would not be permissible for one of them to pray behind the other, but it would be permissible for each of them to pray behind a follower of Mālik, because the Mālikī believes that the garment is pure for purposes of ritual. The reason for this is that the two followers of Shāfiʿī agree in the first case insofar as they reject Mālik's view regarding the purity of these droppings. Furthermore, a ritual prayer led by a prayer leader who is wearing a garment contaminated with these droppings but does not adhere to the doctrine that they are pure for ritual purposes is invalid by consensus. Accordingly, one of the Shāfiʿīs cannot defer to the view of the other regarding the purity of the garment that is suspected to have been contaminated by animal droppings because he has a probable belief that his colleague is in contravention of consensus.

The same principle applies to impure water whose manifest characteristics have not changed, except that it was drawn from a source of water having less than two *qulla*s.[6] If the persons disagreeing about whether the water is pure for purposes of performing ritual ablutions prior to prayer are Shāfiʿīs, neither may defer to the other, but if one is a Mālikī and the other a Shāfiʿī, it would be permissible for the Shāfiʿī to defer to the Mālikī.[7] The basic principle of this topic is that whenever the object of deference leads to a result that is contrary to consensus in the opinion of a follower of a master jurist, deference is prohibited, but if not, deference is permitted. This is the secret to understanding this case, so pay heed [231].

Question 39. "Which rules, found in the doctrines of al-Shāfiʿī, Mālik, and others that were founded on customs and usages which were current at the time those master jurists made such rulings, continue to be valid today? And if these customs and usages have changed, or have come to indicate the opposite of what they had indicated previously, do these opinions recorded in the books of the jurists become invalid, and instead legal opinions should be given in accordance with today's prevailing customs and usages? Or should we say, 'We practice deference to the teachings of the master jurists, and we lack the authority to introduce a new rule on account of the fact that we do not have the capacity to engage in independent legal interpretation'? Should we then give legal opinions in accordance with what is in the books containing the transmitted views of the master jurists?"

The Answer

Giving effect to rules grounded in customs and usages, after changes in those customs and usages, is contrary to consensus and constitutes ignorance in religion. Indeed, everything in [232] the revealed law that is derived from customs and usages changes when the customs and usages underlying such rules change so that the rule is made to conform with the new custom and usage. This does not represent a case of independent legal interpretation (*ijtihād*) on the part of jurists who defer to the teachings of master jurists such that competence to engage in independent interpretation of the revealed law is a prerequisite to engage in this kind of legal interpretation. Rather, the follower of a master jurist in this case would be acting in accordance with what is an established universal legal rule that the master jurists themselves derived through their own interpretations and one with respect to which they reached a consensus. Accordingly, we defer to them with respect to such rules without any need to undertake independent interpretation of the law, relying exclusively on the aforementioned principle.

Consider the fact that the master jurists all agreed that if the genus of the price is not explicitly stated in the contract, the price term of the contract is taken as referring to the preponderant coinage then in use in the location of the contract. So, if the custom and usage at the time of the contract involved a particular coinage, we would interpret indeterminate contractual language in light of the prevailing custom and usage of that locale, and when the custom and usage in that locale changes to another coinage, we specify whatever coinage is used in accordance with the new custom and usage, and we ignore the prior custom and usage on account of the subsequent change in custom and usage.

The same principle applies to the interpretation of wills, oaths, and all chapters of substantive law in which customs and usages are relevant in interpretation: when the relevant customs and usages change, the rulings of those areas of substantive law also change. So, too, when the judge, in reliance on the circumstantial evidence provided by custom and usage, in connection with specific legal claims, determines which party in a lawsuit is the defendant, and can thus win the case by swearing an oath denying the plaintiff's claim if the plaintiff fails to produce competent evidence, and then the relevant custom and usage changes, in which case the party that would have previously been the defendant in light of the evidence of the previous custom now becomes the plaintiff as a result of the change in the prevailing custom and usage.[1] [233] Indeed, it is not even a requirement that the custom and usage change, for were we to go from one town to another, it may be that their customs and usages could very well be contrary to the customs and usages of the town in which we had been, in which case we would give petitioners from that second town a legal opinion in accordance with their own customs and usages, and we would give no consideration to the customs and usages of town from which we came. So, too, if someone arrives from a different town, and his custom and usage is contrary to the custom and usage of our town, we give him a legal opinion only in accordance with the customs and usages prevailing in his town, not one based on the customs and usages of our town.

An example of this has been transmitted from Mālik: when two spouses dispute whether possession was taken of the dower after marital cohabitation has commenced, the husband is the defendant, even though the last undisputed fact was the wife's nonpossession of the dower. Al-Qāḍī Ismāʿīl[2] said, "This was [234] their custom and usage in Medina, that the man does not cohabitate with his wife until she takes possession of the entirety of her dower, but today, their custom and usage is contrary to that, and as a result, it is the woman who is the defendant. The procedural rule changed because of the change in customs and usages."

Having established this principle, I shall give you examples of legal rules which our colleagues have expressly stated are based on conventions and usages and that the basis of their legal opinions with respect to them is entirely custom and usage, and today's customs and usages are contrary to prior custom and usage. Accordingly, a change in the legal rule is incumbent in accordance with what the new custom entails.

It is necessary to understand that when one speaks of custom and usage with respect to a word's meaning, it is a reference to the fact that when a word is used unqualifiedly, the prevalent meaning among the speakers of that language which impresses itself on their mind immediately when they hear that word is something other than the word's original denotative meaning. This is how custom and usage apply to a particular word, and this word's new meaning is referred to as its customary denotative meaning, and it is also the preponderant metaphorical meaning [235], viewed from the perspective of the word's original linguistic denotative meaning. This is what the jurists mean when they say, "Custom is given priority to original denotative meaning in language when they conflict," and everything else that is derivative of these expressions.

Some examples from substantive law follow.

The first rule: some of the phrases used in the cost-plus-profit (*murābaḥa*) contract,[3] for example, when the seller says, "I will sell to you everything I purchased at a discount, for every eleven, ten," or "for every twenty, ten," or a discount greater than that.[4] Our Mālikī colleagues said, "This expression entails, by virtue of custom and usage, that the seller takes for every eleven he paid originally, ten from the purchaser, and that he reduce the price by one half in the second expression. They bind the contracting parties to this understanding, simply by virtue of the words, because it is the custom and usage."

This custom, however, no longer exists, and no one at all understands that formula today in this manner. Indeed, most jurists do not understand it, to say nothing of the general public, because there is no custom or usage with respect to it, nor can it be understood by reference to the phrase's denotative meaning in language. Accordingly, if such a contract were to occur among the common people, it would have to be invalid, because it is in no way part of their custom or usage to use it [236]: we have lived our entire lives and never encountered this formula except in books of law, but not in the actual contractual dealings of the people. And, if the price is unspecified by the language of the parties, and neither custom nor usage specifies it, then the contract must be held to be invalid.

The second rule: in the cost-plus-profit contract, if the seller says, "I will sell to you in accordance with my expenses," our Mālikī colleagues said it is a valid sale, and the seller receives, along with the price which he paid for the goods, the price he paid for the associated services of bleaching, folding, embroidery, sewing, dying, and the like, as long as the service results in something tangible, and he is entitled to receive his share of profit with respect to those expenses in accordance with what he specified in the agreement. If it does not result in something tangible, but it does increase demand for the good, or makes it more valuable in the market, then he is entitled to his costs, but not any profit from that expense, such as the rental of camels to carry the goods to various towns and the like. If it does not increase the marketability of the goods, then he is not entitled to the cost, much less profit, like the wage paid for folding and loading, the cost of lodging, and what he spends on himself.

This explanation, however, cannot be understood from the literal expression "in accordance with my expenses." [237] Instead, this contract of sale is valid using these words if this expression entails these details as a matter of custom and usage, in which case the price is known as a matter of custom and usage so it becomes valid. Today, however, this is not understood from custom and usage, and traders do not use such expressions in the marketplace. Accordingly, there is no custom and usage at this time, so the contract price is unknown and the contract would be invalid as a result of uncertainty of the contract's terms. Accordingly, legal opinions should not be given in accordance with what is in the books of substantive law regarding this expression's validity and what it entails because of the change in custom and usage.

The third rule: one finds in the *Mudawwana*, "If a man says to his wife, 'You are prohibited to me,' or 'You are *khaliyya* [i.e., free of a husband],' or 'You are *barriyya* [i.e., free without obligation to a husband],' or 'I have given you to your family,' an irrevocable triple divorce binds him, if she lives with him in the marital home, and his intention that he intended less than three divorces does not help him." This conclusion is based on the assumption that these phrases in linguistic custom and usage had become well known for terminating the marital tie; had become well known with respect to the number of divorces intended, which is three; had become well known for both the termination of marriage and the number of divorces; and that their literal sense had been displaced by a customary meaning, for had the statement "she is unlawful to me" continued to be used in its literal sense, it would most certainly be a lie, because by consensus, she, insofar as she is his wife, is lawful to him. Accordingly, a declarative statement that she is forbidden is necessarily false [238]. The literal signification of this expression is nothing other than a declarative statement that she is forbidden and that the prohibition had already taken place sometime in the past before he uttered his formula. That is, without doubt, false, so one is required to say that this phrase's signification changed as a result of custom and usage to mean three things: termination of the marital tie, the number three, and the origination of divorce. The formulas of divorce, if they are not an origination, or are intended to be an origination, cannot terminate the marital tie in any fashion.

It is this principle that is responsible for the controversy between the moderns and the ancients with respect to this issue. Having established this principle, one should know that people do not use these previously mentioned expressions with that purpose in mind. Indeed, lifetimes will pass and no one will be heard saying to his wife when divorcing her, "You are *khaliyya*," nor will anyone ever hear someone say, "I have given you to your kin." No one uses these expressions, either for the termination of the marital relationship or to specify the number of divorces intended to be exercised. Accordingly, there is no doubt that no custom or usage exists with respect to these expressions, and since no custom or usage exists, nothing remains to be understood from them except their literal denotative meaning, for here we are talking about cases in which the speaker's subjective intent and the context of the speech are not taken into account [239, 240].

It is impossible to deny that these utterances were not coined originally in the Arabic language to bear the meanings which Mālik assigned to them in the *Mudawwana*, nor would anyone claim that these are the denotative meanings of these utterances except someone who does not understand the Arabic language. Because these utterances do not produce these meanings, whether denotatively or through contemporary usage and custom, and neither the speaker's intention nor the context is relevant, these rulings [241] lack any foundation, and a legal opinion without a foundation is invalid as a matter of consensus and sinful with respect to one who communicates it or believes it.

Certainly, in our age, the expression "forbidden" is used to dissolve the marital tie, but without any signification regarding number. It is well known for this, in contrast to what was discussed with respect to the other expressions. This entails that the legal opinion with respect to a man who says to his wife, "You are forbidden," is that it produces one revocable divorce, nothing else, and that if other expressions are used, he is to be asked what his intention was with regard to those other expressions. Accordingly, if there was no intention to dissolve the marital tie or a context suggesting intent to dissolve the marital tie, then no legal consequences arise because these are cases of oblique expressions lacking a legally clear meaning, as the preceding analysis makes clear.

Unfortunately, most of our Mālikī colleagues and our contemporaries do not agree with this analysis and reject it, even though it is my conviction that their position is contrary to the consensus of the master jurists. This explanation is clear to anyone who considers it with sound reason and fair deliberation, free from the partisan attachment to historical doctrines which is not consistent with the morality of those who are mindful of God, sublime is He. It is certainly strange that, when they are told that a man said to his wife, "You are divorced," and are asked whether it is necessary to inquire about his intention, they will say:

> No, because this phrase is expressed as a matter of denotative linguistic meaning for the dissolution of the marital tie, because the letters, *ṭāʾ*, *lām*, and *qāf* are used literally for the removal of a restriction, and for that reason one says "an

unrestricted [*lafẓ muṭlaq*] expression," and "purely lawful [*ḥalāl ṭilq*]," and "a bright face [*wajh ṭalq*]," [242] and "so-and-so has been released from jail [*uṭliqa fulān min al-ḥabs*]," and "he has diarrhea [*istaṭlaqat baṭnuhu*]."[5] The marriage contract is one form of a restriction, so when restriction is removed without qualification as in the expression "You are divorced," which is literally "You are free of restriction," the restriction of marriage is necessarily removed.

But, if one says to them, "What if he says to her, 'You are free [*munṭaliqa*],' for it shares the very same triconsonantal root as the word *ṭāliq*," they will have no answer as to why this other phrase does not result in a divorce other than the fact that it is not used, as a matter of custom and usage, to effect a divorce. Accordingly, that phrase could result in a divorce only if there were a specific intention to use it for that purpose. And, if it is said to them, "Were it to happen that the expression *munṭaliqa* comes to be widely used at some time or in some city to terminate the marital tie, and the expression *anti ṭāliq* is not well-known, what is the legal ruling?" they are required to say, "Divorce is effective with the use of *munṭaliqa* but not *ṭāliq* unless he specifically intended to terminate the marital tie by using *ṭāliq*, in contrast to our present situation." Then one would say to them, "So too, the utterance 'forbidden,' legal opinions with respect to it and phrases related to it, ought to be a function of usage and custom, positively and negatively." [243] Any expression which is in widespread use for the termination of the marital tie must be deemed effective in so doing without regard to the specific intent of the speaker, but any phrase that is not widely used to effect a divorce must not be deemed effective in the absence of a specific intent on the part of the speaker to terminate the marital tie.

Moreover, proof that an expression is widespread is not satisfied simply by the mufti's belief that it is widespread, for that belief is likely to be a result of his reading of law books, his assiduous study of it, and his debates in defense of it. Instead, proof that a linguistic custom and usage is widespread consists exclusively in the fact that the people of a particular town do not understand anything when the expression is used without qualification, other than that particular meaning. That is the kind of usage and custom which is sufficiently widespread to justify interpreting a word according to custom and usage rather than its original denotative meaning in the language [244].

Question 40. And it consists of important practical reminders which a mufti should keep in mind when answering people's questions about the law. I will discuss ten of them, with God's permission, sublime is He.

The First Reminder

A mufti must pay careful attention to the difference between an intention to particularize a word's meaning and an intention to confirm the word's meaning. A speaker's intention confirms a word's meaning when the speaker's intention is consistent with the utterance's literal meaning. A speaker's intention particularizes a word's meaning when it is contrary to part of the utterance's literal meaning.

An example will clarify the difference. Suppose someone says, "By God, I shall not wear any garment today!" If he intended thereby all kinds of garments, then his intention is confirmatory and is synonymous with the utterance's literal meaning. In this case we hold that he breaks his oath and must expiate regardless of what kind of garment he wears, because that is what his utterance and his intention entail [245]. Were the oath taker to say, "I had intended linen garments and nothing else crossed my mind when I took my oath," we would still find that he broke his oath and that he must expiate; if he wore linen garments, by virtue of his utterance and his intention, and if he wore other kinds of garments, by virtue of the plain sense of his utterance, which his stated intention did not contradict. His disregard for garments made of materials other than linen is not evidence of an intent either to include them in the oath or to exclude them. Accordingly, the utterance remains completely free of any contrary indicator, in which case wearing a garment of any kind suffices to break the oath. The intention in this case, therefore, confirms part of the utterance's meaning, but not its entirety. In no case, however, does it particularize or limit the scope of the word's meaning.

Suppose he were to say, "I explicitly considered garments not made of linen and I intended to exclude them from my oath when I swore it." In this case we would say, "This intention contradicts and opposes the plain sense of the utterance with respect to some of its meaning, so it is a particularizing intent." It is a condition of a particularizing term or an abrogating term that it be contrary to the plain sense of the utterance. In this circumstance the oath taker must say regarding the particularizing intention, "I intended to exclude such and such from my oath." His statement "I intended linen garments," without mention that he intended to exclude garments made from materials other than linen, is of no help to him. What is helpful is the intent to exclude, not the specific intent to include one or more of the utterance's meanings.

Most jurists who give legal opinions, however, ask those who seek their legal opinions regarding oaths, "What did you intend by your statement?" so he tells them, "I meant by it such and such," so they give him a legal opinion that by doing something other than that which he specifically intended, such as wearing a cotton garment rather than a linen garment, he has not broken his oath and need not expiate. This is an error. Rather, it must be the case that he says, "I intended [246] to exclude the specific meaning from my intention," in order for a specifying intention to be ascertained. If they were to say, "He did not intend by his statement 'I intended linen garments' anything other than the exclusion of all other garments," we would say that this is extremely implausible. The difference between a particularizing intention and a confirming intention is something understood only by a select group of jurists, so how can it be claimed that the uneducated masses intend to particularize when the evidence is an utterance whose literal sense is inconsistent with it? Is this nothing other than distortion of speech? Instead, when a commoner expressly tells a mufti that he used a particular phrase, and its plain sense is clear, the mufti should investigate the commoner's circumstances, and the facts of his case to determine whether there is anything in those facts that contradict the express sense of his language. How can we be satisfied by his claim that he intended a particular meaning when he used an expression that was not particular, saying, 'His intent when he used it was particular'? No, with respect to the general public, we are certain that the contrary is the case, and that when they use a word, only part of its meaning occurs to them, and they ignore the rest. This, however, is not particularization as a matter of consensus.

It is obligatory for the mufti, then, to pay heed to this and proceed carefully to confirm what kind of intention the oath taker expressed and only after that reply to his question. Speed in giving legal opinions without first becoming certain about this is sinful, and we mean by certainty only probable opinion [247].

The Second Reminder

When someone comes to a mufti, saying, "What is your opinion about such and such, according to the doctrine of Mālik? Does it bind me or not? I am a follower of al-Shāfiʿī, but I have undertaken to follow Mālik's doctrine in this case," the Mālikī mufti should take care, and not provide him a legal opinion, either affirmatively or negatively, based on the doctrine of Mālik, even in circumstances where Shāfiʿī doctrine contradicts it, because of his statement, "I am a follower of al-Shāfiʿī." The rule that is used in connection with giving legal opinions in the doctrine of Mālik is to prohibit a Mālikī from adopting the view of al-Shāfiʿī in a particular case, and likewise, a Shāfiʿī from adopting the view of Mālik in a particular case.

If the legal opinion to be given in this case prohibits abandoning the opinion of one school for the opinion of another, that view is derived from Mālikī doctrine, on the basis that it is binding on all persons; however, this view, in fact, is not binding from the Shāfiʿī perspective, and as a result, this rule does not bind the questioner, for nothing that contradicts Shāfiʿī doctrines can bind him. Likewise, what is permissible for the followers of Mālik's teachings is not permissible for a follower of al-Shāfiʿī, if al-Shāfiʿī prohibited it, because moving from one opinion to another is forbidden, and continued adherence [248] to the doctrine to which that person bound himself is obligatory. The rule of God, sublime is He, with respect to him is what his teacher said, not what others have said.

This type of question is a ruse which is rarely detected. Indeed, Mālikī muftis provide legal opinions in accordance with the doctrine of Mālik, even if the questioner says, "I am a follower of al-Shāfiʿī." Likewise, muftis who follow the doctrine of al-Shāfiʿī provide the questioner opinions based on the doctrine of al-Shāfiʿī, even if he says, "I am a follower of Mālik." Be aware of this.[1] [249]

The Third Reminder

When a petitioner comes to the mufti, seeking his legal opinion, and he does not know whether the petitioner is from the same town as the mufti or whether the legal opinion will be applied in the same place as the mufti's town, he must take care not to give him a legal opinion in accordance with what he would ordinarily say before first asking him about where he lives, whether there is a particular custom and usage in that town with respect to the expression which is the subject of the petitioner's question and, if the expression which is the subject of the question has a particular meaning derived from custom and usage, whether the custom and usage of the petitioner's town is or is not in accordance with the custom and usage of the mufti's own town, and so on.

This matter is obligatory and a duty; no scholars dispute it because all agree that, when the customs and usages in two towns are different, the applicable particular legal rulings must be different, even if they are applications of the same general rule. The scholars have disagreed only with respect to which is to be given greater priority when the two, literal language and linguistic custom, are in conflict—is linguistic custom to be given greater weight than literal language, or the opposite? The correct opinion is that linguistic custom is given greater weight because it abrogates the literal meaning, and the universally recognized rule in interpretation is that the second, abrogating text controls the meaning of the prior, abrogated text. The same principle should apply here [250].

The Fourth Reminder

If a mufti permits a petitioner to follow the doctrine of a master jurist other than the one the petitioner ordinarily follows in particular instances, it is obligatory that the mufti take care that the answer he gives does not otherwise contradict the master jurist's doctrine from which the petitioner is departing in that particular case.

An example is a Shāfiʿī mufti who permits a Mālikī to abandon a particular doctrine of Mālik in favor of Shāfiʿī's view, and a Mālikī petitioner asks him whether it is permissible for the petitioner, as a Mālikī, to omit rubbing his limbs during ritual ablutions. In this case it becomes obligatory for the Shāfiʿī mufti not to permit this for his Mālikī petitioner, because the Mālikī does not utter the invocation "in the Name of God, the Merciful, the Compassionate" as part of his prayer. Accordingly, Mālik would hold that this petitioner's prayer is invalid because he omitted rubbing his limbs during his ablutions prior to prayer—proper ablutions being a condition precedent to a valid prayer according to Mālik—and al-Shāfiʿī would also invalidate this petitioner's prayer on other grounds, namely, because the petitioner failed to utter the invocation "in the Name of God, the Merciful, the Compassionate"—a fundamental constituent element of the ritual prayer's validity according to al-Shāfiʿī.[2]

I was asked once about the performance of ritual ablutions while wearing a Persian sandal sewn [251] using pig hair, and whether it was permissible to pray in places where water from that thread had fallen. The questioner was a follower of al-Shāfiʿī, so I told him, "As for Mālik's doctrine, pig hair is pure for ritual purposes, but you are a follower of al-Shāfiʿī, so you wipe only part of your head during ablutions, so both master jurists would agree that your prayer is invalid: Mālik because you did not wipe the entirety of your head, and al-Shāfiʿī because he believes that pig hair is impure for ritual purposes." One must pay careful attention to such issues, for they occur with some frequency [252].

The Fifth Reminder

The mufti should not take the words of a member of the public at their face value when he asks for a legal opinion until he ascertains his intent. Nonjurists sometimes express themselves using phrases in a fashion that is contrary to their ordinary sense, and when one of them uses an expression or a concept which is not consistent with his personal background, that constitutes a cause for suspicion which should cause the mufti to investigate the petitioner's background to determine the petitioner's true identity and circumstances, and not to rely solely on the petitioner's formulation of the question. Once the mufti is satisfied that he knows the real background of the question, he may give him a legal opinion, but if he cannot, he should not reply to the petitioner's questioner as long as the initial suspicion remains. The same is true if the expression concerns a topic about which the questioner would not ordinarily inquire. In this case the mufti must investigate and not give a legal opinion based on the petitioner's verbal expression alone. It is likely that the petitioner in these circumstances has a hidden agenda, and had he expressed it openly, he would not have obtained the legal opinion he desires.

Once I was asked about whether a marriage contract concluded in Cairo was valid. I became suspicious so I asked him, "I will not give you a legal opinion until you explain to me [253] why you are asking me this question, for everyone knows that a marriage contract concluded in Cairo is valid." I continued to ask him until he said, "We had intended to contract the marriage outside of Cairo, but we were prevented, because it was a marriage contract whose goal was to circumvent the legal prohibition against a woman remarrying her previous husband, so we came to Cairo to contract it." I said to him, "This is not permissible, whether in Cairo, or elsewhere."[3] [254]

The Sixth Reminder

It is necessary for the mufti, if there is empty space at the end of a line or a gap on the petition, to fill it with something appropriate. Blank space in the questioner's petition presents an easy opportunity for malicious sorts to attack the reputation of scholars and muftis, and provides an easy opportunity for fraud and forgery [255]. Once, a famous scholar was asked about a man who died, leaving his mother, and a half brother from the same mother. The scribe who wrote the question left a blank space at the end of the line, and then he said, "And a male paternal first cousin." The mufti then wrote, "The mother receives a third; the half brother one-sixth; and the remainder goes to the first cousin." When the petitioner took the legal opinion, he added to the petition, in the omitted space, "and a father." He then circulated the legal opinion publicly in Kūfa,[4] and said, "Look at so-and-so, how he excluded the father from inheritance through the paternal cousin." His colleagues told him, "The likes of him would not be ignorant of this rule," but he said, "This is his handwriting, testifying against him." As a result strife occurred between two great groups of jurists.

Accordingly, the mufti should be careful about things like this and make sure to fill in the blank spaces of the petitioner's document, just as scribes do when writing out endowment deeds and documents recording other transactions, out of fear of forgery. And if he finds an incomplete line at the end of his opinion he should fill it in, using his own handwriting in accordance with what he has written in the legal opinion.

And if the petitioner mentions in his expression a qualification that is part of the question and materially changes the ruling, he should write, in his own hand, between the lines of the legal opinion, or he should say, "The petitioner said, using his own words, 'such and such,'" so that he is not subject to criticism on account of his legal opinion. These precautionary steps should not be ignored, because prudence demands circumspection and caution toward others, and blocking the means to untoward consequences is among the best legal doctrines. The Prophet, upon him be peace, said, "Shun [256] that which gives you suspicion for that which does not make you suspicious."[5] [257]

The Seventh Reminder

The mufti should not give a legal opinion except in accordance with the legal question presented to him, after due investigation of any suspicion regarding it. He should not depart from it and adopt another expression, writing it as an addition to the text of the petitioner's question, and then give his legal opinion in accordance with the addition that he himself inserted, such as when a petitioner writes in his petition, "What do you say about someone, a Muslim, who purchases wine?" and then he says in his legal opinion, "If he has drank it after purchasing it, the mandatory penalty for drinking applies to him." In this case the petitioner will say, "The jurists have given me the legal opinion that so-and-so, the one who purchased wine, should be subject to the mandatory penalty," in reliance on what he wrote. In this case the mufti would have given his legal opinion based upon what he, himself, had inserted into the legal question, resulting in confusion. Accordingly, the mufti should reply only to what he finds written down. For this reason, one of the scholars said in this respect, "A mufti should not act as a volunteer."

The only exception to this is when the phrasing of the legal question is ambiguous and can bear more than one meaning, and as a result, is ambiguous, and in need of qualifications and additions before a sensible answer can be given. In this case, he may insert additions, such as when they say [258], "What is your opinion regarding someone who has divorced his wife, twice. May he rescind the divorce?" The mufti then says, "If he is a free man, and there has not been a divorce prior to this double divorce, nor has she separated from him as a result of divorce through payment of consideration, and she remains in her waiting period, and she has cohabitated with the husband in the marital home, then he may rescind the divorce, but if not, no."

The text of the legal question might be clear, but it may give rise to suspicion in light of the petitioner's identity, as is the case when an oppressor asks, "Is it permissible to take property as a loan?," and the mufti realizes that he is seeking a pretext through this legal question for the immediate misappropriation of someone else's property, with only a remote possibility that he might return it in the future, assuming that such a thing were even to cross his mind. Accordingly, the mufti should say, "If the borrowing takes place from its owner with his consent, without compulsion or duress, in accordance with the conditions of the law, then it is permissible, but if not, no." Or, he may refrain from giving him an answer entirely, and that is the best course of action, because the petitioner's goal in seeking the legal opinion is assistance in the commission of injustice.

Alternatively, a usurer, or someone who regularly trades using invalid contracts, may ask, "Is it permissible to sell merchandise for cash?" If the mufti were to say to him, "It is permissible," he will sell a trifle and a silver coin in exchange for one thousand silver coins, in reliance on this legal opinion. In this case, the mufti should qualify his response in a manner that will prevent the harmful consequences that are suspected to result from the petitioner, or he may refrain from answering entirely, the latter being the best course of action.

A mufti needs to be keenly aware of such pretexts [259], for many rights are sought for the sake of injustice, and it is reported that the Messenger of God, may God bless him and grant him peace, said, "Jurists are God's trustees over His creation."[6] Accordingly, a jurist should not betray his trust, and when people wish to make him a path to the commission of sins, he ought not to assist them in that. Rather, he must be like a clever judge investigating the truth in accordance with his ability [260].

The Eighth Reminder

When a mufti is asked about a novel case, and he wishes to derive a solution in accordance with the principles of the legal doctrine to which he adheres, he must think carefully in light of universal rules and the established doctrinal principles of his school about whether or not there is something in the question that requires recognition of a difference between the novel case and the original case. Whenever he notices a difference, and that there is some factor in the original case which is missing in the novel case, one which the master jurist to whose teachings he defers—the one who has established that principle in his legal doctrine—would have taken into account, he must refrain from deriving a new rule based on the original case, because analogy between dissimilar cases is void. In addition, the relationship of the mufti to the legal principles of the master jurist whose teachings he follows is like the relationship of a master jurist to the indicants of the revealed law. Just as it is impermissible for a master jurist to perform analogy based on the express texts of the revealed law when there is a difference between the novel case and the original case, so, too, the mufti cannot perform an analogy in light of the general principles of the master jurist whose opinions he follows when there is a difference between the novel case and the original one.

On the basis of the foregoing, it is not permissible for a mufti to derive a rule for a novel case in light of an express rule unless he is intimately familiar with the rules of the master jurist whom he follows and the universal rules, and in accordance with his weakness in respect of that, it may be more appropriate for him to refrain from deriving a rule for the novel case. Indeed, in this case he should not give a legal opinion except in accordance with the express rules of his doctrine, on the condition that he is sufficiently well grounded in the legal doctrines of the master jurist whose teachings he defers to, that he can reach a probable conclusion that there is nothing in those doctrines [261] which requires qualification of the unqualified rule which forms the basis of his legal opinion, nor is there anything that requires narrowing its universality.

If he has neither this capacity nor this level of knowledge, he should refrain from giving legal opinions in all circumstances, whether or not he knows the express rule governing the case. This is because the unqualified rule which he knows might, in fact, be qualified according to the view of the master jurist which he follows, with respect to a qualification that has been omitted from the legal question. In this case it would be sinful for him to give a legal opinion. This entails that anyone who is ignorant of theoretical jurisprudence is not permitted to give legal opinions, because he is ignorant of the principles governing differences between cases, particularization, qualification, and the different types within these categories. No one understands these considerations except for someone who has studied theoretical jurisprudence and practiced it.

A Case

Universal legal principles seem to require that a legal opinion which is attributed to a master jurist should be invalid unless it was transmitted from one credible narrator to another until it reaches the master jurist whom the mufti takes as his authority so that the mufti is convinced that the report's attribution to the master jurist is valid, as is the case with reports about the Prophet in the mind of the master jurist, because both cases involve transmission of God's religion [262], sublime is He, and that unless this condition is satisfied, reliance on the reported legal opinion should be forbidden. It is certainly the case, however, that the people of our age have not been strict in this regard, and accordingly, they give legal opinions based on books which they read without consideration of the validity of transmission. This represents a grave danger to religion and a departure from normal rules.

The possibility of errors and forgeries in the well-known books of jurisprudence, is, however, on account of their fame, quite remote, and for this reason, people rely on them simply for the fact of their widespread use, which suggests that they are reliable. This is the same reason that has led to the failure to narrate, with attribution, books of the Arabic language and Arabic grammar through explicit chains of transmission by credible narrators, in reliance on the implausibility of error, even though the Arabic language is the foundation of revelation in the Quran and the Sunna. This omission with respect to the books of language, grammar, and morphology, both in ancient times and in contemporary ones, supports the present practice of ignoring the formal rules pertaining to transmission with respect to books of law, given that they share the common characteristic that error in their transmission is unlikely.

But, in light of this explanation, it is impermissible to give a legal opinion in accordance with teachings found in books which are not well known, until such time as there is agreement regarding the content of their teaching and the extent to which such content is valid. The same principle applies to books of recent authorship, if their asserted citations to well-known books have not become widely known, unless it is known that its author relied on the conception of validity discussed above and that he is known to be trustworthy. So, too [263], it is prohibited to give legal opinions in accordance with what is set out in the marginalia of legal texts, because of their invalidity with respect to attribution and their unreliability [264].

The Ninth Reminder

With respect to that which relates to the form of the legal question and the document on which the petition is written, the mufti should use the same kind of pen, neither too thick nor too slender, to write his legal opinion and use the same script. Variation in the pen and script makes forgery easier, using that or another script, for one might say, "It is his script," because his script is not consistent.

The mufti's pen should not be too thick, lest his answer consume the entirety of the petitioner's document, nor should it be too slender, lest reading it be too difficult. Rather, it should be between these extremes, with clear writing for ease of reading. He should not take shortcuts such as using abbreviations, notes, or summaries for some of the phrases.

The mufti should observe decorum if others who have a superior rank to him are included in the legal opinion. If the one who answered prior to him is at the apex of scholarly rank, he should say, "Like that is my answer," if he agrees with the view of the one who answered before him. Less modest than that would be for him to say, "My answer is like that," because in mentioning his answer prior to the other, he is giving precedence to his answer over the answer of the one who preceded him and to whom he is mentioned [265] in comparison. If he says, "Like that is my answer," use of the demonstrative *that* which is preceded by *like*, references the answer of the one who preceded him. In this case he gives greater precedence to the previous answer before mentioning his own. Mentioning something first is a way of according it respect and singling it out for concern. It is thus more respectful.

A less respectful form, and one closer to a stance of superiority, would be to write a response that is similar to the previous answer, but one that uses a different expression, combined with a complete failure to reference the similarity of his reply to that of his predecessor. Yet more haughty and immodest than that is for him to say, "The answer is correct," or "The answer is valid." This should not be used unless he is in a position to authorize the person who gave the previous answer to provide a legal opinion or to confirm the integrity of his statement, and that the predecessor is in the position of his student and his follower because he discloses that the predecessor's answer is in the form of one for whom the second must attest to its soundness and its correctness. This is the least deferential form, because it lacks any expression connoting the gravity and rank of the preceding opinion's author.

That is from the perspective of its verbal form. As for the position on the document where the legal opinion should be written, he should write his answer beneath that of the first, if he is of lesser rank than the author of the preceding opinion. If he deems himself to be superior in rank to the first, he should write his answer across from the first, whether to its right or to its left, although the right side is more noble than the left [266]. Accordingly, the modest mufti will write on the left, and one who is uninterested in modesty but desires to magnify his own station, will write on the right, on account of its being the blessed direction, and place his reply there.

It is important for the mufti, whenever a legal question comes to him, and it contains the written response of someone who is not qualified to give a legal opinion, to refrain from writing his opinion on that document. Writing his opinion on the same document with it amounts to recognizing the validity of the first's action, and the validity of circulating that view when it should not be given any assistance, even if the answer provided was correct in itself. The ignorant, from time to time, might be correct, and the greatest calamity is when unqualified persons give legal opinions about God's religion, whether their lack of qualifications is on account of their limited learning, their limited piety, or both.

It is important that the mufti not include in his written response to the petitioner more than what the petitioner needs. The paper is the petitioner's property, and he did not authorize its use except to the extent that it was for his benefit, and therefore to write beyond that is sinful, so he should not exceed it, unless custom permits simple additions, in which case they become permissible as a matter of custom and usage, such as when a mufti says at the conclusion of his legal opinion, "And God knows best," and things similar to that [267].

It is not appropriate that he use this expression, and ones similar to it, unless he intends thereby to remember God, sublime is He, for the use of expressions of remembrance not for purposes of remembrance of God and glorifying Him, sublime is He, is a manifestation of poor etiquette with God, sublime is He, so it is forbidden. Instead, he must intend, through these phrases, their established linguistic and theological meanings.

If the mufti finds an error in the response already given to the petitioner's question, whether in a matter governed by consensus or in a controversial matter, and the answer provided is an error according to the view of the mufti, or a falsehood, it must be addressed, even if the petitioner resents this, because providing a legal opinion that is contrary to his own convictions is sinful. If the mufti's doctrine entails that it is valid, but it is not an opinion that may be followed because it contradicts universal legal rules, express texts, or manifest analogy, and there are no valid countervailing considerations in its favor, it, too, is a falsehood which must be addressed. If, however, it is something that may legitimately be followed, he should not criticize it, even if it contradicts his own view.

He should also, if he finds the previous opinion to be erroneous in one aspect, and he knows that its author, were the opinion to be returned to him, would not be insulted thereby, and that he would correct it without giving rise to any kind of rancor, send it back to him. That is safer for him, and more protective of his colleague's honor. Doing so prevents the error from becoming notorious, and prevents a bitter opponent or envious colleague from discovering it and using it for his own purposes. Preventing disorder and conflict [268] before it occurs is the best course. But, if it is only an error that resulted from a slip of the pen or a spelling error, he should correct it himself and not return it to the author; this reconciles the goals of preserving the benefit of the legal opinion, saving its author from the pain of embarrassment, and aids in quickly removing any harm that could result from the error.

It is not appropriate for the mufti to discuss any controversies among the jurists on the question asked, so that he does not cause the petitioner to become confused as to which of the views he should follow. Nor should he mention the proof for his opinion in revelation, or where the opinion has been transmitted in the books of substantive law. That is wasteful of the petitioner's paper unless he knows that certain jurists will reject his opinion, and his opinion will result in controversy. In this case, he can mention the relevant proofs and citations to books of law, intending thereby to demonstrate to other jurists whom he imagines will oppose him why his opinion is correct. By doing this he may guard his own reputation from attack and allow others to take guidance from it. Whenever it is only a matter of the personal direction of the questioner, however, he should limit himself to the answer without any additions [269].

When the petition concerns a particular event that relates to a crucial matter of religion or the public good of the Muslim community, and it implicates public officials, it is appropriate for the mufti to provide a lengthy answer, with detailed explanation, and what would otherwise be excessive language in order to clarify the truth of the issue at hand, using expressions which can be grasped easily, warning the unjust and encouraging a speedy resolution to achieve the public good. In these circumstances it is proper for the mufti to mention the textual proofs which call to the achievement of these legal goods; it is also proper to expose the evil of those involved in sins whose prohibition and vileness is a matter of consensus. With the exception of these circumstances, however, it is important for him not to go beyond the answer.

When the legal question which is the subject of the petition involves many conditions and details, some of which are commonplace and others that are remote, the mufti must mention the commonplace conditions and omit the remote ones. If he is asked, for example, whether a man who has divorced his wife may rescind the divorce or not, he should mention conditions such as its occurrence after she entered the marital home; that it be either the first or second divorce, for otherwise an intervening marriage to another man would be required; that her waiting period should not have come to an end; and similar matters. He should omit, however, something like the possibility that either spouse might, in the interim, have apostatized, for such matters are extremely rare [270]. In this fashion, he should always mention the commonplace while omitting the rare and unlikely. Were it the case that a mufti is under an obligation to mention every issue that is connected to the petition, including all conditions and the details related thereto, even if their likelihood is extremely implausible, his response would approach a lengthy volume. This would be extremely injurious, and a waste of time, paper, and thought.

It is not appropriate for the mufti, in cases where there are two opinions, one of which is stern and the other lenient, to provide the stern response to the common folk while providing the lenient response to the elite who constitute the political class. That is almost the essence of immorality, betrayal of true religion, manipulation of the Muslims, proof that his heart is empty of reverence for God, sublime is He, recognition of His majesty, or fear of Him, and proof that it is busy with triviality, love of power and ingratiation to God's creatures instead of God. We seek protection from God, sublime is He, from the traits of the heedless [271].

The Tenth Reminder

It is important for the mufti to be handsomely dressed, in accordance with the rules of the law. It is in people's natures for them to honor outward appearances, and if they do not honor him on account of his shabby appearance, they will not hasten to his teachings or accept his views. He should also carry himself outwardly and inwardly in a blameless manner. Whoever intends something in the depths of his soul, God causes him to be cloaked outwardly in it. He should always seek in all that the means to give effect to truth and to guide people to it, in which case all of these matters become great acts of religious devotion. He should take heed of what God, sublime is He, related from Abraham, upon whom be peace, when he prayed, "Give me a reputation for truth among those who come after me."[7] The scholars explained this, saying its meaning is "worthy praise so that others may follow my example." This is similar to ʿUmar b. al-Khaṭṭāb's statement "I prefer to see the reciter of the Quran wearing white garments," meaning that he may be honored in the people's sight, so that the truth he possesses is also honored [272, 273].

He should also be fearless in speaking the truth to the mighty and the imposing, not fearing to incur the blame of censurers for the sake of God.

He should always strive to do justice with a light touch, wherever possible, for that is more appropriate [274], in accordance with the Prophet's statement, may God bless him and grant him peace, "Whoever among you calls others to the good, let him choose means that are themselves good."[8] God, sublime is He, said to Moses, "Speak to him [i.e., Pharaoh] gently, that he may be reminded or come to fear God."[9] This is the basic principle, even if in certain circumstances, it becomes necessary to be harsh and excessive in criticism if gentleness threatens to undermine the truth or defeat it entirely. In brief, he should pursue the most effective means for the truth to become manifest in light of that case's circumstances.

He should covet little, and he should be exceptional in his scruples. No one who is excessive in his desire for the profane world, or given to glorify its people and their vanities, is successful.

He should begin with himself with respect to every type of virtue to which he counsels others in his legal opinions, in his own conduct and speech; in this lies people's righteousness. God, sublime is He, said, "Do you command the people to righteousness, but neglect yourselves?"[10]

When the mufti is mindful of God, sublime is He [275], God places blessings in his speech and facilitates its acceptance by those who listen to him [276–282].

If the mufti is asked about things such as the nature of God's Messenger, or something connected to the nature of the Divinity, which are not in accord with the station of the questioner, because he is one of the uneducated masses, or he is asked about extremely difficult and subtle theological points, the ambiguous verses of the Quran, or questions which only the most learned scholars debate, knowing that what motivated the question is only excessive free time, idle speculation, or a desire to challenge things beyond his capacity, he should not [283] provide an answer at all, but instead should criticize the questioner for that, saying to him, "Busy yourself with what concerns you, like asking about how to improve the performance of your prayer or how to conform your business transactions to the law's requirements, and do not dive into questions which might cause you to perish given your lack of intellectual preparation."

If, however, the motive is occasioned by genuine doubt or confusion in the questioner's mind, then he should hasten to him and through gentle discussion remove the petitioner's doubt by means that are satisfactory to the questioner's intelligence, for providing guidance is an obligation imposed on anyone who is asked. It is better in these cases for the guidance to be provided orally rather than in writing because speech is more articulate than the pen; the tongue is alive while the pen is dead. The people are God's dependents, and the closest to Him are those who are of greatest benefit to His dependents, particularly with respect to matters of religion and what relates to religious dogma.

This is the conclusion of the book, "The Criterion for Distinguishing Legal Opinions from Judicial Rulings [284] and the Administrative Acts of Judges and Rulers." I wrote this for you, dear brothers in God, sublime is He, and upon you is peace, the mercy of God, and His blessings. He suffices us and He is the best trustee. We ask Him to envelop us, all of us, with His forgiveness and His mercy.

Notes

Translator's Introduction

1. Several works have been published that challenge the traditional conception of *taqlīd* as simply a decadent form of jurisprudence. See, for example, Sherman Jackson, "Taqlid, Legal Scaffolding and the Scope of Legal Injunctions in Post-Formative Theory: *Mutlaq* and *ʿAmm* in the Jurisprudence of Shihab al-din al-Qarafi," *Islamic Law and Society* 3, no. 2 (1996): 165–92; Mohammad Fadel, "The Social Logic of *Taqlīd* and the Rise of the *Mukhtaṣar*," *Islamic Law and Society* 3, no. 2 (1996): 193.

2. Muḥammad b. Idrīs al-Shāfiʿī, *Islamic Jurisprudence: Shāfiʿī's* Risāla, trans. Majid Khadduri (Baltimore: Johns Hopkins Press, 1961). More recently, Joseph Lowry has prepared a translation of the *Risāla*. See Muḥammad b. Idrīs al-Shāfiʿī, *The Epistle on Legal Theory*, ed. and trans. Joseph E. Lowry (New York: New York University Press, 2013).

3. Bernard Weiss, *The Search for God's Law* (Salt Lake City: University of Utah Press, 1992).

4. There are three printed editions of the Criterion in its original Arabic. The first was edited by Maḥmūd ʿArnūs and published in 1938 in Cairo by Maktab Nashr al-Thaqāfa al-Islāmiyya. The second was edited by ʿAbd al-Fattāh Abū Ghudda and published in Aleppo

in 1967 by Maktab al-Maṭbūʿāt al-Islāmiyya. A second edition of the Abū Ghudda version was published in Beirut in 1995 by Dār al-Bashāʾir al-Islāmiyya. The third was edited by Abū Bakr ʿAbd al-Razzāq and published in Cairo in 1989 by al-Maktab al-Thaqāfī li'l-Nashr wa'l-Tawzīʿ. I have relied primarily on the 1967 Abū Ghudda Aleppo edition; however, in some cases where the Abū Ghudda text was unintelligible, I looked to these other two editions for guidance. I have noted such instances in the notes to the translation. Bracketed page numbers in the translation refer to the Abū Ghudda Aleppo edition of the text.

5. This section draws largely from Jackson's discussion of al-Qarāfī's life and works as found in the introduction of *Islamic Law and the State: The Constitutional Jurisprudence of Shihāb al-Dīn al-Qarāfī*. Sherman Jackson, *Islamic Law and the State: The Constitutional Jurisprudence of Shihāb al-Dīn al-Qarāfī* (New York: Brill, 1996).

6. The ʿAbbāsids, following the sack of Baghdad, lost all pretense of effective sovereignty. Nevertheless, an ʿAbbāsid "shadow" caliphate continued in Cairo throughout the Mamlūk period, serving to preserve the political order's symbolic legitimacy. The symbolic importance of the "shadow" ʿAbbāsid caliphate is reflected in, among other things, statements in legal works of the period (and even into the Ottoman period) that it was "preferred" that the caliph hail from the ʿAbbāsid family if possible. See, for example, *Sharḥ al-Zurqānī ʿalā Mukhtaṣar Khalīl* (Beirut: Dār al-Fikr, n.d.), 7:124.

7. Marshall Hodgson, *The Venture of Islam*, vol. 2, *The Expansion of Islam in the Middle Periods* (Chicago: University of Chicago Press, 1977).

8. Abu'l-Ḥasan ʿAlī b. Muḥammad al-Māwardī, *al-Aḥkām al-Sulṭāniyya* (Beirut: Dār al-Kutub al-ʿIlmiyya, n.d.); Abū Yaʿlā Muḥammad b. al-Ḥusayn al-Farrāʾ, *al-Aḥkām al-Sulṭāniyya* (Beirut: Dār al-Kutub al-ʿIlmiyya, 1983).

9. Mona F. Hassan, *Longing for the Lost Caliphate: Transregional Imaginaries of State and Muslim Community* (Princeton, NJ: Princeton University Press, 2017), 177–220.

10. For an overview of the various theories regarding the establishment of the system of four chief judges in the Mamlūk state, see Yossef Rappoport, "Legal Diversity in the Age of Taqlīd: The Four Chief Qāḍīs under the Mamluks," *Islamic Law and Society* 10, no. 2 (2003): 210–28; Sherman Jackson, "The Primacy of Domestic Politics: Ibn Bint al-Aʿazz and the Establishment of the Four Chief Judgeships in Mamluk Egypt," *Journal of the American Oriental Society* 115 (1995): 52–65; Joseph Escovitz, "The Establishment of Four Chief Judgeships in the Mamluk Empire," *Journal of the American Oriental Society* 102 (1982): 529–31; Jorgen Nielsen, "Sultan al-Ẓāhir Baybars and the Appointment of Four Chief *Qāḍīs*, 663/1265," *Studia Islamica* 60 (1984): 167–76; E. Tyan, *Histoire de l'organisation judiciare en pays d'Islam*, 2nd rev. ed. (Leiden: E. J. Brill, 1960), 138–42.

11. Al-Qarāfī wrote a multivolume commentary on al-Rāzī's text of theoretical jurisprudence, *al-Maḥṣūl fī ʿIlm al-Uṣūl.* Shihāb al-Dīn al-Qarāfī, *Nafāʾis al-Uṣūl fī Sharḥ al-Maḥṣūl*, 9 vols., ed. ʿĀdil Aḥmad ʿAbd al-Mawjūd and ʿAlī Muḥammad Muʿawwaḍ (Mecca: Maktabat Nizār Muṣṭafā al-Bāz, 1997).

12. Shihāb al-Dīn al-Qarāfī, *al-Dhakhīra*, 14 vols., ed. Muḥammad Ḥajjī (Beirut: Dār al-Gharb al-Islāmī, 1994).

13. Al-Qarāfī, *al-Dhakhīra*, 10:23–58.

14. Compare to the common law doctrine of the law of the case. Wright and Miller, "Law of the Case," *Federal Practice & Procedure* § 4478 (Eagan, MN: Thomson/West).

15. A fatwa, or a legal opinion, is universal by its formal terms because it addresses every person who is a potential subject of the law (*mukallaf*).

16. For more on this theological and jurisprudential debate, see Baber Johansen, "Truth and Validity of the Qadi's Judgment: A Legal Debate among Sunnite Muslim Jurists from the Ninth to the Thirteenth Centuries," *Recht van de Islam*, no. 14 (1997): 1–26. See also Mohammad Fadel, "Adjudication in the Mālikī Madhhab: A Study of Legal Process in Medieval Islamic Law" (PhD diss., Department of Near Eastern Languages and Civilizations, University of Chicago, 1995), 104–17; Mohammad Fadel, "Authority in Ibn Abī Zayd al-Qayrawānī's *Kitāb al-Nawādir wa-l-Ziyādāt ʿalā Mā fī al-Mudawwana min ghayrihā min al-Ummahāt:* The Case of the Chapter of Judgments (*Bāb al-Aqḍīya*)," in *The Heritage of Arabo-Islamic Learning: Studies Presented to Wadad Kadi*, ed. Maurice Pomerantz and Aram Shahin (New York: Brill Academic Publishers, 2016), 207–26.

17. See, for example, Qāsim b. ʿAbd Allāh b. Muḥammad Ibn al-Shāṭṭ, *Tahdhīb al-furūq on the margin of al-Furūq* (Beirut: ʿĀlam al-Kutub, n.d.), 4:50–51.

18. Such textual indicants are universal by virtue of their linguistic form, which addresses all legally competent members of the class identified by the universal term.

19. The act at issue need not even be lawful. For example, were a person to impose upon him- or herself an obligation, unless he or she commits a sinful act (e.g., were a man to say to his wife, "You are thrice divorced unless I give you a severe beating [*ḍarb mubarriḥ*])," the obligation is deemed to arise immediately because the condition cannot be legally fulfilled.

20. Such rules or principles are universal insofar as they formally apply by their terms to all members who fall within their domain.

21. Al-Qarāfī argues that all the schools of law have adopted some rules that are unreasonable interpretations of revelation insofar as they contradict either univocal text, universal rules, or manifest analogy without the existence of a valid countervailing consideration justifying the contravention of these other sources of the law.

22. This last element is relevant only to those rules of Islamic law that are amenable to judicial enforcement.

23. For an introduction to the theological distinction between mental speech and audible speech, see Harry Austryn Wolfson, *The Philosophy of the Kalam* (Cambridge, MA: Harvard University Press, 1976). For a discussion of how this distinction was incorporated into theoretical jurisprudence, see Ebrahim Moosa, "Allegory of the Rule (*Ḥukm*): Law as Simulacrum in Islam?" *History of Religions, Islam and Law* 38, no. 1 (1998): 1–24, 15–20; Bernard Weiss, "Exotericism and Objectivity in Islamic Jurisprudence," in *Islamic Law and Jurisprudence*, ed. Nicholas Heer (Seattle: University of Washington Press, 1990), 53–71.

24. Anver Emon, "*Ḥuqūq Allāh* and *Ḥuqūq al-ʿIbād*," *Islamic Law & Society* 13, no. 3 (2006): 325–91.

25. See Fadel, "Adjudication in the Mālikī Madhhab," 76.

26. Johansen, "Truth and Validity of the Qadi's Judgment," 8–9.

27. Sherman Jackson, "From Prophetic Actions to Constitutional Theory: A Novel Chapter in Medieval Muslim Jurisprudence," *International Journal Middle East Studies* 25, (1993): 72.

28. The normative practice of the Prophet consists of the Prophet's statements (*aqwāl*), his actions (*afʿāl*), and his knowing confirmation of acts of others (*iqrār*).

29. Ibn Ḥajar, *Fatḥ al-Bārī Sharḥ Ṣaḥīḥ al-Bukhārī*, 5:361.

30. Jackson, "Prophetic Actions," 84.

31. Ibid.

32. "In short, a *tasarruf* [*bi'l-imāma*] or discretionary opinion (or action, if it issues from a judge or a government official) is binding, in the sense that it carries the capacity to confer legal rights or impose legal obligations. But it is not unassailable in that it is not protected and may be legally challenged or adjusted." Jackson, *Islamic Law and the State*, 133.

33. Al-Qarāfī, *al-Dhakhīra*, 3:388.

34. Jalāl al-Dīn ʿAbdallāh b. Najm b. Shās, *ʿIqd al-Jawāhir al-Thamīna fī Madhhab ʿĀlim al-Madīna*, ed. Muḥammad Abū al-Ajfān and ʿAbd al-Ḥafīz Manṣūr (Beirut: Dār al-Gharb al-Islāmī, 1995), 1:464 (*jihād* can become an individual obligation if the imam launches a campaign against the enemy and orders a particular person to participate in the campaign).

35. For the details of Jackson's argument, see chapters 4–6 from his work *Islamic Law and the State.*

36. That al-Qarāfī continues to accept the basic premises of the constitutional order outlined by al-Māwardī is evidenced by, among other things, the fact that he continues to use the operative language of delegation (*tafwīḍ*) as set out in al-Māwardī's description of the contract of the caliphate to explain how the office of the caliph or imam is filled (question no. 25). His answer to the thirty-third question, when he explains that only the particular persons to whom the judicial authority has been delegated have the authority to originate particular legal rules, is also consistent with the conclusion that he continues to assume the continued validity of the constitutional scheme outlined by al-Māwardī in his *al-Aḥkām al-Sulṭāniyya.* This is also consistent with his discussion of public offices in *al-Dhakhīra*, where in his chapter on adjudication (*qaḍāʾ*) he makes numerous express references to al-Māwardī's *al-Aḥkām al-Sulṭāniyya* and essentially summarizes its descriptions of various public offices. Al-Qarāfī, *al-Dhakhīra*, 10:23–58.

37. Shihāb al-Dīn al-Qarāfī, *al-Furūq* (Beirut: ʿĀlam al-Kutub, n.d.), 1:128–29.

38. Al-Qarāfī points out that while the material sources of the law and the kinds of evidence that a judge may admit in litigation are both specified by the Lawgiver, the ways in which we understand, as an empirical matter, whether legal causes, prerequisites, conditions, or obstacles have taken place are indefinite and potentially infinite. Ibid., 1:128.

39. Fadel, "Adjudication in the Mālikī Madhhab," 104–17.

40. ʿAlāʾ al-Dīn ʿAlī b. Khalīl al-Ṭarābulsī, *Muʿīn al-Ḥukkām fī Mā Yataraddadu Bayna al-Khaṣmayn min al-Aḥkām* (Beirut: Dar al-Fikr, n.d.) (Ḥanafī jurist who cited to al-Qarāfī twenty times in his work on adjudication). Of course, his influence on Mālikī authors was greater. See, for example, Ibrāhīm b. ʿAlī b. Muḥammad Ibn Farḥūn, *Tabṣirat al-Ḥukkām fī Uṣūl al-Aqḍīya wa Manāhij al-Aḥkām* (Cairo: Maktabat al-Kulliyyāt al-Azhariyya, 1986) (Mālikī jurist who cited to al-Qarāfī seventy-five times in his work on adjudication).

41. See, for example, *Tuḥfat al-Muḥtāj* and *Nihāyat al-Muḥtāj*, both of which cite al-Qarāfī in support of his position regarding the circumstances in which a judicial decision can be overturned and when it is impermissible to give effect to a legal opinion. Aḥmad b. Muḥammad b. ʿAlī Ibn Ḥajar al-Haytamī, *Tuḥfat al-Muḥtāj fī Sharḥ al-Minhāj* (Cairo: al-Maktaba al-Tijāriyya al-Kubrā, 1983), 10:144; Shihāb al-Dīn al-Ramlī, *Nihāyat al-Muḥtāj Ilā Sharḥ al-Minhāj* (Beirut: Dār al-Fikr, 1984), 8:258.

42. Tāj al-Dīn ʿAbd al-Wahhāb b. ʿAlī al-Subkī, *al-Ashbāh wa'l-Naẓāʾir*, ed. ʿĀdil Aḥmad ʿAbd al-Mawjūd and ʿAlī Muḥammad ʿAwaḍ (Beirut: Dār al-Kutub al-ʿIlmiyya, 1991), 2:285–86. Al-Subkī did not even bother to mention al-Qarāfī's name, despite the fact that not only his analysis, but even his examples, came directly from the Criterion.

Introduction

1. ʿAdnān is the legendary progenitor of the northern Arabian tribes from whom the Prophet Muḥammad was said to have descended.

2. For an overview of classical rules determining the Islamic calendar, and the debate regarding the acceptability of calculation to determine the Islamic lunar calendar, see Ebrahim Moosa, "Shaykh Aḥmad

Shākir and the Adoption of a Scientifically-Based Lunar Calendar," *Islamic Law & Society* 5, no. 1 (1998): 60–64.

3. In Islamic procedural law, only witnesses deemed to possess "integrity" or "good character" (*ʿadāla*) were permitted to testify in court.

4. The distinction between mental speech (*kalām nafsānī*) and audible speech (*kalām lisānī*) has its origins in the theological controversy regarding the createdness of the Quran. Whereas the Muʿtazilite theologians insisted on the createdness of the Quran to emphasize its distinctness from the divine essence, traditionalist theologians insisted that the Quran, as divine speech, must be coexistent with God, and therefore it must be uncreated. Ashʿarī theologians, in contrast, affirmed the uncreated nature of divine speech and thus of the Quran, but in so doing stated that its uncreatedness was limited to its existence in God's mind as mental speech, whereas the Quran, as audible speech in the Arabic language, was necessarily contingent on the empirical characteristics of Arabic speech and was thus created. The distinction between mental speech and audible speech therefore corresponds to the binary division between idea and expression, or content and form, with audible speech functioning to manifest to the external world already-existing ideas in the mind of the speaker. Hence, according to al-Qarāfī, and other Ashʿarī, audible speech is simply a communication or manifestation of the contents of the speaker's ideas. For an introduction to the theological distinction between mental speech and audible speech, see Harry Austryn Wolfson, *The Philosophy of the Kalam* (Cambridge, MA: Harvard University Press, 1976). For a discussion of how this distinction was incorporated into theoretical jurisprudence, see Ebrahim Moosa, "Allegory of the Rule (*Ḥukm*): Law as Simulacrum in Islam?" *History of Religions, Islam and Law* 38, no. 1 (1998): 1–24, 15–20; Bernard Weiss, "Exotericism and Objectivity in Islamic Jurisprudence," in *Islamic Law and Jurisprudence*, ed. Nicholas Heer (Seattle: University of Washington Press, 1990), 53–71.

5. I have translated the plural Arabic term *a'imma* (s. *imām*) non-literally as "public officials" in this case, even though *imām* literally applies to the head of the Muslim political community. As al-Qarāfī subsequently explains, many public officials of lesser rank share some of the same rule-making powers that the imam enjoys, and the same standards that govern the legitimacy of decisions made by the imam also apply to public officials of lesser rank. Muslim legal texts regularly refer to lesser public officials using the term *imām* or *khalīfa*, another term that applies literally to the head of the Muslim political community. See Mohammad Fadel, "Public Authority (Sulṭān) in Islamic Law," in *The Oxford International Encyclopedia of Islamic Law*, ed. Stanley N. Katz (New York: Oxford University Press, 2009).

Question 1

1. Muḥammad b. Idrīs al-Shāfiʿī (d. 204/820), the putative founder of the Shāfiʿī school of law, one of the four generally recognized Sunni schools of law.

2. Mālik b. Anas (d. 179/795), the putative founder of the Mālikī school of Islamic law, one of the four generally recognized Sunni schools of law. For a history of the origins of the Mālikī school, see Umar F. Abd-Allah Wymann-Landgraff, *Mālik and Medina: Islamic Legal Reasoning in the Formative Period* (Boston: Brill, 2013).

3. Abū al-Qāsim ʿAbdallāh b. Aḥmad al-Kaʿbī al-Balkhī (d. 317/929) was a Central Asian Muʿtazalite theologian.

4. Islamic ethical theory recognizes five ethical categories: the obligatory (*al-wājib*), the forbidden (*al-ḥarām* or *al-maḥẓūr*), the recommended (*al-mandūb*), the disfavored (*al-makrūh*), and the permitted (*al-mubāḥ*). The permitted is defined as an act the performance or nonperformance of which is a matter of indifference to the Lawgiver.

Question 2

1. *Al-Māʾida*, 5:3.

2. For example, giving charity in excess of the amount owed under the duty of *zakāt* is considered recommended, but a person may vow to pay an excess amount of his wealth as charity, in which case it becomes obligatory. In contrast, a vow to eat steak every day, for example, because eating steak is a matter of moral indifference, would not become obligatory despite the taking of a vow to do so.

3. Consensus (*ijmāʿ*) is one of the material sources of Islamic law in Sunni jurisprudence, and where it exists, it is deemed to be conclusive and infallible.

4. I have translated al-Qarāfī's term *al-aʾimma*, by which he means the eponyms of the legal schools, as "master jurists" insofar as they are all *mujtahids*, meaning, they have the authority to derive rules of law directly from revelatory sources. The four master jurists according to Sunni tradition are Abū Ḥanīfa (d. 148/767), Mālik b. Anas (d. 179/795), Muḥammad b. Idrīs al-Shāfiʿī (d. 204/820), and Aḥmad b. Ḥanbal (d. 241/855).

Question 3

1. *Al-Naḥl*, 16:60.

2. The Sunna is the normative practice of the Prophet Muḥammad, and consists of his statements, his actions, and those matters that he confirmed, implicitly or explicitly. The Sunna is documented in historical reports known as hadith, which in turn were collected in various collections. The Sunni tradition developed numerous doctrines intended to judge the historical reliability of these reports and to separate those reports that were reliable from those that were not.

Question 4

1. In this context al-Qarāfī is speaking of the caliph, the nominal head of the Muslim community, as evidenced by his use of the adjective *al-aʿẓam*, "the greatest." A literal rendering of the term, then, would be "the administrative acts and decrees of the greatest public official."

2. ʿAlī b. Abī Ṭālib (d. 40/661), was the Prophet Muḥammad's cousin, son-in-law, fourth of the rightly guided caliphs of the Sunnis, and the first imam of the Shiʿa.

3. Muʿādh b. Jabal (d. 18/639) was a prominent companion of the Prophet Muḥammad with a reputation for being an expert in the revealed law.

4. Abū Bakr al-Ṣiddīq (d. 13/634) was one of the earliest converts to Islam and one of the most esteemed of the Prophet Muḥammad's companions in the estimation of the Sunnis, and the first of the rightly guided caliphs after the death of Prophet.

5. Al-Qarāfī in this context is distinguishing between a policy that entails both benefits and harms, but its beneficial aspect exceeds the harmful aspects and a policy that includes only beneficial elements. The former represents the common good in a preponderant sense, whereas the latter represents the common good in a pure sense.

6. Quraysh was the tribe of the Prophet Muḥammad, and considered the most prestigious Arab tribe prior to Islam on account of its custodianship of the Kaʿba in Mecca and its role in organizing the annual Arabian pilgrimage to that shrine.

7. *Al-Rūm*, 30:21.

8. A reference to the two types of unlawful gain prohibited in Islamic contract law, *ribā al-faḍl* and *ribā al-nasīʾa*. For more details on these doctrines, see Mohammad Fadel, "*Ribā* Efficiency and Prudential Regulation: Preliminary Thoughts," *Wisconsin Journal of International Law*, no. 25 (2008): 655.

Question 6

1. Al-Qarāfī is referring to various rules of Islamic law that, instead of specifying a specific act, set out different options for fulfilling the obligation. An example would be the punishment for highway robbery, at least within the Mālikī school of law, which interprets *al-Māʾida*, 5:33, as giving the relevant public official the right to choose among the various punishments specified in the verse.

2. The optative mood is a grammatical mood that expresses a wish or a hope.

Question 10

1. The Arabic term is *al-muḍāriʿ*.

2. "Divorced" in Arabic takes the form *ṭāliq*, which is linguistically the active participle from the root, *ṭalaq*, to be untethered. A divorced woman is *ṭāliq* because the tie binding her to her husband has been removed.

Question 13

1. ʿAbd al-Fattāḥ Abū al-Ghudda, editor of the 1967 Aleppo edition of the *Iḥkām*, accuses al-Qarāfī of misunderstanding the Ḥanafī position on this issue, which he asserts is similar to those of the Mālikīs and the Shāfiʿīs.

2. Shihāb al-Dīn Aḥmad b. Idrīs al-Qarāfī, *al-Umniyya fī Idrāk al-Niyya*, ed. Musāʿid b. Qāsim al-Fāliḥ (Riyadh: Maktabat al-Ḥ aramayn, 1988).

Question 15

1. Al-Qarāfī's point is that although from a denotative perspective there is no difference between the first utterance, *anti ṭāliq*, and the

second utterance, *anti muṭlaqa* (because they are both derived from the same root), only the first has the legal effect of originating divorce.

2. In the original Arabic, al-Qarāfī listed questions 6–15 seriatim, and then answered them. For ease of presentation, I placed the answer for each question immediately after the question, which is the format found in manuscript for all the questions other than questions 6–15.

Question 16

1. The Islamic law of divorce gives the husband unilateral power to divorce his wife (*ṭalāq*). In the ordinary case of divorce, after the husband pronounces the formula of divorce, the wife observes a "waiting period" (*ʿidda*) in the marital home, which usually lasts up to three months. During the waiting period, the divorce is subject to revocation (*rajʿa*), which means that the husband is entitled to revoke his divorce and resume marital relations with his wife without a new marriage contract. This divorce is described as a revocable divorce (*ṭalāq rajʿī*). If he does not retract his divorce, at the end of the waiting period the divorce matures into a divorce of separation (*ṭalāq bāʾin*). In this case, because the husband may remarry his wife pursuant to a second marriage contract, it is known as the "minor separation" (*al-baynūna al-ṣughrā*). A husband is entitled to divorce his wife twice, and retract his divorce twice, or allow them to become divorces of separation and then remarry twice pursuant to new marriage contracts. Upon the pronouncement of a third divorce, he loses the right to retract the divorce or remarry her pursuant to a new contract, however, and upon conclusion of her waiting period following the third divorce, an absolute separation (*baynūna kubrā*) between the spouses takes place. In this case, the husband may not remarry his former wife until she has married and consummated a marriage with another man and is subsequently divorced or widowed from that second husband.

The issue in this hypothetical is that if the conditional divorce undertaken by the man is legally valid, as the Mālikīs believe, his subsequent marriage to the woman would be invalid because he would have divorced her three times immediately upon his marriage to her. According to the Shāfiʿīs, however, this conditional divorce, because it occurred prior to the time of the first marriage, is invalid, and thus poses no obstacle to the validity of the first or second marriage; in other words, the conditional divorce is a legal nullity. By upholding the validity of the second marriage contract, the Shāfiʿī judge's decision in this case, by necessary implication, rejects the Mālikī view that the husband's conditional divorce prohibited the marriage of the parties from the outset.

2. Al-Qarāfī in this argument is invoking a well-established hermeneutical principle from theoretical jurisprudence (*uṣūl al-fiqh*), namely that in the event of a conflict between a specific revealed indicant (*dalīl khāṣṣ*) and a universal one (*dalīl ʿāmm*), effect is given to the specific textual indicant.

Question 17

1. These three rules of evidence are all taken from Mālikī law but are rejected by one or more of the other Sunni schools of law.

Question 18

1. Muslim jurists used the term *ṭard* to indicate a legal cause that was sufficient to produce a legal effect, meaning that its presence was also consistently found with the legal ruling at issue. A legal cause was necessary and sufficient, *ʿaks*, if in its absence, the legal ruling at issue was never found. Aron Zysow, "The Economy of Certainty" (PhD diss., Harvard University, 1984), 367–68.

2. Under Islamic law, persons who have nursed from the same woman are not permitted to marry each other, but jurists disagree on how many times the child must nurse before the prohibition comes into force. All schools of Islamic law agree, however, that two just witnesses are sufficient to establish the fact that nursing has taken place.

3. The Mālikīs consider this formula for a conditional divorce valid and effective, whereas the Shāfiʿīs do not.

4. *Al-Māʾida*, 5:103. The Quranic verse is a condemnation of a pre-Islamic practice that involved consecrating livestock to the exclusive benefit of pagan deities. Abū Ḥanīfa analogized the immobilization of an endowment's capital to this pre-Islamic institution, and so concluded that an endowment could be capitalized only with immobile property in order to avoid falling under the condemnation expressed in this verse of dedicating animals to pagan gods.

5. A report with wording similar to that cited by al-Qarāfī is narrated in the collection of Ibn Māja, but in connection with the question of whether a slave has an exclusive right to divorce his wife, or whether the slave's master may divorce the slave's wife from him against his will. Muḥammad Fuʾād ʿAbd al-Bāqī, ed., *Sunan Ibn Māja*, hadith no. 2081 (Beirut: Dār al-Kutub al-ʿIlmiyya, n.d.), 1:672.

6. *Khiyār al-majlis* (the option of the bargaining session) is based on a report of the Prophet Muḥammad, narrated by Mālik, among others, that he said that "the buyer and seller are free to cancel their agreement until they part ways." Ibn Ḥajar al-ʿAsqalānī, *Fatḥ al-Bārī Sharḥ Ṣaḥīḥ al-Bukhārī* (Beirut: Dār al-Kutub al-ʿIlmiyya, 1989), 4:412.

7. A hadith is a report that includes a statement (*qawl*) of the Prophet Muḥammad, an action (*fiʿl*) of the Prophet Muḥammad, or his knowing acquiescence (*iqrār*) to an action. For an overview of the voluminous hadith literature, and the different kinds of hadith collections produced throughout Islamic history, see Jonathan Brown, *Hadith: Muhammad's Legacy in the Medieval and Modern World*

(Oxford, UK: Oneworld, 2009). This particular hadith is narrated in the highly regarded collections of al-Bukhārī and Muslim, as well as in Mālik's *Muwaṭṭa'*. Its plain meaning is that the buyer and seller are free to rescind their agreement until such time as they physically separate and thus bring to a close the bargaining session. Mālik did not incorporate this into his own legal doctrine of sales, despite his acceptance of the validity of the report's attribution to the Prophet Muḥammad, because it was not consistent with the practice of the people of Medina. Jalāl al-Dīn al-Suyūṭī, *Sharḥ Tanwīr al-Ḥawālik Muwaṭṭa' al-Imām Mālik* (Cairo: Maktabat wa Maṭba'at Muṣṭafā al-Bābī al-Ḥalabī, 1951), 2:79.

Question 19

1. Al-'Izz b. 'Abd al-Salām, *Qawā'id al-Aḥkām fī Maṣāliḥ al-Anām* (Beirut: Dār al-Ma'rifa, n.d.), 2:57.

2. Each of these contracts is deemed exceptional for one reason or another but is upheld because of textual evidence deemed reliable by the jurists that the Prophet permitted them, despite their exceptional nature.

Question 24

1. *Al-Mā'ida*, 5:49.

Question 25

1. One of God's proper names in the Islamic tradition is "the Truth."

2. Ibn Ḥajar, *Fatḥ al-Bārī Sharḥ Ṣaḥīḥ al-Bukhārī*, 5:361.

3. *Maryam*, 19:19.

4. *Āl ʿImrān*, 3:45.

5. "Friend in God," means that their friendship was grounded in a mutual love for and worship of God.

6. Muḥammad b. Khalīfa al-Washtiyānī al-Abī, *Ikmāl Ikmāl al-Muʿallim bi Sharḥ Ṣaḥīḥ Muslim*, ed. Muḥammad Sālim Hāshim (Beirut: Dār al-Kutub al-ʿIlmiyya, 2008), 8:520–21.

7. *Al-ʿAlaq*, 96:1–2.

8. *Al-Muddaththir*, 74:1–2.

9. *Al-Aʿrāf*, 7:158.

10. Ibn Ḥajar, *Fatḥ al-Bārī Sharḥ Ṣaḥīḥ al-Bukhārī*, 5:22.

11. On Mālikī doctrine regarding common property surrounding a town, see Aḥmad b. Muḥammad b. Aḥmad al-Dardīr, *al-Sharḥ al-Ṣaghīr*, ed. Muṣṭafā Kamāl Waṣfī (Cairo: Dār al-Maʿārif, n.d.) 4:88–89; for Mālikī doctrine regarding divorce on account of the husband's insolvency, see al-Dardīr, 2:747.

12. Hind bt. ʿUtba was married to Abū Sufyān b. Ḥarb. Both were bitter opponents of the Prophet Muḥammad and leaders of pagan opposition to Islam in Mecca. They eventually embraced Islam, however, after the Prophet's successful return to Mecca.

13. Ibn Ḥajar, *Fatḥ al-Bārī Sharḥ Ṣaḥīḥ al-Bukhārī*, 9:634.

14. Ḥamad b. Muḥammad b. Ibrāhīm al-Khaṭṭābi (d. 388/998), a scholar of hadith and a jurist.

15. Abū ʿĪsā Muḥammad b. ʿĪsā al-Tirmidhī, *Sunan al-Tirmidhī*, ed. Aḥmad Muḥammad Shākir et al., 2nd ed. (Cairo: Maktabat wa Maṭbaʿat Muṣṭafā al-Bābī al-Ḥalabī, 1975), 3:556.

16. In other words, one group of jurists interpreted the story of Hind as entailing a judicial ruling, whereas the other group understood it as a legal opinion that was particular to her. For this second group, the general rule against self-help was set forth in the tradition "Do not betray those who betray you."

17. *Al-Anfāl*, 8:41.

18. This group of Arabs was from the tribe of Musaylama al-Kadhdhāb ("the Liar") who claimed prophecy and led a rebellion against the Islamic state in Medina shortly after the death of the Prophet Muḥammad. His forces were defeated by Muslim armies during the reign of Abū Bakr al-Ṣiddīq, the first caliph of Islam.

Question 26

1. ʿAbdallāh b. Najm b. Shās, *ʿIqd al-Jawāhir al-Thamīna* (Beirut: Dār al-Gharb al-Islamī, 1995). The leading Egyptian Mālikī jurist of his generation (d. 616/1219), Ibn Shās's *Jawāhir* was considered an authoritative statement of Mālikī doctrine.

2. In other words, the judge ruled on the basis of erroneous evidence, and the prevailing party has reason to know the evidence is false. Otherwise, if the prevailing party has no reason to know that the evidence was erroneous, he is entitled to believe that he is morally entitled, as well as legally entitled, to the judgment given to him by the judge.

3. Abū Bakr Muḥammad b. ʿAbdallāh b. Yūnus al-Tamīmī (d. 451/1059) was a highly respected Mālikī jurist and considered by later Mālikī jurists an authoritative source of the school's doctrines.

4. Abū Marwān ʿAbd al-Malik b. ʿAbd al-ʿAzīz Ibn al-Mājishūn (d. 212/827), an early Mālikī jurist from Medina who studied directly with Mālik.

5. This case, known as *istisʿāʾ*, involves a jointly owned slave whose bankrupt owner manumits his share of the slave. Ordinarily, if a joint owner of a slave manumits his share in the slave, he is required to compensate his partner in order to perfect the act of manumission. This solution is not available here because the manumitting partner is bankrupt and unable to compensate his partner. The Mālikīs refuse to recognize one possible solution to this case, namely, that the judge

order the slave to work and earn sufficient funds to compensate the nonmanumitting partner.

6. "The practice of the people of Medina (*'amal ahl al-madīna*)" is an authoritative source of law according to the Mālikīs, but not to other schools of law.

7. The alms tax, known as *zakāt*, is a scripturally mandated tax payable on certain kinds of property, including gold and silver, certain agricultural products, and livestock.

8. A person must own a minimum of forty sheep before he becomes liable to pay the alms tax in respect of them. In this hypothetical, the Mālikīs pay no heed to the fact that the forty individuals commingled their animals into one flock (*khulṭa*) and accordingly hold that no tax is payable in respect of these sheep, since, when viewed from the perspective of individual ownership, each person owns less than the required minimum. They will treat commingled livestock as though it were owned by a single person for purposes of assessing liability for the alms tax only if the following conditions are satisfied: (1) there was an intent to commingle; (2) each of the associates, separately, would be liable for the alms tax for his share of the commingled flock; and (3) the associates jointly own (whether outright, lease, or hold the right to use what is public land) the factors incidental to livestock husbandry (e.g., pasture, water, barns). Aḥmad b. Muḥammad b. Aḥmad al-Dardīr, *al-Sharḥ al-Ṣaghīr*, 1:602–3. Commingling is distinguished from a partnership insofar as whether, after a common herd is formed, it is still possible to identify which individuals own which animals, for example, by a distinguishing mark, such as a brand. If they are able to distinguish them, Mālikīs deem this a commingling arrangement but not a partnership. Only if it becomes impossible for the individual associate to distinguish his animals from his associate's is the arrangement a partnership (*sharika*). The Shāfi'īs, in contrast, always treat a commingled flock as though it were owned by a single

person. In the hypothetical case of a commingled flock of forty sheep with forty individual owners, therefore, they conclude that tax is due on the entirety of the commingled flock, even though none of the individual owners would have been personally liable for tax. Shams al-Dīn Muḥammad b. Muḥammad al-Khaṭīb al-Shirbīnī, *Mughnī al-Muḥtāj*, ed. ʿAlī Muḥammad Muʿawwaḍ and ʿĀdil Aḥmad ʿAbd al-Mawjūd (Beirut: Dār al-Kutub al-ʿIlmiyya, 2009), 1:508.

9. The author of the *Ṭirāz* is Abū ʿAlī Sanad b. ʿInān al-Asadī (d. 541/1146).

10. Under the rules of the alms tax, a person is not obliged to pay until he owns at least forty sheep. If he owns between 40 and 120 sheep, he must pay one sheep as alms tax. If he owns 121 sheep, however, he is obliged to pay two sheep as alms tax. The question here turns on whether the law considers the beneficial interest of the associates as the relevant measure for the tax due, or whether the commingled flock in its entirety is the relevant basis for calculating tax liability. Under the Mālikī rule, only one sheep would be collected in this case out of the total of 121 sheep. The first associate owns eleven sheep and thus does not owe any alms tax. The second associate owns 110 sheep, which, because it is less than 121, results in liability for only one sheep. Mālik b. Anas, *al-Mudawwana al-Kubrā* (Beirut: Dar al-Fikr, 1986), 1:279. Under the Shāfiʿī rule, two sheep would be collected from the same commingled flock in this case, even if one associate owned only 1 sheep and the other partner owned 120. Shams al-Dīn Muḥammad b. Muḥammad al-Khaṭīb al-Shirbīnī, *Mughnī al-Muḥtāj*, 1:508.

11. *Al-Mudawwana*, 3:141–42.

12. Ibid., 3:376.

13. Ibid., 3:377.

14. In this case, when the creditors of the bankrupt debtor-manumitter, or when the bankrupt debtor-manumitter, sold the slaves

whom the bankrupt debtor had manumitted, the sale was invalid because whether the slaves were a legitimate object of sale had yet to be resolved. Subsequently, once the bankrupt debtor became solvent, the manumission automatically became effective because the effectiveness of the manumission was in doubt only because of the manumitter's insolvency. Where the judge, however, sells the bankrupt debtor-manumitter's slaves, his sale of the slaves, by necessary implication (a free person can never be enslaved pursuant to Islamic law in Islamic territory), entails an invalidation of the bankrupt debtor's attempt to manumit his slaves. Accordingly, the subsequent solvency of the bankrupt is legally irrelevant to the status of the slaves whom he had previously attempted to manumit.

15. I could not find this case in the *Mudawwana*; however, Mālik discusses the case of a man who dies after his dates have been estimated but before they have been harvested. Had he lived, the harvested amount of dates would have exceeded the minimum amount required to establish liability for the alms tax; however, with his death, the amount the heirs receive from the estate result in each heir owning an amount that does not result in individual liability for the alms tax. In this case, because the amount had been estimated by the tax collector prior to the owner's death, liability is established for the alms tax despite his death. As Mālik puts it, "If the dates have been estimated, the alms tax becomes obligatory" (*idhā khuriṣat fa-qad wajabat fīhā al-zakāt*). Mālik b. Anas, *al-Mudawwana*, 1:284.

16. In Mālikī law the owner of a well has the right to prevent anyone else from digging an adjoining well if doing so would substantially harm the flow of water in his well. The area of land adjoining the well in which digging is foreclosed is known as *ḥarīm al-biʾr*, or the well's enclosure. The enclosure need not be part of the well owner's private property. Aḥmad b. Muḥammad b. Aḥmad al-Dardīr, *al-Sharḥ al-Ṣaghīr*, 4:89–90.

17. *Al-Mudawwana*, 1:267. For Mālik, only payment of a healthy animal can discharge the taxpayer's obligation to pay the alms tax due on livestock.

18. This is another case in which tax liability is a function of whether commingling is deemed material to the calculation of tax liability or not. Under the Mālikī view, because the commingled flock is only 120 sheep, only one sheep ought to be paid as tax. Under the Ḥanafī view, because each of the three owns the legal minimum of forty sheep, each owner owes one sheep as alms tax. Where the tax collector takes three without relying on a legal opinion, one sheep is deemed to be in payment of the alms tax, and the other two are deemed to have been misappropriated by the tax collector, and it falls on the individual taxpayer to seek redress from the tax collector for his action. Accordingly, he can seek contribution from his partners only for their two-thirds' share of the one sheep that was lawfully collected as tax. If, however, the tax collector consciously acted pursuant to the Ḥanafī view, then the taxpayer is entitled to full indemnification from his partners insofar as he paid on their behalf taxes lawfully assessed and collected.

Question 29

1. This is a reference to the notion of *al-barāʾa al-aṣliyya*, the presumption in Muslim ethical thought that no ethical obligations exist in the absence of revelatory proof of an obligation.

2. Premodern Islamic law understood the witness (*al-shāhid*) as exercising a kind of public power (*wilāya*). See Mohammad Fadel, "Two Women, One Man: Knowledge, Gender and Power in Medieval Sunnī Legal Thought," *International Journal of Middle East Studies* 29 (1997): 185.

Question 31

1. Abū ʿAbdallāh ʿAbd al-Raḥmān b. al-Qāsim b. Khālid al-ʿUtaqī (d. 191/806). Ibn al-Qāsim was Imām Mālik's most prominent student and his views are considered the most authoritative source of Mālik's teachings.

2. Abū Bakr Muḥammad b. Aḥmad b. ʿAbd al-Raḥmān al-Zuhrī al-Balansī, d. 655/1257.

3. Ibn Shās, *al-Jawāhir*, 3:115.

4. In this case, there is no dispute that the divorce may not be rescinded by the husband and that separation between the husband and wife takes place. The issue in dispute is whether the wife's decision to elect divorce constitutes one divorce, in which case she may remarry her former husband without an intervening marriage to another man, or whether it constitutes three divorces, in which case she may not.

5. This is a reference to the controversial procedure of group oaths to establish liability for intentional or accidental homicide accepted by the Mālikīs known as *qasāma*. This is used in cases where circumstantial evidence both suggests that a person was murdered and establishes the likely guilt of the accused. In this case, the heirs of the deceased are required to swear fifty oaths, alongside the circumstantial evidence, in order to establish the defendant's guilt. Aḥmad b. Muḥammad b. Aḥmad al-Dardīr, *al-Sharḥ al-Ṣaghīr*, 4:406–23.

6. Al-Qarāfī suggests that the position attributed to ʿAbd al-Malik on this question by Ibn Yūnus is contrary to the position that Ibn Shās attributed to Ibn Yūnus in *al-Jawāhir*, although the basis for this claim is not clear.

Question 32

1. This is known as *īlāʾ*. In Mālikī jurisprudence, a husband who swears such an oath is required, by judicial order if need be, to break

his oath and resume marital relations with his wife, upon pain of judicial divorce if he refuses.

2. According to Mālikī jurisprudence, a slave who is abused by his master is entitled to a judicial declaration of freedom.

3. Because it is illegal to perform an immoral oath, the person taking such an oath is deemed to have violated it from the moment he made the oath. An oath by the master to administer an abusive beating upon a slave, therefore, results in the slave's immediate emancipation.

4. For al-Shāfiʿī, the debt owed to the creditors in this case is generic and can be satisfied with money, whereas the slave's right to emancipation is particular and unique to him (or her). Accordingly, in his view, the slave should be manumitted and the creditors be obliged to seek repayment from the debtor's other property, whether in his current possession or gained in the future.

5. Ashhab b. ʿAbd al-ʿAzīz b. Dāwūd al-Qaysī (d. 204/819), an Egyptian student of Mālik and who, along with Ibn al-Qāsim, was one of the most important transmitters and expositors of Mālik's legal doctrines.

6. One of the prerequisites for the validity of the Friday congregational prayer according to the Ḥanafīs is the permission of the imam, a point the Mālikīs reject.

Question 33

1. The text of the first paragraph of al-Qarāfī's response to this question is clearly garbled in the Abū Ghudda edition. The third sentence of this paragraph, "Some . . . capacity," is not found in either the ʿArnūs edition or the Azhar edition.

2. Abū ʿAbdallāh Muḥammad b. Saʿīd Ibn Bashīr al-Maʿāfirī al-Andalusī, d. 198/813.

3. Al-Qāḍi ʿIyāḍ b. Mūsā al-Sabtī al-Yaḥṣubī, d. 544/1149, a Mālikī judge, scholar of hadith, and historian.

4. ʿAbd al-Malik b. Marwān b. al-Ḥakam, the founder of the Marwānid branch of the Umayyad caliphate, who introduced various significant administrative reforms, including Arabizing the official language of the state and Islamizing the caliphate's coinage (r. 65/685–85/705).

5. Idrīs b. Ṣabīḥ al-Awadī is counted among the third generation of Muslims (a "successor of the Successors" (*atbāʿ al-tābiʿīn*)) who was reported to have transmitted a few hadiths about the Prophet Muḥammad, including one in the respected collection of Ibn Māja. His precise death date is unknown.

6. Saḥnūn b. Saʿīd b. Ḥabīb al-Tanūkhī (d. 240/854), an early Mālikī scholar from Qayrawān in present-day Tunisia. Saḥnūn studied with Ibn al-Qāsim and compiled the *Mudawwana*. The *Mudawwana* is the most important source for Mālik's legal teachings and formed the doctrinal foundations for the Mālikī school.

7. The Saḥnūn quote is corrupted in both the Abū Ghudda edition of the *Iḥkām* and the Azhar edition. I have reconstructed the quote on the basis of other Mālikī sources.

8. This official would estimate the amount of dates an orchard would produce before harvest in order to assess the cultivator's liability on harvest day.

9. This example is illustrative of the Mālikī principle of *sadd al-dharīʿa*, or blocking the means to illegality. Here, Mālik recognizes that owners of date palms face a moral hazard were *zakāt* to be calculated after the crop was actually harvested inasmuch they could consume some of their crop prior to the time on which the tax due is collected. To solve this problem, liability for the alms tax is determined on the basis of a binding estimate of the future crop before it ripens. As al-Qarāfī explains, this rule benefits the owners of date

palms because the alternative solution would be to prevent them from accessing their property until the dates were harvested, measured, and the tax paid, a much more intrusive result than under Mālik's rule.

10. Bailees in Islamic law, as a general rule, are liable for property that perishes while in their possession only if it can be shown that the property perished on account of their negligence.

Question 34

1. In other words, the repealing judge is correcting only the factual error, not the applicable rule of law.

Question 36

1. The Abū Ghudda edition has *murtaddīn* (i.e., apostates), whereas the ʿAbd al-Razzāq edition has *musrifīn* (i.e., profligates). Abū Ghudda's reading makes no sense, and so I have adopted ʿAbd al-Razzāq's reading.

2. Al-Qarāfī is making a reference to the institution of the *murṣad*, pursuant to which a ruler dedicates the proceeds of certain public lands for a designated public purpose in the manner of an endowment. For more background on the *murṣad*, and its role in the political economy of Egypt and Syria, see Kenneth M. Cuno, "Ideology and Juridical Discourse in Ottoman Egypt: The Uses of the Concept of Irṣād," *Islamic Law & Society* 6 (1999): 136.

3. Usāma b. Zayd, the son of Zayd b. al-Ḥāritha, the onetime adopted son of the Prophet until the Quran abrogated adoption (d. 54/674). Usāma grew up in the Prophet's household as a virtual grandson of the Prophet, and the Prophet Muḥammad appointed him to lead an expedition to Syria against the Byzantines shortly before the Prophet's death. After the Prophet died, Abū Bakr affirmed

Usama's command of the expedition against the advice of some of the Prophet's more senior companions who objected to Usama's youth at the time of the campaign.

4. Under this opinion, the imam may compel the prisoners of war to accept the status of protected persons (*ahl al-dhimma*) in the Islamic state, and accordingly, they become obliged to pay the poll tax (*jizya*).

Question 37

1. Muslim theology did not permit deference (*taqlīd*) in matters of dogma or theoretical jurisprudence (*uṣūl al-fiqh*), and instead held that each person had to affirm the propositions set forth in those disciplines through the independent exercise of reason (*ijtihād*).

2. Islamic law recognizes a special category of kinship, the "milk sibling," which arises when two persons, otherwise unrelated by blood, suckle from the breast of the same woman. The dispute is how many times the individuals must suckle before the legal relationship comes into existence and the maximum age before which the suckling must take place.

3. *Ribā*, which is customarily but erroneously translated as "usury," applied only to sales involving specific contracts involving commodities subject to the rules of *ribā*. Other commodities could be traded without regard to these rules.

4. A *qulla* was a measure of weight that has been estimated to be approximately 95.6 kilograms, according to the definition of most Muslim schools of law, and 101.6 kilos, according to the Ḥanafīs. Two *qulla*s, then, would be between approximately 191.2 and 203.2 kilos. In terms of volume, then, it would be between approximately 191 and 203 liters of water. ʿAlī Jumuʿa Aḥmad, *Al-Makāyīl wa'l-Mawāzīn al-Sharʿiyya* (Cairo: al-Quds li'l-Iʿlān wa'l-Nashr wa'l-Taswīq, 2001).

5. The commenda is the Latin equivalent of the Arabic term *qirāḍ* (in the case of the Mālikīs) or *muḍāraba* (in the case of the other legal schools), and describes an investment contract pursuant to which the investor entrusts a sum of capital to an entrepreneur who invests it, with profits from the venture being shared pursuant to a preagreed formula, with the investor bearing the entire risk of loss to the venture's capital.

6. The *witr* prayer is a special prayer offered typically at the end of the nighttime prayer. It consists of one unit (*rakʿa*).

7. A person could testify before a Muslim judge (*qāḍī*) only if the judge first determined that the witness was of sufficiently good character (*ʿadl*).

8. The story of Māʿiz's confession of adultery, and the Prophet Muḥammad's decision to stone him to death—following repeated requests from the Prophet to Māʿiz for him to withdraw his confession—is well known in the hadith literature. Ibn Ḥajar, *Fatḥ al-Bārī Sharḥ Ṣaḥīḥ al-Bukhārī*, 12:162–63; Jalāl al-Dīn al-Suyūṭī, *Tanwīr al-Hawālik Sharḥ Muwaṭṭaʾ Mālik*, 2:165–66.

9. Jalāl al-Dīn al-Suyūṭī, *Tanwīr al-Hawālik Sharḥ Muwaṭṭaʾ Mālik*, 2:166–67.

10. Ibid., 2:174.

11. Historical reports of Prophetic legal precedent, before they were accepted by Sunni jurists as a valid source of revealed law, had to meet certain minimum requirements of credibility, including, that it was narrated from a credible source. Here, the point is that all jurists are in agreement that if the narrator of the Prophetic precedent is a credible scholar of the law, his transmission of the report is sufficient to establish a legal precedent, even if he is the only source who reported that precedent.

12. *Ẓihār* refers to a pre-Islamic formula for divorce, pursuant to which a man would say to his wife, "You are to me like the back of my mother."

13. This is a reference to Abū al-Walīd Muḥammad b. Aḥmad b. Rushd al-Jadd (d. 520), grandfather of the celebrated Ibn Rushd, the philosopher known as Averroës in Latin Europe. The *Muqaddimāt* is an introduction to Mālikī law.

14. Al-Layth b. Sa'd (d. 175/791) was a prominent Egyptian religious scholar and a contemporary of Mālik.

Question 38

1. Qarāfī's point here is that each school of law has two rules for every controversial doctrine. The first rule is that which it holds to be the substantively correct rule, which is the view of the master jurist that it follows, and that binds all those who defer to the views of that master jurist, such as Mālik for the Mālikīs and al-Shāfi'ī for the Shāfi'īs. The second rule, which is derived from consensus, is that, in cases of legal controversy, the master jurist and those who follow him are obliged to follow the rule that the master jurist believes to be the applicable rule of God. Accordingly, if a follower of Mālik asks a Mālikī mufti for the rule governing, for example, the wiping of the head in preparation for proscribed prayers, he will tell him that he must wipe the entirety of his head, but if the questioner is a follower of al-Shāfi'ī, the Mālikī mufti should tell him that he need wipe only part of his head, in reliance on the principle established by consensus that a follower of Shāfi'ī is obliged to follow the views of al-Shāfi'ī in all controversial questions of law, even though the Mālikīs believe, as a substantive matter, that al-Shāfi'ī's view on this question was mistaken.

2. Abū Ḥāmid Muḥammad b. Muḥammad al-Ghazālī (d. 505/1111). Al-Ghazālī, known as Algazel in the Medieval Latin West, was the author of numerous works in Shāfi'ī law, theoretical jurisprudence (*uṣūl al-fiqh*), mysticism (*taṣawwuf*), and philosophy (*falsafa*). His *Mustaṣfā fī Uṣūl al-Fiqh* is his most famous work in theoretical jurisprudence.

3. According to the Mālikīs, wiping the entirety of the head and rubbing the limbs while washing them with water are essential to the correct performance of the ablutions. Proper performance of ablutions, moreover, is a condition for the valid performance of the ritual prayer. Accordingly, if one fails to do these things, his prayer would be invalid. Likewise, the Shāfiʿīs believe that the invocation "In the name of God, the Merciful, the Compassionate" is a part of the *Fātiḥa*, the first chapter of the Quran, which must be recited in every cycle of every proscribed ritual prayer. Failure to recite the *Fātiḥa* properly would result in an invalid prayer. Mālikīs do not consider that phrase to be part of the *Fātiḥa*, and accordingly omit it from their prayers, something that the Shāfiʿīs believe renders the prayer invalid. Despite these material differences in the rules governing the proper performance of prayer, Mālikīs are permitted to pray behind a Shāfiʿī imam who follows Shāfiʿī doctrine regarding the performance of ablution, and Shāfiʿīs are permitted to pray behind a Mālikī imam who follows Mālikī doctrine and omits "In the Name of God, the Merciful, the Compassionate" from his recitation of the *Fātiḥa*.

4. The first set of disputed questions, in other words, involves disputed questions of law, and each master jurist can point to some basis in revelation that justifies his position, whereas in the second set of disputed questions (e.g., direction of prayer), they are each following the same rule but disagree regarding the empirical question of which direction is correct. Accordingly, if A were to follow B's determination of the prayer direction, even though he believed it to be incorrect, he would not be acting under a countervailing revelatory indicant, as he would be in the first set of disputed *legal* questions.

5. Al-Qarāfī here references the debate in theoretical jurisprudence regarding whether there is a uniquely correct answer for each legal question. Those who believed that there was such a solution believed that in cases of legal disagreement, only one answer was correct. They

were opposed by a group of jurists who held that in matters of legal reasoning, God had not decreed a specific rule for each legal question, but instead imposed an obligation to engage in legal reasoning. Under this doctrine, so long as the master jurist exerted his utmost efforts in a good-faith effort to find an answer, his obligation toward God was satisfied by adhering to the conclusion reached by those good-faith efforts.

6. A unit of volume between 191 and 203 liters. See question 37, n. 4.

7. The Mālikī position with respect to a body of water whose volume is less than two *qulla*s is that it remains pure so long as the water's objective characteristics—taste, color, and odor—have not changed, even if it has been contaminated by ritually impure substances.

Question 39

1. In Islamic procedural law, the plaintiff is not necessarily the party who initiated the lawsuit, nor is the defendant necessarily the party summoned to court by the party initiating the suit. Instead, Muslim jurists developed a system of presumptions that they used to determine which party bore the burden of proof in a particular case. One method that jurists used, particularly Mālikī jurists, was to consider the evidence of custom and usage with respect to a specific claim: if the claim was contrary to custom, the claimant bore the burden of proof, but if the claim was consistent with custom, the party summoned to court would bear the burden of proof. See Mohammad Fadel, "Adjudication in the Mālikī Madhhab: a Study of Legal Process in Medieval Islamic Law" (PhD diss., Department of Near Eastern Languages and Civilizations, University of Chicago, 1995), 143–51.

2. Abū Isḥāq Ismāʿīl b. Isḥāq b. Ḥammād al-Baghdādī (d. 282/895), a prominent Mālikī judge who served in Baghdad.

3. The cost-plus-profit (*murābaḥa*) contract is one in which the seller offers to sell his merchandise to the purchaser at an agreed markup or discount to the seller's costs. The seller must disclose to the purchaser his costs at the time of delivery.

4. Al-Qarāfī discusses this case in another of his works. See Shihāb al-Dīn Aḥmad b. Idrīs al-Qarāfī, *al-Furūq* (Beirut: ʿĀlam al-Kutub, n.d.), 3:287.

5. The printed editions of the *Iḥkām* read *inṭalaqat baṭnuhu.* I could not find, however, such an expression in any Arabic dictionary. Accordingly, I have corrected it to *istaṭlaqat baṭnuhu*, which is found in Arabic dictionaries.

Question 40

1. Al-Qarāfī appears here to reject strongly the doctrine of *takhayyur* (alternatively, *takhyīr*), which permits a person who is not a master jurist to pick and choose among the various opinions articulated by the various master jurists. Elsewhere, however, he tolerates and even defends it. See, for example, Shihāb al-Dīn al-Qarāfī, *Nafāʾis al-Uṣūl fī Sharḥ al-Maḥṣūl*, ed. ʿĀdil Aḥmad ʿAbd al-Mawjūd and ʿAlī Muḥammad Muʿawwaḍ (Riyadh: Maktabat Nizār Muṣṭafā al-Bāz, 1997), 9:4134. Note his direction to muftis in the fourth reminder about the special precautions that are warranted if they approve of the doctrine of *takhyīr* and respond to petitioners' questions in accordance with that doctrine.

2. This doctrine of picking and choosing, known as *talfīq*, literally means "to patch up." Al-Qarāfī's concern in this context is that in certain circumstances, permitting the petitioner to practice *talfīq* easily results in a form of prayer that no master jurist would consider valid. That is the case in the hypothetical he raises. If the Mālikī who adopts the particular doctrine of the Shāfiʿī school with regard to how to per-

form ritual ablutions continues to adhere to other Mālikī doctrines of prayer, his prayer becomes invalid according to both the Shāfiʿīs and the Mālikīs: according to the Shāfiʿīs, his omission of the invocation "In the Name of God, the Merciful, the Compassionate" invalidates his prayer because it undermines the performance of what the Shāfiʿīs consider a constitutive element of the prayer; and according to the Mālikīs, his failure to rub his limbs during ritual ablutions invalidates his prayer because valid ablutions are a condition precedent for the validity of the ritual prayer.

3. Such a marriage is known as the *istiḥlāl* marriage because its explicit goal is to permit a thrice-divorced woman to remarry her original husband by entering into a sham marriage with a second man, who then divorces her.

4. Kūfa is a town in southern Iraq founded by the Arab conquerors of Iraq, and an early center of Islamic law and Arab literary culture.

5. This hadith is found in numerous well-regarded hadith collections, including *Sunan al-Tirmidhī*, *Sunan al-Nasāʾī*, *Musnad Aḥmad b. Ḥanbal*, and *Ṣaḥīḥ Ibn Ḥibbān*. Ibn Ḥajar *Fatḥ, al-Bārī Sharḥ Ṣaḥīḥ al-Bukhārī*, 4:366–67.

6. A report with similar wording is found in Jalāl al-Dīn al-Suyūṭī's *al-Jāmiʿ al-Ṣaghīr*. Zayn al-Dīn ʿAbd al-Raʾūf al-Munāwī, *al-Taysīr bi-Sharḥ al-Jāmiʿ al-Ṣaghīr* (Riyadh: Maktabat al-Imām al-Shāfiʿī, 1988), 2:301.

7. *Al-Shuʿarāʾ*, 26:84.

8. *Al-Munāwī*, 2:785.

9. *Al-Dukhān*, 44:20.

10. *Al-Baqara*, 2:44.

Glossary of Names

ʿAbd Allāh b. Aḥmad al-Kaʿbī al-Balkhī, Abū'l-Qāsim (d. 317/929): A Central Asian Muʿtazilī theologian.

ʿAbd al-Malik b. Marwān (d. 85/705): The founder of the Marwānid branch of the Umayyad caliphate who introduced various significant administrative reforms, including Arabizing the official language of the state and Islamizing the caliphate's coinage (r. 65/685–85/705).

Aḥmad b. Ḥanbal (d. 241/855): Eponym of the Ḥanbalī school of law, Aḥmad b. Ḥanbal lived in Baghdad, where he gained fame as a traditionist, his vehement rejection of theological rationalism, and his torture during the infamous inquisition al-Miḥna, when he refused to endorse the rationalist theology espoused by the early ʿAbbāsid caliph, al-Maʾmūn (r. 813/197–833/217).

ʿAlī b. Abī Ṭālib (d. 40/661): The Prophet Muḥammad's cousin, son-in law, fourth of the rightly guided caliphs of the Sunnis, and the first imam of the Shiʿa.

al-Āmidī, Sayf al-Dīn (d. 630/1233): A Shāfiʿī theologian and author of the well-known work in theoretical jurisprudence *al-Iḥkām fī Uṣūl al-Aḥkām.*

Ashhab b. ʿAbd al-ʿAzīz b. Dāwūd al-Qaysī (d. 204/819): One of the leading Egyptian students of Mālik b. Anas.

Abū Bakr al-Ṣiddīq (d. 13/634): One of the earliest converts to Islam and the first of the rightly guided caliphs after the death of the Prophet. He led the so-called Wars of Apostasy against those Arab tribes that had attempted to assert their independence from the nascent Islamic state in Medina after the Prophet's death, paving the way for the successful Muslim conquests of the Near East under the rule of his two successors, ʿUmar b. al-Khaṭṭāb (d. 23/644) and ʿUthmān b. ʿAffān (d. 36/656).

Fakhr al-Dīn al-Rāzī, Muḥammad b. ʿUmar (d. 606/1209): A Central Asian Shāfiʿī theologian and jurist who wrote numerous works on theology and theoretical jurisprudence. Al-Qarāfī authored summations and commentaries on al-Rāzī's work in theoretical jurisprudence.

Al-Farrāʾ, Abū Yaʿlā Muḥammad b. al-Ḥusayn (d. 458/1066): An eleventh-century Baghdādī Ḥanbalī judge and jurist who was a contemporary of al-Māwardī. Al-Farrāʾ also wrote a work on constitutional law, also titled (as is al-Māwardī's) *al-Aḥkām al-Sulṭaniyya*, which in many respects mirrored al-Māwardī's work but explicitly incorporated the teachings of Aḥmad b. Ḥanbal.

Al-Ghazālī, Abū Ḥāmid Muḥammad b. Muḥammad (d. 505/1111): Known as Algazel to medieval Latin scholars, al-Ghazālī was a prolific author who wrote numerous works that enjoyed enduring influence in Shāfiʿī substantive law, theoretical jurisprudence, philosophy, ethics, and Sufism (Islamic mysticism).

Abū Ḥanīfa, al-Nuʿmān b. Thābit (d. 148/767): Eponym of the Ḥanafī school of law, Abū Ḥanīfa lived in the Iraqi garrison town of Kūfa.

Ibn Bashīr, Abū ʿAbdallāh Muḥammad b. Saʿīd al-Maʿāfirī al-Andalusī (d. 198/813): An early Andalusian Mālikī jurist.

Ibn Bint al-A'azz, Taqī al-Dīn (d. 665/1267): The Shāfiʿī chief judge of Egypt during the waning days of the Ayyūbid state whose fanatic adherence to Shāfiʿī doctrine has been identified as one of the reasons that led al-Qarāfī to write the Criterion.

Ibn al-Mājishūn, Abū Marwān ʿAbd al-Malik b. ʿAbd al-ʿAzīz (d. 212/827): A prominent early student of Mālik b. Anas.

Ibn Muḥriz, Abū Bakr Muḥammad b. Aḥmad b. ʿAbd al-Raḥmān al-Zuhrī al-Balansī (d. 655/1257): An Andalusian and North African Mālikī jurist and traditionist.

Ibn al-Qāsim, Abū ʿAbdallāh ʿAbd al-Raḥmān b. al-Qāsim b. Khālid al-ʿUtaqī (d. 191/806): The most prominent student of Mālik b. Anas, Ibn al-Qāsim lived and taught in Egypt. His transmissions of Mālik's teachings in the *Mudawwana* are considered the foundational sources of Mālikī legal doctrine.

Ibn Shās, ʿAbd Allāh b. Najm (d. 616/1219): An Egyptian Mālikī jurist and author of *al-Jawāhir*, an important treatise consolidating the mature doctrines of the Mālikī school.

Ibn al-Subkī, Tāj al-Dīn ʿAbd al-Wahhāb b. ʿAlī b. ʿAbd al-Kāfī (d. 771/1369): A prominent Shāfiʿī theologian, jurist, and historian of the Shāfiʿī school of law. He was born in Egypt but traveled to Damascus as a young man. He served in several offices in the Mamlūk state, eventually becoming the Shāfiʿī chief judge in Damascus, where he died.

Ibn Yūnus, Abū Bakr Muḥammad b. ʿAbd Allāh al-Tamīmī (d. 451/1059): A leading Mālikī jurist who lived in Sicily and North Africa.

Idrīs b. Ṣabīḥ al-Awadī (precise death date unknown): From the third generation of Muslims (a "successor of the Successors" (*atbāʿ al-tābiʿīn*)), he was reported to have transmitted a few hadiths about the Prophet Muḥammad, including one in the respected collection of Ibn Māja.

Abū Isḥāq Ismā'īl b. Isḥāq b. Ḥammād al-Baghdadi (d. 282/895): A leading Mālikī jurist of Baghdad commonly known as al-Qāḍī Ismā'īl.

'Iyāḍ b. Mūsā al-Sabtī al-Yaḥṣubī (d. 544/1149): A Moroccan traditionist and Mālikī jurist and judge, and commonly referred to as al-Qāḍī 'Iyāḍ, he authored numerous works in hadith and the history of the Mālikī school. A collection of his legal opinions, *Madhāhib al-Ḥukkām fī Nawāzil al-Aḥkām*, has also been published.

Al-'Izz, 'Abd al-'Azīz b. 'Abd al-Salām (d. 660/1262): A prominent Shāfi'ī jurist of the late Ayyūbid and early Mamlūk period who lived in Syria and Egypt, and one of al-Qarāfī's most important teachers.

Al-Khaṭṭābī, Ḥamad b. Muḥammad b. Ibrāhīm (d. 388/998): A traditionist and a jurist.

Al-Layth b. Sa'd (d. 175/791): An early Muslim jurist who lived in Egypt and was a contemporary of Mālik b. Anas, with whom he had a famous exchange regarding the jurisprudential status of the practice of the people of Medina (*'amal ahl al-madīna*) as an authoritative source of Islamic law.

Mālik b. Anas (d. 179/795): Eponym of the Mālikī school of law, Mālik b. Anas lived his life in the town of Medina, site of the original Muslim community.

Al-Māwardī, Abū'l-Ḥasan 'Alī b. Muḥammad (d. 450/1058): An eleventh-century CE Baghdadi Shāfi'ī jurist and polymath who wrote numerous works in Shāfi'ī substantive law, including a widely cited work on constitutional law, *al-Aḥkām al-Sulṭāniyya*, theoretical jurisprudence (*uṣūl al-fiqh*), and secular works on statecraft in the Mirror-for-Princes genre and political wisdom. Al-Māwardī also had an active political career in which he served as chief judge of the 'Abbāsid caliphate.

Mu'ādh b. Jabal (d. 18/639): A companion of the Prophet Muḥammad who was reportedly dispatched by the Prophet to Yemen to serve as a judge.

Saḥnūn b. Sa'īd b. Ḥabīb al-Tanūkhī (d. 240/854): An important Mālikī legal scholar who served as chief judge of what is now Tunisia under the Aghlabids. He compiled the foundational Mālikī legal text, *al-Mudawwana*, which consists primarily of a series of dialogues he had with Ibn al-Qāsim regarding Mālik's views on a series of legal questions (*masā'il*).

Sanad b. 'Inān al-Asadī, Abū 'Alī (d. 541/1146): An Egyptian Mālikī jurist from Alexandria.

Al-Shāfi'ī, Muḥammad b. Idrīs (d. 204/820): Eponym of the Shāfi'ī school of law, author of the *Umm*, a work in substantive law, and *al-Risāla* (*The Epistle*), the first written work of theoretical jurisprudence in Islamic legal history.

'Umar b. al-Khaṭṭāb (d. 23/644): The second of the rightly guided Sunni caliphs who oversaw the dramatic expansion of the Islamic state into the Fertile Crescent, Egypt, Iraq, and Persia.

Usāma b. Zayd (d. 54/674): The son of Zayd b. al-Ḥāritha. Zayd had been the onetime adopted son of the Prophet until the Quran abrogated adoption.

'Uthmān b. 'Affān (d. 36/656): Third of the rightly guided Sunni caliphs who oversaw the final conquest of the Persian Empire but whose reign concluded in his assassination, triggering a series of civil wars that led to the eventual rupture between Sunni Muslims and Shi'a Muslims.

Glossary of Terms

'*Adāla*: The quality of integrity. A witness must be found to possess the legal qualifications of integrity before a Muslim judge can accept his testimony in a judicial proceeding. In the transmission of normative reports, the narrator must also be deemed to possess integrity as a condition to acceptance of the report by an expert jurist as evidence of God's law.

Āḥād: The plural of *aḥad*, meaning "one" or "singular." In Islamic jurisprudence it is usually used as the second noun of the compound noun *ḥadīth āḥād*, or a report transmitted by a specific (and delimited) number of individual narrators. Even when the narrators of such reports possess integrity, such a report produces only probable (*ẓann*) knowledge of its truth.

Aḥkām furū'iyya: The detailed rules of Islamic law regulating both the conduct of ritual and human interactions. These rules are contrasted with the methodological rules of Islamic law, *al-aḥkām al-uṣūliyya*, from which the former are said to derive.

'*Āmm*: A term that denotes a universal set of individuals, such as "All men" in the phrase "All men are obliged to pray." Books of Islamic jurisprudence typically include lengthy discussions of the various structures the Arabic language uses to communicate a universal set, as well as lengthy debates regarding the denotative meaning of a universal term, that is, whether it applies denotatively to all putative members of its set, or only some, and whether it does so in a conclusive fashion (*qaṭʿī*) or only presumptively (*ẓannī*).

Amr: An affirmative command as in the phrase, "Open the door!"

ʿAqd al-dhimma: The contract of protection granted by the Muslim state to non-Muslims who are permanently resident in the Muslim state in exchange for their payment of a special tax, known as *jizya*, and their agreement to be bound by the rules of Islamic law except in connection with what is deemed to be religious, such as the observance of Muslim rituals and the formation and dissolution of marriages.

Bayʿ al-Salam: A forward sale pursuant to which the purchaser pays the purchase price in advance of the seller's delivery of the goods that are the object of the contract. This is considered an exceptional contract because it contradicts the ordinary principle of Islamic contract law that requires the seller to sell only what is in his possession at the time of the contract.

Dalīl (p. *adilla*): In Islamic jurisprudence, evidence for God's law. This evidence might be textual in character, such as a verse of the Quran, a report from the Prophet Muḥammad, or consensus, or it might be discursive, such as an analogical or nonanalogical argument.

Fāsiq: An immoral, dissolute person who flouts the norms of divine law. A *fāsiq* lacks the moral integrity necessary for his testimony to be accepted before a Muslim judge or for his narrations of normative reports to be accepted by a master jurist as evidence of God's law.

Fatwā: A nonbinding opinion from a qualified jurist that communicates the content of divine law with respect to a particular question of law. A *fatwā* is based on legal reasoning and represents the probable judgment of the jurist issuing the *fatwa*.

Hadith: In Islamic jurisprudence, hadith is a normative report, usually concerning an incident from the life of the Prophet Muḥammad, which may include a report of his direct words, his actions, or his omissions. Such reports, if they are considered historically sound, generally serve as probable evidence of God's law.

***Ḥākim* (p. *ḥukkām*)**: A Muslim judge (also called *qāḍī*; p. *quḍāt*). The word is the active participle of the verb meaning "to exercise judgment." Conventionally, it is used for the person who exercises judgment in order to resolve a particular dispute between two or more parties. Although commonly used specifically for the Muslim judge, it can also be used for any public officeholder who exercises the function of dispute resolution.

Ḥawāla: A contract pursuant to which a debtor assigns to his creditor the right to collect a debt belonging to the debtor from a third person in satisfaction of the first debtor's obligation to the creditor. It is considered an exceptional contract that contravenes ordinary principles of Islamic commercial law insofar as it involves trading of debts, not tangible property.

***Ḥimā* (p. *aḥmiya*)**: A portion of public lands that was once part of the commons, but became reserved for the use of the state by decree of the ruler.

Ḥisba: Literally, "holding accountable." In Islamic constitutional law, it may be applied to a broad array of public offices that exercise regulatory power with the power to intervene in conduct without waiting for a specific complaint. The best known such office is that of the market inspector, called the *muḥtasib*, who had jurisdiction to investigate allegations of fraud in the market, as well as other kinds of public violations of the law, but lacked any jurisdiction to resolve disputes arising out of contractual relations.

***Ḥudūd* (s. *ḥadd*)**: In Islamic law, a reference to a limited number of crimes with fixed scriptural penalties, including theft (amputation of the right hand), wine drinking (forty or eighty lashes), fornication (one hundred lashes) and adultery (stoning to death), slander (eighty lashes), highway robbery (various punishments depending on the severity of the conduct), rebellion, and apostasy (death unless the apostate repents). Unlike other crimes in Islamic law known as *taʿzīr*, the punishment for a *ḥadd* crime, if proved before a public official having jurisdiction over the matter with competent evidence, could not be waived and had to be enforced against the criminal. Accordingly, numerous legal doctrines arose that were intended to preclude findings of guilt, particularly for crimes such as wine drinking, theft, and illicit sexual intercourse.

***Ḥujja* (p. *ḥijāj*)**: Fact evidence used by a Muslim judge in the course of resolving a dispute. Islamic evidentiary law recognized three broad classes of evidence: eyewitness testimony, admissions against the party's interest, and oaths in affirmation of one's claim or the refusal to swear an oath to affirm the truth of one's claim.

Ḥukm: Literally, "a judgment." It can be used to refer to a general rule of law as communicated by a master jurist in the form of a legal opinion (*fatwā*), or it can refer to the particular judgment of a judge resolving a particular dispute between two parties.

***ʿIbāda* (p. *ʿibādāt*)**: Means "worship." Islamic law is divided into two broad categories, ritual law and transactional law. Ritual law covers the fundamental aspects of Muslim public ritual: daily prayer, fasting, paying alms, and pilgrimage, as well as the rules of purity that are applicable to the performance of ritual acts. Unsurprisingly, ritual law constitutes the first topic of Islamic law, and later jurists, who would divide Islamic law into quarters, made ritual law the first of the four quarters constituting Islamic law.

ʿIdda: The waiting period a divorced or widowed woman must observe before she may remarry.

Iḍmār: Means "elision." Muslim jurists often assume that many revealed texts elide phrases that must be restored by the master jurist in order to understand divine intent properly. For example, the verse stating, "The punishment of those who wage war against God and His Messenger and bring strife to the land" (*al-Mā'ida*, 5:33) is understood by the jurists to include the elided noun *servants*, such that the proper meaning of the verse is "those who wage war against the *servants* of God." The jurists argue that there must be an elided noun in this case because of the rational impossibility of a human being waging war against God.

Ijāra: A lease contract or an employment contract.

Ijmā': Consensus, one of the substantive sources of Islamic law. Although there is agreement that consensus is a material source of Islamic law, there is profound disagreement on what constitutes a consensus—that is, does it require the agreement of the entire Muslim community, or alternatively, the agreement, explicit or implicit, of the master jurists of the Muslim community of one generation?

Ijtihād: Literally, "the exertion of effort." In Islamic jurisprudence, it is the good-faith exercise of moral and intellectual diligence in seeking the content of God's law. The rules of Islamic law are divided, from a hermeneutical perspective, into those rules knowledge of which do not require specialized training and intellectual skill and those that do. The former are known as the "necessary rules of religion," or "that of religion which is known by necessity," and the latter are known as the "rules derived through the exertion of effort." While the necessary rules are universal and do not admit of dispute, those derived through effort are plural and often contradictory as a result of the different good-faith conclusions reached on the same question by different master jurists.

Ikhbār: The communication of a historical report.

Īlā': An oath by a husband to refrain from sexual relations with his wife with the intent of expressing his anger toward her. This is considered a sinful oath, and the husband is required to repudiate it upon pain of suffering a judicial divorce of his wife.

Ilzām: A judicial order obliging one party to perform a certain act, such as a judicial order commanding a man to pay his ex-wife a specific sum for her expenses in taking care of their minor child.

***Imām* (p. *a'imma*)**: In the generic sense, *imam* is the head or leader of any group. In the political context, *imam* refers to the head of the community. The term *khalīfa* (caliph) is synonymous, at least in the Sunni context, with *imam.* In the context of ritual prayer, *imam* means the prayer leader whom the congregation follows during the prayer.

Imāma: The status of being a leader. In the political context, it therefore means the state in an unrestricted sense. When Muslim jurists and theologians describe establishment of the *imāma* as an obligation, it is in reference to this generic use of the term.

Inshā': To bring something into existence where it had not existed previously. Jurists use the term to describe certain verbal formulas that by their own terms create specific legal consequences, such as formulas of marriage or divorce or manumission. I have translated it in this book as *origination.* Jurists contrast originations to propositional statements (*akhbār*), which, by virtue of their structures, are amenable to acceptance or rejection. A propositional statement requires the listener to determine the truthfulness of the predication, whereas an origination requires the listener to apply the relevant legal consequences of the statement.

Iqṭā': In Islamic law, the grant of the usufruct of public property to a specific person enabling him to exploit it for his private ends for a period of time and for a certain fee.

Ithbāt: The establishment of facts in a judicial proceeding.

I'tiqād: A belief or doctrine.

Jāhiliyya: The pre-Islamic Arabian period of paganism.

Kalām lisānī: Speech that is made manifest on the tongue of a speaker in the form of a natural human language.

Kalām nafsānī: Speech that is confined to the mental processes of a human being (or God) and has not become manifest on the tongue of a speaker in the form of a natural human language.

Khāriṣ: A tax collector who estimated the quantity of fruit that an orchard would yield for purposes of assessing liability for the alms tax (*zakat*).

Khāṣṣ: A text that applies to particular members of an otherwise universal set. In Islamic jurisprudence, indicants are either universal (*ʿāmm*) in their applicability to their members or particular (*khāṣṣ*), insofar as it applies to only one or some of the members of the universal set.

Khiṭāb al-taklīf: In the usage of the Muslim jurists, revelatory speech that establishes the moral status of the actions of those subject to the law, that is, mature human beings of sound mind. In Muslim jurisprudence, human action falls into one of five moral categories: obligatory (*wājib* or *farḍ*), prohibited (*maḥẓūr* or *ḥarām*), recommended (*mandūb*), disfavored (*makrūh*), and permitted (*mubāḥ*).

Khiṭāb al-waḍʿ: In the usage of the Muslim jurists, revelatory speech that establishes a rule whose effect comes into being as a consequence of a certain state of affairs in the world. For example, the rule that a valid contract of sale results in the transfer of ownership of the good sold to the purchaser, or that a valid marriage contract renders sexual intercourse between the spouses lawful.

Kināya: An oblique expression. Particularly important in oaths, an oath may be express (*ṣarīḥ*), in which case the oath taker's subjective intent is irrelevant, or it may be oblique, in which case his subjective intent is legally relevant.

***Lafẓ* (p. *alfāẓ*)**: A word in a natural human language.

***Madhhab* (p. *madhāhib*)**: A view or opinion, and in the usage of Islamic law, the aggregate legal opinions of a master jurist and his followers, such as the Mālikīs, the Ḥanafīs, the Shāfiʿīs and the Ḥanbalīs.

Maḥẓūr: Also called *ḥarām*, one of the five moral categories of Islamic jurisprudence meaning "prohibited." If an act is prohibited with respect to a person, he or she deserves praise if he refrains from performing it and blame if he performs it.

Majāz: In Muslim hermeneutics, the nonliteral use of a word or phrase.

Makrūh: One of the five moral categories of Islamic jurisprudence meaning "disfavored." If an act is disfavored with respect to a person, he or she deserves praise if she refrains from performing it, but does not incur blame if she performs it.

Mandūb: One of the five moral categories of Islamic jurisprudence, meaning "recommended." If an act is recommended with respect to a person, he deserves praise if he performs it but does not incur blame if he fails to perform it.

***Māniʿ* (p. *mawāniʿ*)**: Literally, "obstacle," and in the usage of Muslim jurists, a circumstance that prevents the operation of rule even though all of its positive elements have been satisfied. For example, if a thief steals property having value in excess of the minimum amount necessitating amputation of the hand, the punishment nevertheless cannot be applied if it turns out that the stolen item belonged to the thief's son.

Maṣlaḥa ʿāmma: Literally, "a universal good," and in Islamic law, the common or public good.

Maẓālim: The plural of *maẓlama*, meaning, "unjust action," and in Islamic law, referring to a specific forum designed in the first instance to redress the wrongdoing of government officials but that could also entertain private lawsuits.

Mubāḥ: One of the five moral categories of Islamic jurisprudence, meaning "permitted." If an act is permitted with respect to a person, he deserves neither praise nor blame, whether or not he performs it. As a term of property law, it means property that lacks an owner and may be used or appropriated through an appropriate act of possession.

Muḍāri': In Arabic grammar, the term for the imperfect mood of a verb, or in combination with the appropriate particle, for the negation of the past tense.

Mujtahid: Literally, "someone who exerts effort." In Islamic law, it refers to a person who has mastered the various sciences necessary and possesses the necessary moral integrity to allow him or her to deduce God's law directly from revelation without deferring to the opinions of others. Accordingly, such a person can be referred to as a master jurist.

Muqallid: Literally, "someone who places a necklace or other insignia around the neck of another." In Islamic law, it refers to a jurist who has not mastered the various sciences necessary to allow him or her to deduce God's law directly from revelation, and as a result, he defers to the opinions of a master jurist in order to acquire knowledge of divine law. According to theoretical jurisprudence, the law of God for a *muqallid* is derivative of the *fatwā* of the master jurist. Accordingly, the *muqallid* satisfies the obligation to comply with divine law through adherence to the teachings of a master jurist.

Musāqāt: A kind of labor partnership for the cultivation of an orchard depending on an irrigated source of water. It is considered an exceptional contract insofar as it contravenes ordinarily applicable principles of Islamic contract law.

Mutawātir: A mass-transmitted historical report whose provenance is incontestable because it has been independently corroborated via the transmission of an innumerable number of independent transmitters at each generation such that it becomes inconceivable in the mind of a present recipient of the report that the report is mistaken or a forgery.

Nadhr: A vow, and in Islamic law, a vow to perform a recommended act or refrain from committing a disfavored act for the sake of God.

Nahy: A prohibition.

Nā'ib: A delegate or representative authorized by a principal to act on his behalf with respect to some domain of action.

Naskh: In Muslim theoretical jurisprudence, the abrogation, partial or complete, of an earlier rule of divine law by a subsequent rule of divine law.

Naṣṣ: In Muslim theoretical jurisprudence, the term used to describe a text of such clarity that it bears only one meaning.

Nubuwwa: "Prophecy," which as defined by al-Qarāfī, occurs when a human being receives from God revelation that instructs him to do, or to refrain from, a particular act.

Qaḍā': The exercise of the judicial power entailed in the act of resolving a particular dispute between two particular parties.

***Qā'ida* (p. *al-qawā'id*)**: Literally, "foundation," and in the context of Islamic law, a rule that applies to a universal set of cases sharing a common feature; for example, "every claim for the payment of money against another person can be proved by the direct testimony of two male witnesses possessed of sufficient integrity."

Qawl: An "opinion" or "view."

Qirāḍ: An exceptional contract pursuant to which an investor lends money to an entrepreneur in exchange for a predetermined share of the profit. If no profit is realized, the entrepreneur is obliged to repay only the principal amount of the loan.

Qiṣāṣ: The principle of proportional retaliation for wrongs that lies at the foundation of the Islamic law of torts. Pursuant to this principle, the victim of an intentional tort (or in the case of murder, the victim's next of kin) has the private right of retaliation in kind, or to accept compensation in exchange of waiver of this right. In the case of nonintentional torts, Islamic law provided a schedule of damages, known as *diya*, for various specified injuries. If the compensation for an injury was not specified by the law, the judge was obliged to exercise judgment to determine the value of the injury. As a general rule, the family of the tort-feasor, known as *al-ʿāqila*, was obliged to contribute to the payment of compensation to the victim of the tort committed by their family member. Special rules for accelerated payment of compensation applied in the case of torts committed recklessly (*diya mughallaẓa*).

Qiyās Jalī: An a fortiori analogy.

Rājiḥ: Literally, "weightier," and in the usage of Islamic law, in a case admitting of several solutions, the solution that, given the relative strength of the argument in its support in the mind of the interpreter, outweighs the other possible solutions, and therefore ought to be deemed the likely rule of God.

Risāla: Literally, "message," and in Islamic theology, the status of being a messenger of God. According to al-Qarāfī, messengership is distinguished from prophecy insofar as a messenger is commanded by God to convey to others the message that God has revealed to him.

Riwāya: The narration of something occurring in the past. In Islamic jurisprudence, transmission of the Quran and prophetic and other precedents is the means by which the indicants of the divine law reach master jurists.

***Sabab* (p. *asbāb*)**: A cause, and in Islamic law, the elements that must be satisfied for an obligation to come into existence; for example, the existence of a valid contract of sale produces the obligation on the part of the seller to deliver the object of the sale and the obligation on the part of the purchaser to deliver the price.

Shahāda: The testimony of a witness in a court. In Islamic jurisprudence, testimony is contrasted with narration, insofar as testimony, because of the particular interests involved in a legal dispute, requires substantive corroboration before it is accepted.

***Shakk* (p. *shukūk*)**: Means "doubt." In Muslim theoretical jurisprudence, an implausible inference, but one not considered impossible or absurd.

Sharīʿa: The revealed law of Islam.

***Sharṭ* (p. *shurūṭ*)**: A condition for the performance of a legal obligation, such as the obligation to purify oneself before performing ritual prayer, or in the case of sales, for receiving the benefit of the transaction, for example, that the object of the sale be property that is ritually pure and thus usable in the hands of a Muslim.

Shufʿat al-jār: A legal doctrine of the Ḥanafī school of law rejected by the Mālikīs that gives a neighbor a right of first refusal upon the sale of adjoining real property.

Siyāsa ʿāmma: The general police power, which authorizes the ruler to make generally applicable rules for the public good.

Tablīgh: Communication of an idea from its source to its recipient through the mediation of a messenger. Accordingly, the function of the messenger is to communicate God's words that he receives from the angel to humanity. Likewise, the function of a master jurist is to communicate the legal concepts that he deduces from the words of revelation to the public, and that of a jurist who defers to a master jurist is to communicate the views of the master jurist to the public.

Taḥkīm: Arbitration.

Takhṣīṣ: In Islamic jurisprudence, it is the hermeneutical technique by which the scope of a universal term is made particular. According to jurisprudential principles, when there is both a universal indicant and a particular one, priority is given to the particular indicant. Accordingly, the verse "As for the thief, whether male or female, cut their hands" (*al-Mā'ida*, 5:38) is by its terms universal insofar as it applies to all thieves. A hadith of the Prophet Muḥammad, however, states that a thief, to be eligible for Quranic punishment, must steal something with a value in excess of one-quarter of a gold dinar. This latter report has the effect of particularizing the Quranic rule so that it applies to only some, instead of all, thieves.

Ṭalāq bā'in: A divorce that has become final and thus necessitates the departure of the wife from the marital home.

Ṭalāq raj'ī: A revocable divorce that permits the husband to retract it at any time prior to the expiration of the wife's waiting period.

Ta'līq: An oath whose performance is conditional upon the occurrence of some fact in the world, for example, the wife's departure from the marital home, as in "If my wife leaves the home, she is divorced."

Taqlīd: In Islamic jurisprudence, the practice of jurists who are not capable of deriving the rules of Islamic law directly from revelation to defer to the opinions of master jurists.

Taṣarruf al-imām: The administrative acts and decrees of the head of state and lesser public officials, in furtherance of the good of those under their authority.

Uṣūl al-dīn: The dogmatic elements of religion.

Uṣūl al-fiqh: The theoretical foundations of Islamic law. The discipline of theoretical jurisprudence includes topics such as the material sources of divine law, hermeneutics (i.e., the rules of language that govern the interpretation of those sources), and the inferential techniques that are to be used in interpreting the material sources of the law. It also includes topics of theology and the nature of moral obligation.

Waḍʿ: In theoretical jurisprudence, a reference to some primordial time in human history when each linguistic community posited the original meanings of all the words in their language.

Wājib: Also called *farḍ*, one of the five moral categories of Islamic jurisprudence, meaning "obligatory." If an act is obligatory with respect to a person, he or she deserves praise if he performs it and blame if he fails to perform it.

Wazīr al-istishāra: A minister whose role is limited to providing advice.

Wazīr al-tafwīḍ: A minister who has policy-making, judicial, and enforcement powers.

Wazīr al-tanfīdh: An executive minister whose power is limited to enforcement of decisions made by others.

Ẓāhir: Literally, "obvious," and in Islamic jurisprudence, the inference that is supported by the obvious or plain sense of the law.

Zakāt: The alms tax. One of the five pillars of Islam, it is an obligation imposed on anyone owning property in excess of certain legally specified minima.

***Ẓann* (p. *ẓunūn*)**: Literally, "opinion," and in Islamic law, an opinion that is the product of rational deliberation and represents a probable conclusion about the object of reasoning (e.g., God's law) or a fact about the external world (e.g., that a person holding a knife dripping with blood and standing over a corpse that has been repeatedly stabbed is a responsible for the murder).

Bibliography

Arabic Sources

Aḥmad, ʿAlī Jumuʿa. *Al-Makāyīl wa-l-Mawāzīn al-Sharʿiyya*. Cairo: al-Quds li-l-Iʿlān wa-l-Nashr wa-l-Taswīq, 2001.

Al-Abī, Muḥammad b. Khalīfa al-Washtiyānī. *Ikmāl Ikmāl al-Muʿallim bi Sharḥ Ṣaḥīḥ Muslim*. Edited by Muḥammad Sālim Hāshim. 8 vols. Beirut: Dār al-Kutub al-ʿIlmiyya, 2008.

Al-ʿAsqalānī, Ibn Ḥajar. *Fatḥ al-Bārī Sharḥ Ṣaḥīḥ al-Bukhārī*. Edited by ʿAbd al-ʿAzīz b. Bāz. 13 vols. Beirut: Dār al-Kutub al-ʿIlmiyya, 1989.

Al-Dardīr, Aḥmad b. Muḥammad b. Aḥmad. *Al-Sharḥ al-Ṣaghīr*. Edited by Muṣṭafā Kamāl Waṣfī. 4 vols. Cairo: Dār al-Maʿārif, n.d.

Al-Farrāʾ, Abū Yaʿlā Muḥammad b. al-Ḥusayn. *al-Aḥkām al-Sulṭāniyya*. Beirut: Dār al-Kutub al-ʿIlmiyya, 1983.

Al-Haytamī, Aḥmad b. Muḥammad b. ʿAlī Ibn Ḥajar. *Al-Fatāwā al-Kubrā al-Fiqhiyya*. 4 vols. Beirut: Dār Ṣādir, 2000.

———. *Tuḥfat al-Muḥtāj fī Sharḥ al-Minhāj*. 10 vols. Cairo: al-Maktaba al-Tijāriyya al-Kubrā, 1983.

Al-Māwardī, Abu'l-Ḥasan ʿAlī b. Muḥammad. *al-Aḥkām al-Sulṭāniyya*. Beirut: Dār al-Kutub al-ʿIlmiyya, n.d.

Al-Munāwī, Zayn al-Dīn ʿAbd al-Raʾūf. *Al-Taysīr bi-Sharḥ al-Jāmiʿ al-Ṣaghīr*. 2 vols. Riyadh: Maktabat al-Imām al-Shāfiʿī, 1988.

Al-Qarāfī, Shihāb al-Dīn. *al-Dhakhīra,* Edited by Muḥammad Ḥajjī. 14 vols. Beirut: Dār al-Gharb al-Islāmī, 1994.

———. *Al-Furūq.* 4 vols. Beirut: ʿĀlam al-Kutub, n.d.

———. *Nafāʾis al-Uṣūl fī Sharḥ al-Maḥṣūl.* Edited by ʿĀdil Aḥmad ʿAbd al-Mawjūd and ʿAlī Muḥammad Muʿawwaḍ. 9 vols. Riyadh: Maktabat Nizār Muṣṭafā al-Bāz, 1997.

———. *Al-Umniyya fī Idrāk al-Niyya.* Edited by Musāʿid b. Qāsim al-Fāliḥ. Riyāḍ: Maktabat al-Ḥaramayn, 1988.

———. *Al-Iḥkām fī Tamyīz al-Fatāwa ʿan al-Aḥkām wa Taṣarrufāt al-Qāḍī wa-l-Imām.* Edited by Maḥmūd ʿArnūs. Cairo: Maktab Nashr al-Thaqāfa al-Islāmiyya, 1938.

———. *Al-Iḥkām fī Tamyīz al-Fatāwa ʿan al-Aḥkām wa Taṣarrufāt al-Qāḍī wa-l-Imām.* Edited by ʿAbd al-Fattāḥ Abū Ghudda. Aleppo: Maktabat al-Maṭbūʿāt al-Islāmiyya, 1967.

———. *Al-Iḥkām fī Tamyīz al-Fatāwa ʿan al-Aḥkām wa Taṣarrufāt al-Qāḍī wa-l-Imām.* Edited by Abū Bakr ʿAbd al-Razzāq. Cairo: al-Maktab al-Thaqāfī li-l-Nashr wa-l-Tawzīʿ, 1989.

Al-Qazwani, Muḥammad b. Yazīd Ibn Maja. *Sunan Ibn Māja.* Edited by Muḥammad Fuʾād ʿAbd al-Bāqī. Beirut: Dār al-Kutub al-ʿIlmiyya, n.d.

Al-Ramlī, Shihāb al-Dīn. *Nihāyat al-Muḥtāj Ilā Sharḥ al-Minhāj.* 8 vols. Beirut: Dār al-Fikr, 1984.

Al-Rāzī, Fakhr al-Dīn. *al-Maḥṣūl fī ʿIlm al-Uṣūl.* 2 vols. Beirut: Dār al-Kutub al-ʿIlmiyya, 1999.

Al-Shirbīnī, Shams al-Dīn Muḥammad b. Muḥammad al-Khaṭīb. *Mughnī al-Muḥtāj.* Edited by ʿAlī Muḥammad Muʿawwaḍ and ʿĀdil Aḥmad ʿAbd al-Mawjūd. 2nd ed. 4 vols. Beirut: Dār al-Kutub al-ʿIlmiyya, 2009.

Al-Suyūṭī, Jalāl al-Dīn. *Sharḥ Tanwīr al-Ḥawālik Muwaṭṭaʾ al-Imām Mālik.* 2 vols. Cairo: Maktabat wa Maṭbaʿat Muṣṭafā al-Bābī al-Ḥalabī, 1951.

Al-Ṭarābulsī, ʿAlāʾ al-Dīn ʿAlī b. Khalīl. *Muʿīn al-Ḥukkām fī Mā Yataraddadu Bayna al-Khaṣmayn min al-Aḥkām*. Beirut: Dar al-Fikr, n.d.

Al-Tirmidhī, Abū ʿĪsā Muḥammad b. ʿĪsā. *Sunan al-Tirmidhī*. Edited by Aḥmad Muḥammad Shākir et al. 3rd ed. 3 vols. Cairo: Maktabat wa Maṭbaʿat Muṣṭafā al-Bābī al-Ḥalabī, 1975.

Al-Zurqānī, 'Abd al-Bāqī. *Sharḥ al-Zurqānī ʿalā Mukhtaṣar Khalīl*. 8 vols. Beirut: Dār al-Fikr, n.d.

Ibn ʿAbd al-Salām, al-ʿIzz. *Qawāʿid al-Aḥkām fī Maṣāliḥ al-Anām*. 2 vols. Beirut: Dār al-Maʿrifa, n.d.

Ibn Farḥūn, Ibrāhīm b. ʿAlī b. Muḥammad. *Tabṣirat al-Ḥukkām fī Uṣūl al-Aqḍīya wa Manāhij al-Aḥkām*. Cairo: Maktabat al-Kulliyyāt al-Azhariyya, 1986.

Ibn Shās, Jalāl al-Dīn ʿAbdallāh b. Najm. *ʿIqd al-Jawāhir al-Thamīna fī Madhhab ʿĀlim al-Madīna*, ed. Muḥammad Abū al-Ajfān and ʿAbd al-Ḥafīz Manṣūr. 3 vols. Beirut: Dār al-Gharb al-Islāmī, 1995.

Ibn al-Shāṭṭ, Qāsim b. ʿAbd Allāh b. Muḥammad. *Tahdhīb al-furūq* on the margin of *Al-Furūq*. 4 vols. Beirut: ʿĀlam al-Kutub, n.d.

Ibn al-Subkī, Tāj al-Dīn ʿAbd al-Wahhāb b. ʿAlī. *Al-Ashbāh wa'l-Naẓāʾir*. Edited by ʿĀdil Aḥmad ʿAbd al-Mawjūd and ʿAlī Muḥammad ʿAwaḍ. 2 vols. Beirut: Dār al-Kutub al-ʿIlmiyya, 1991.

Mālik ibn Anas. *al-Mudawwana al-Kubrā*. 4 vols. Beirut: Dar al-Fikr, 1986.

Non-Arabic Sources

Al-Shāfiʿī, Muḥammad b. Idrīs. *The Epistle on Legal Theory*. Edited and translated by Joseph E. Lowry. New York: New York University Press, 2013.

———. *Islamic Jurisprudence: Shāfiʿī's* Risāla. Translated by Majid Khadduri. Baltimore: Johns Hopkins Press, 1961.

Brown, Jonathan. *Hadith: Muhammad's Legacy in the Medieval and Modern World*. Oxford, UK: Oneworld, 2009.

Cuno, Kenneth M. "Ideology and Juridical Discourse in Ottoman Egypt: the Uses of the Concept of Irṣād." *Islamic Law & Society*, no. 6 (1999): 136–63.

Emon, Anver. "*Ḥuqūq Allāh* and *Ḥuqūq al-ʿIbād.*" *Islamic Law & Society* 13, no. 3 (2006): 325–91.

Escovitz, Joseph. "The Establishment of Four Chief Judgeships in the Mamluk Empire." *Journal of the American Oriental Society* 102 (1982): 529–31.

Fadel, Mohammad. "Adjudication in the Mālikī Madhhab: A Study of Legal Process in Medieval Islamic Law." PhD diss., Department of Near Eastern Languages and Civilizations, University of Chicago, 1995.

———. "Authority in Ibn Abī Zayd al-Qayrawānī's *Kitāb al-Nawādir wa-l-Ziyādāt ʿalā mā fī al-Mudawwana min ghayrihā min al-Ummahāt:* The Case of the Chapter of Judgments (*Bāb al-Aqḍīya*)." In *The Heritage of Arabo-Islamic Learning: Studies in Honor of Wadad Kadi,* edited by Maurice Pomerantz and Aram Shahin, 207–26. New York: Brill Academic Publishers, 2016.

———. "Public Authority (Sulṭān) in Islamic Law." In *The Oxford International Encyclopedia of Legal History*, edited by Stanley N. Katz. New York: Oxford University Press, 2009.

———. "Ribâ Efficiency and Prudential Regulation: Preliminary Thoughts." *Wisconsin Journal of International Law*, no. 25 (2008): 655–702.

———. "The Social Logic of *Taqlīd* and the Rise of the *Mukhtaṣar.*" *Islamic Law and Society* 3, no. 2 (1996): 193–233.

Hassan, Mona F. *Longing for the Lost Caliphate: Transregional Imaginaries of State and Muslim Community.* Princeton, NJ: Princeton University Press, 2017.

Hodgson, Marshall. *The Venture of Islam.* Vol. 2, *The Expansion of Islam in the Middle Periods.* Chicago: University of Chicago Press, 1977.

Jackson, Sherman. "From Prophetic Actions to Constitutional Theory: A Novel Chapter in Medieval Muslim Jurisprudence." *International Journal of Middle East Studies* 25, no. 1 (1993): 71–90.

———. *Islamic Law and the State: The Constitutional Jurisprudence of Shihāb al-Dīn al-Qarāfī.* New York: Brill, 1996.

———. "The Primacy of Domestic Politics: Ibn Bint al-Aʿazz and the Establishment of the Four Chief Judgeships in Mamluk Egypt." *Journal of the American Oriental Society* 115 (1995): 52–65.

———. "Taqlid, Legal Scaffolding and the Scope of Legal Injunctions in Post-Formative Theory: *Mutlaq* and *ʿĀmm* in the Jurisprudence of Shihāb al-Dīn al-Qarāfī." *Islamic Law and Society* 3, no. 2 (1996): 165–92.

Johansen, Baber. "Truth and Validity of the Qāḍī's Judgment: A Legal Debate among Sunnite Muslim Jurists from the Ninth to the Thirteenth Centuries." *Recht van de Islam* 14, (1997): 1–26.

Moosa, Ebrahim. "Allegory of the Rule (Ḥukm): Law as Simulacrum in Islam?" *History of Religions, Islam and Law* 38, no. 1 (1998): 1–24.

———. "Shaykh Aḥmad Shākir and the Adoption of a Scientifically-Based Lunar Calendar." *Islamic Law & Society* 5, no. 1 (1998): 57–89.

Nielsen, Jorgen. "Sultan al-Ẓāhir Baybars and the Appointment of Four Chief *Qāḍīs*, 663/1265." *Studia Islamica* 60 (1984): 167–76.

Rappoport, Yossef. "Legal Diversity in the Age of Taqlīd: The Four Chief Qāḍīs under the Mamluks," *Islamic Law and Society* 10, no. 2 (2003): 210–28.

Tyan, E. *Histoire de l'organisation judiciare en pays d'Islam.* 2nd ed. Leiden: E. J. Brill, 1960.

Weiss, Bernard. "Exotericism and Objectivity in Islamic Jurisprudence." In *Islamic Law and Jurisprudence*, edited by Nicholas Heer, 53–71. Seattle: University of Washington Press, 1990.

———. *The Search for God's Law.* Salt Lake City: University of Utah Press, 1992.

Wolfson, Harry Austryn. *The Philosophy of the Kalam.* Cambridge, MA: Harvard University Press, 1976.
Wright, C., and A. Miller & E. Cooper. "Law of the Case." *Federal Practice & Procedure* § 4478. Eagan, MN: Thomson/West.
Wymann-Landgraff, Umar F. Abd-Allah. *Mālik and Medina: Islamic Legal Reasoning in the Formative Period.* Boston: Brill, 2013.
Zysow, Aron. "The Economy of Certainty." PhD diss., Harvard University, 1984.

Index